FROM A CAUSE TO A STYLE

Also by Nathan Glazer

The Lonely Crowd
(with David Riesman and Reuel Denney)

Faces in the Crowd (with David Riesman)

American Judaism

The Social Basis of American Communism

Beyond the Melting Pot (with Daniel P. Moynihan)

*Remembering the Answers:
Essays on the American Student Revolt*

*Affirmative Discrimination:
Ethnic Inequality and Public Policy*

Ethnic Dilemmas, 1965–1982

Clamor at the Gates: The New American Immigration (editor)

The Public Face of Architecture (editor, with Mark Lilla)

The Limits of Social Policy

Conflicting Images: India and the United States
(editor, with Sulochana Raghavan Glazer)

We Are All Multiculturalists Now

Sovereignty under Challenge: How Governments Respond
(editor, with John D. Montgomery)

FROM A CAUSE TO A STYLE

Modernist Architecture's Encounter
with the American City

NATHAN GLAZER

Princeton University Press
Princeton and Oxford

Library of Congress Cataloging-in-Publication Data

Glazer, Nathan.
From a cause to a style : modernist architecture's encounter
with the American city / Nathan Glazer.
p.   cm.
Includes bibliographical references and index.
ISBN-13: 978-0-691-12957-0 (hardcover : alk. paper)
ISBN-10: 0-691-12957-6 (hardcover : alk. paper)
1. Architecture and society—United States—History—20th century.
2. City planning—United States—History—20th century. 3. City
planning—Social aspects—United States. 4. Modernism
(Aesthetics)—United States—History—20th century. I. Title.
NA2543.S6G59 2007
720.973'0904—dc22   2006028071

British Library Cataloging-in-Publication Data is available

This book has been composed in Méridien with Frutiger Display
Printed on acid-free paper. ∞
press.princeton.edu
Printed in the United State of America

10 9 8 7 6 5 4 3 2 1

Contents

Acknowledgments   vii

INTRODUCTION   1

PART ONE
The Public Face of Architecture   21

CHAPTER ONE
Building for the Public: What Has Gone Wrong?   23

CHAPTER TWO
The Prince, the People, and the Architects   48

CHAPTER THREE
"Subverting the Context": Olmsted's Parks
and Serra's Sculpture   67

CHAPTER FOUR
Monuments in an Age without Heroes   93

CHAPTER FIVE
Modernism and Classicism on the National Mall   117

CHAPTER SIX
Daniel P. Moynihan and Federal Architecture   146

PART TWO
The New York Case   163

CHAPTER SEVEN
What Happened in East Harlem   165

CHAPTER EIGHT
Amenity in New York City   192

CHAPTER NINE
Planning for New York City: Is It Possible?   228

PART THREE
The Professions: From Social Vision
to Postmodernism   253

CHAPTER TEN
What Has Happened to the City Planner?   255

CHAPTER ELEVEN
The Social Agenda of Architecture   271

Index   293

Acknowledgments

Many of these essays have been previously published, but all have been edited and revised, and some have been substantially rewritten, and appear in a form quite different from the original place of publication. Chapter 1 was presented as a paper in the Boston, Melbourne, Oxford Conversazione on "The Public Face of Architecture" in 1991, was published in their proceedings, edited by Claudio Veliz, and also published in the Australian journal *Quadrant* (December 1991). Chapter 2 was published in *The American Scholar* (Autumn 1990). Chapter 3 was delivered as the Benjamin C. Howland lecture at the University of Virginia, and published in *The Public Interest* (Fall 1992). Chapter 4 was presented in the Boston, Melbourne, Oxford Conversazione on "Monuments for a World without Heroes," 1995, published in the proceedings of the Conversazione, edited by Claudio Veliz, and also in *The Public Interest* (Spring 1996). A different version of chapter 5 appears in *The Mall and the Nation*, edited by Nathan Glazer and Cynthia Field (Baltimore: Johns Hopkins University Press, 2007). This paper was commissioned by the Newington-Cropsey Cultural Studies Center, which also funded the research for it. Chapter 6 appeared in *Celebrating the Courthouse*, edited by Steven Flanders (New York: W. W. Norton, 2006). Chapter 7 was published in *City Journal* (Autumn 1991). Sections of chapter 8 have appeared in the *American Arts Quarterly* (Summer 2002); *City Journal* (Winter 1995); *The Public Interest* (Fall 1996). Chapter 9 was published in

City Journal (Spring 1992). Chapter 10 appeared in *The Profession of City Planning*, edited by Lloyd Rodwin and Bishwapriya Sanyal (New Brunswick, N.J.: Center for Urban Policy Research, Rutgers University, 2000). Chapter 11 was presented at Princeton University at a conference in honor of Robert Gutman, and has not been previously published.

I would like to express my appreciation to Tim Sullivan, my editor at Princeton University Press, who saw the possibilities of this book, and shepherded it through the various stages leading to publication with rare understanding and imagination; to Lauren Lepow, at Princeton University Press, who gave the manuscript a meticulous reading and has helped to improve it; and to Sulochana Raghavan Glazer, my wife, who read the manuscript closely twice with sustained enthusiasm, discovered errors and inconsistencies, and proposed changes that helped make it a better book.

FROM A CAUSE TO A STYLE

INTRODUCTION

In the 1980s, the Prince of Wales, who has adopted a number of surprising causes for a prince in the course of his life, became for a time the most influential critic of architecture, urban design, and planning in Great Britain. Both modernist architecture and modernist city planning had been very successful in Britain—as indeed they have been almost everywhere—in shaping new towns and rebuilding the centers of old cities and towns. But ordinary people often looked on the results with dismay. The prince's interventions and criticisms received wide publicity, and were effective in derailing some high-profile projects by modernist architects.

Leading architects, who by the end of World War II had pretty much been fully captured by modernism in architecture and urban design and planning, were outraged by the prince's unprofessional intervention in their work and practice. They had been criticized before; but never by someone whose comments had such resonance in the public media.

The architects, to their disgruntlement, were portrayed as arrogant, unresponsive to what ordinary people wanted, indifferent to their interests, as they pursued their own visions as to what was appropriate and suitably contemporary or advanced in the design of major structures and in the shaping of town and city. Ordinary people, it seems, endorsed the prince's taste for more traditional features in major public buildings and more traditional layouts of towns and cities.

But what was most shocking to modernist architects was how easy it was to portray them as distant from the people and their interests. For at the origins of modernism in architecture and urban design and planning, the visionary architects and planners were, in their minds, leagued with the people against what they saw as archaic, overblown, extravagant, and inefficient architecture and design, the taste of princes. Some of the architects who launched modernism were socialists, close to the movements of the working class. Modernism in architecture and planning spoke for the people and their interests—in good sanitary housing, in green space, in access to air and light, in more living space, in an urban environment adapted to their needs and interests—and against the interests of princes, or merchant princes, or profit-minded developers. Modernism, in its origins, was a cause, not simply another turn in taste. What, then, had happened, that a prince could better represent the people, their interests and tastes, than the architects?

Something odd and unexpected seems to have happened to modernism in architecture and planning: it had broken free from its origins and moorings, drifted away from the world of everyday life, which it had hoped to improve, into a world of its own. From a cause that intended to remake the world, it had become a style, or a family of styles. Modernism had, it is true, produced masterpieces, but it had been incapable of matching the complex urbanity that the history of building, despite its attachment to the historical styles decried by modernism, had been able to create in so many cities. As the older parts of cities were swept away in a wave of urban renewal, as nineteenth-century courthouses and city halls were demolished for modern replacements, more and more people wondered whether what they had lost was matched by the new world being created by modernism. The essays collected in this book reflect the growing disenchantment of an early enthusiast of modernism in architecture and planning—and who when young is not?— with the failures of modernist architects and planners in dealing with contemporary urban life. Of course it is giving architects too much power, too much credit, to ascribe the ills of urban life to them; architects are only one player in shaping urban life. What becomes of our cities is a matter that in varying degrees involves us all: developers, elected officials, government agencies, the variety of interest groups among "the people" and what they will tolerate or protest in urban development.

But the architects and planners also have a role. Major architects—like Frank Gehry, Renzo Piano, Rem Koolhaas, Richard Meier, Santiago Calatrava, Zaha Hadid, Daniel Liebeskind, and some others—have recently attained remarkable prominence in popular perception and popular media. These "starchitects" are often presented as potential saviors of declining cities through exciting advanced design, and their role is well worth exploring.

II

Disaffection with the precepts and practice of successful modernism, following its triumph over traditional approaches to architecture and urban design after World War II, surfaced early. Catherine Bauer, who had first brought the news of how European cities after World War I were building a new kind of housing for the working classes—government subsidized or built, with more access to air and light and greenery—and who played a role in launching our own public housing, was disappointed by the results as early as the late 1950s. Robert Venturi, a modernist architect, launched the first effective blast against the chief design precepts of modernism in 1966, with his *Complexity and Contradiction in Modern Architecture*. "Less is more," one of the shapers of modernism, Mies van der Rohe, had sagely pronounced; Venturi indicated his displeasure with modernism's rejection of historical architecture's complexity by countering memorably, "Less is a bore." He became even more outrageous, finding some virtue in garish popular architectural taste, when he wrote, with Denise Scott-Brown and Stephen Izenour, *Learning from Las Vegas* in 1972. (After the Prince of Wales denounced a proposed modernist addition to London's National Gallery of Art, the gallery turned to Venturi to design the new extension.) Peter Blake, another modernist architect and architectural critic, spelled out his disappointment at length in 1974 in *Form Follows Fiasco*, turning another precept of modernism—"Form follows function"—on its head. The French translation was intriguingly titled *L'Architecture moderne est morte à Saint-Louis (Missouri) le 15 juillet 1972 a 15h 32 ou à peu près*

. . . (Modern architecture died in St. Louis, Missouri, on July 15, 1972, at 3:32 p.m. or thereabouts . . .). The reference is to one of the most poignant dates in the history of architecture, when the towers of the Pruitt-Igoe housing project in Saint Louis, designed by a leading modernist architect, were demolished by dynamite charges. In 1981 the ingenious journalist and novelist Tom Wolfe published his satirical send-up of modernism in *From Bauhaus to Our House*. And there were more.

Noel Annan, in his masterful account of postwar British intellectual and cultural life, *Our Age*, set out the problem well:

Perhaps no profession faced the future [after World War II] with such confidence as did the architects. The destruction of wartime bombing gave them their chance. . . . The modernists captured one after the other the university architectural schools. . . . The Oxbridge colleges became their patrons.

Yet it was among Our Age [he means those who fought World War II and became the leaders of British art and thought in the postwar years] that the movement emerged that was to undermine the reputation of . . . the leading architects. [John] Betjeman evoked on television the beauties of Victorian churches and commercial exchanges and denounced the vandalism of planners and property developers who blithely demolished them. . . . The conservationists . . . hunted the modernists in full cry, demanding an end to concrete fortresses, glass boxes and tower blocks approached by windswept walkways, an arena for prowlers and muggers. Why design buildings of elephantine dimensions that neglected their unobtrusive neighbors? Why did so many buildings, specifically designed to meet the functions which those who were going to use them were going to perform, end being inhuman?[1]

The story, of course, was the same in the United States, and in varying degrees in all the countries recovering from the war and participating in the great postwar expansion. In time modernism was to dominate all contemporary building, erasing traditional design in countries with grand architectural and planning traditions of their own.

It may seem odd and out of time to tell this story when major architects and their amazing productions—museums, concert halls, office towers, striking residential and academic complexes—seem to herald a new age of architectural creativity and achievement, and perhaps that age is at hand. Some of the remarkable architecture we now see may well have been influenced by the barrage of criticism I have referred to, which early gave rise to the term "post-modernism," a word first used in connection with architecture, subsequently naturalized without its hyphen. One of the implications of postmodernism was to favor a looser stance in regard to the sober and radically stripped-down and dehistoricized forms demanded by early, we might say "classic," modernism. Postmodernism suggested that one could perhaps accept the incorporation in contemporary buildings of hints of architectural elements used in the past. Postmodernism also fostered, if the client could be persuaded, an extrava-

[1] Noel Annan, *Our Age* (London: Weidenfeld and Nicolson, 1990), p. 291.

gance in forms and materials—if you will, a sensation-
alism—that has made stars of many architects, and that
is far from the sober unornamented surfaces of modernism's greatest practitioners. Style has become more personal, idiosyncratic, sometimes fantastic, and that certainly has attracted attention.

But the central issue in modernism was not really, to
begin with, style. Modernism was not simply a new style
in architecture, succeeding neo-Gothicism, neoclassicism,
Art Nouveau, or what you will. Modernism was a movement, with much larger intentions than replacing the
decorated tops of buildings with flat roofs, molded window frames with flat strips of metal, curves and curlicues
with straight lines. It represented a rebellion against historicism, ornament, overblown form, pandering to the
great and rich and newly rich as against serving the needs
of a society's common people. But when architects compete with each other in imposing forms on museums and
concert halls and residential towers that bear no resemblance to their functions, the movement in its larger sense
is dead. One element of continuity with early and classic
modernism persists, the proscribing and elimination of
reference to the history of architecture. Modernism in architecture has abandoned its early intentions and hopes.
It is the promise and the fate of that movement, as it deals
with cities, and buildings, and monuments, that are the
subject of this book.[2]

---

[2] Anatole Kopp titles a book on the early history of modernism *Quand le
moderne n'était pas une style mais une cause* (Paris: École Nationale Supérieure
des Beaux Arts, 1988), and I have adapted that title for the title of this
book. Of course others have noted the shift in what "modernism" means.
A concluding caption for the large exhibit on modernism at the Victoria

III

Modernism in architecture and urban design, emerging from theoretical proposals and some impressive achievements in Austria, Germany, the Netherlands, France, and Italy at the turn of the century, proposed one big and all-embracing ideal for buildings and cities: building should be functional, rational, directly accommodating specific needs, and should eschew the forms and elements that had dominated architecture in the West since the Greeks. It rejected the sculpted, ornamented architecture of major public buildings, and the use of the details and conventions of some past epochs, best expressed in the buildings designed for princes and potentates, secular and sacred. But one could see the modest reflections of these historical styles of the past in the structures that housed families, businesses, manufactories: some columns here, a pediment there, some swirls of classicist ornament. Modernism rejected any use of the styles of building of the past. Modernism called for "the machine for living," as against the home, or the machine for manufacturing, or selling, or praying, or governing, as against the architecturally elaborated factory, or department store, or church, or capitol. And the city was also to be a machine, in which all these forms of action were to be efficiently and directly accommodated.

Modernism responded to very strong forces: the huge scale of growing and expanding cities, and the buildings

---

and Albert Museum in London in 2006 (*Modernism: 1914–1939*) asserts that by the thirties modernism, "stripped of its social ideals, . . . became identified as a style, one among many that designers and consumers could choose from." I would date the shift from cause to style a few decades later, for the social ideals of modernism dominated city rebuilding in the post–World War II period until perhaps the 1970s.

and infrastructure they required for their expanded populations; the new materials and new technologies for building and construction that became available; new forms of transportation, and in particular the automobile; the new power in society of technical economic analyses as against the uneconomic and boundless demands for glorification of state and church. Alongside these pragmatic adaptations to technological change and scientific advance, there were some large cultural changes, the revolution of modernism in the arts, in which symbols, icons, and forms that had served varying Western societies for twenty-five hundred years began to lose their power to communicate.

Modernism approached the growing city of industrial and commercial complexity with the same powerfully rationalizing turn of mind with which it approached building. It expressed and called for direct functional adaptation. When modernists thought of the city, they envisioned ideally an empty expanse of space on which a new conception of the city could be erected without the hindrances of the past. And if the city already existed, the first step was to efface a large stretch of it. In the most extreme version, Le Corbusier's proposal for central Paris in 1925, all its complexity and idiosyncrasy and historical remains were to be swept aside for the great roads and skyscrapers that a new age demanded.[3]

Perhaps early modernism's greatest difficulty was when it came to monumental and memorial architecture. What, after all, was the function of a monument, and did not the monument inevitably have to resort to symbols to move,

[3] See Harry Francis Mallgrave, *Modern Architectural Theory: A Historical Survey, 1673–1968* (Cambridge: Cambridge University Press, 2005), p. 258. Le Corbusier proposed the same for Moscow in 1930 (pp. 315–16), but he was less sweeping in his proposals for other cities.

to speak to, a general populace? How could modernism's prescripts accommodate what monuments needed? And yet the world demanded monuments and memorials— perhaps more in the wake of the unexampled disasters of the twentieth century than in previous periods—and some response was necessary (see chapters 4 and 5).

It was easy to attack modernism's approach to building and the city, and such attacks on its principles, practices, and outcomes accompanied modernism from its origins. But as the history of architecture and urban design during the half century since World War II has shown us, it was not easy to replace it. It was eccentric to propose alternatives that did not express the ethic and aesthetic of modernism, for what else was there, aside from the return to a discredited past, with its columns and pediments and men on horseback? Those who fought against modernism in architecture and urban design had in the end very few victories to point to. The greatest successes of the critics of modernism had less to do with building something new and counter to modernism than with preserving what existed, what had been created in the ages before modernism, when historical styles were innocently copied, revived, revised, adapted to different uses, used even for factories and office buildings, and were allowed to cluster together messily and incongruously in the city. In the most recent decades, we have seen a movement for a "new urbanism," proposing a more traditional arrangement for new residential developments. But its target is less modernism than developer-built suburban housing, which in both design and arrangement has owed little to modernism, but which has rather reflected primarily adaptation to the automobile.

In the United States, as in Britain, modernism captured the schools of architecture and planning. The courthouses and city halls of the late nineteenth and early twentieth centuries were demolished to be replaced by more efficient and rationally designed modernist structures. City centers were leveled and their historic street plans erased for an urban renewal that promised more efficient layouts for traffic and living and work. Working-class quarters were demolished to be replaced by projects that city planners asserted would mark a great improvement in the living conditions of the poor and working classes. We had no Prince of Wales or equivalent public figure to take up the cause against modernism, but in Jane Jacobs's *The Death and Life of Great American Cities* (1961), we had a powerful critique of modern city planning that became enormously influential, not only in the United States, but in Britain, Canada, Germany, and elsewhere.

The critics of modernism in the United States made very much the same points that Noel Annan reports were being made in Britain. Yes, the architecture of the past, despite its aping of historical styles, had much to commend it and was being thoughtlessly destroyed in the 1950s and 1960s. The architecture and urban design of modernism—in particular, the publicly subsidized high-rise housing projects on large cleared sites that became, along with the flat-topped glass and steel skyscrapers of the city center, the very emblems of modernism—soon revealed themselves as inferior in some respects to the working-class housing and commercial districts they replaced.

The challenges to modernism did not lead to its replacement—only to new kinds of modernism, with new labels, a preference for somewhat different shapes and materials every few years. Modernism was so powerful because it had both aesthetic and social roots, working in tandem. Its aesthetic rejected the use of historical styles as models: the world was to be made anew, responsive to new technology, new materials, new ways of living and thinking. It decreed, in the powerful slogans that became the emblems of modernism, "ornament is crime," "less is more," "form follows function." But these canons of modernism were so powerful because they reflected, more than just a commitment to a simpler aesthetic, a commitment to social reform, moderate or radical. Simplicity and directness, the rejection of ornament, the most rational accommodation of needs, would better serve the poor and the working classes. Simpler design would mean easily reproducible forms, suited to the needs for which they were designed, perhaps eventually to be manufactured in factories rather than shaped by skilled craftsmen, and so reducing the cost of housing and making more available for less.

This connection between the aesthetic and the social was shaped early. Hendrik Berlage, a major Dutch pioneer of modernism, called for "material and labor economy, in keeping with the forces pushing toward social equality." The Italian pioneers of modernism were, of course, more extravagant. Antonio Sant'Elia's manifesto of 1914 declares that "the world of the twentieth century demands a reformulated modern city, one devoid of monumentality and decoration. It opposes . . . historical preservation, static lines, and costly materials inconsistent with modern culture." He calls for "the architecture of cold calculation, fearless audacity, and simplicity; the

architecture of reinforced concrete, or iron, glass, card-
board, textiles, and all those surrogates of wood, stone,
and brick that allow us to obtain the maximum elasticity
and lightness." Futurist architecture is to be marked by
"obsolescence and transience."[4]

In effect, modernism decreed that decorated or ornamented architecture, and historic systems of ornamentation, had come to an end. Indeed architecture, if viewed
in these terms, had come to an end, for henceforth architecture would accommodate functions rather than impose itself on them. The transition to modernism was at
first marked by efforts to create new systems of ornament
and decoration that did not directly copy or evoke some
past historic style, as in Art Nouveau and Art Deco. This
transition was reflected in the United States in the work
of Louis Sullivan and Frank Lloyd Wright, but that, too,
came to an end in the face of the power of the fully developed modernist ideal. In any case, to create new systems
of ornamentation not dependent on historic styles was
beyond the talents of any but geniuses.

The last "decorated" or "ornamented" style in architecture was the Art Deco of the 1920s and 1930s. It bowed
to modernism in rejecting classical and established forms
of ornament and decoration in architecture, but trans-
gressed the full doctrine of modernism in creating a new
style of decoration better suited, its practitioners thought,
to the age of electricity and the automobile. It created
some of the most widely recognized images of what it
meant to be modern, in such icons of New York City as

[4] As in ibid., pp. 219, 226. Some of the quotations are in Mallgrave's
paraphrase.

the Chrysler Building and the Empire State Building. Paradoxically these icons of "modernism" do not reflect classical "modernist" architecture, the more rigorous and rational modernism of the "international style." Its practitioners and proponents saw the international style not as a style, to be succeeded by others, but indeed as the end of style in architecture, the conclusion of the history of architecture as style. The last burst of decorated or ornamented architecture was eliminated in the early post–World War II period. Then the full program of modernism came into effect, particularly in the design of commercial office structures, the most characteristic form of building of the modern city. But it soon spread to public buildings, and indeed to almost all building except for private homes, the one major area of construction that has for the most part escaped modernist strictures.

For housing built under public authorities, modernism became the dominant influence after World War II in the United States. It dictated the superblock instead of the repeated blocks of equal size and shape that characterized the common gridiron plan of the American city. The superblock would provide more space for greenery, less for streets, as would the concentration of functions, whether for living or working, in high-rise buildings rather than in low-rise building taking up more ground. The modernist elimination of ornament and decoration suited the economic requirement that public housing for the lower-income classes should be of low cost. But public housing, as I describe in chapters 2 and 11 below, also became the Achilles' heel that undermined the social aims of architectural modernism, and led eventually to a complete divorce between the originally joined social and aesthetic sides of modernist architecture.

Modernism's proposals for the city, and their realization in various urban renewal schemes in the United States and in Britain, also came under severe attack. Reformers in the nineteenth and early twentieth centuries were horrified by the city that industrialism had created, and saw no virtue in a city built up in history of varied elements responding to varied needs jumbled together. Some theorists of urbanism saw in the city not the mess that modernists decried but an adaptation to human needs evolving through time. But modernism had no sympathy for such views. That city was a contradiction to what modernism proposed. Modernism put forth one big and all-embracing idea: the city as the functional envelope of urban needs, which can be designed and implemented in one grand plan. Just as modernism calls for "machines for living," or for manufacturing, or selling, as against the architecturally elaborated structures of the age before modernism, so it calls for the city to be the newly made proper envelope for all these machines.

The historical city suggests something very different. It is not of one time, but of many times, not of one style but of many styles, not of discrete functions accommodated in specific areas but of a jumble of functions that may crowd together in the same area. As an early nineteenth-century writer on the city put it, "the [city] plan must be designed with taste and verve, so that order, whimsy, eurythmy and variety may co-exist in equal measure." Or, another writer of the period: the city "should be a varied picture of an infinity of chance occurrences, with great order in the details and confusion, chaos and tumult in the whole."⁵ A twentieth-century architect in Paris gives us a powerful image: "Build the city on top of the city"⁶—do not wipe out its physical history for some presumed modern advantage; save its past, build in the interstices. What was there should remain and should not be fully effaced. That is quite different from modernism's view of the city, which called for a clear slate on which to build anew.

IV

So we struggle today with how to build capitols, churches, universities, civic centers and gathering places, theaters and opera houses and concert halls and monuments with the new language of modernism. (We struggle less when it comes to homes: as I have indicated above, there the traditional prevails for the most part against anything modernism has to offer.)

We know that a great deal has gone wrong. We ponder today the heritage of the buildings of the half century following World War II, and on the whole we are dissatisfied, despite the excitement that extravagant elaborations of modernist ideas have been able to generate for the last decade or so. The structures of modernism offer tremendous problems of maintenance or restoration as their once-new materials for building have aged and been removed from catalogs, and we argue about whether it is

⁵ Manfred Tafuri, "Toward a Critique of Architectural Ideology," in *Architecture Theory since 1968*, ed. K. Michael Hays (Cambridge: MIT Press, 1998), pp. 7, 11.

⁶ Antoine Grumbach, in *Survival Strategies: Paris and New York* (New Brunswick, N.J.: Transaction Books, 1979).

not simpler to demolish them or strip them down to the anonymous steel so we can hang onto them a currently less objectionable and more presentable curtain (often today of more traditional materials replacing a metal that we now generally find too shiny or vulgar). The variants and offshoots of modernism that prevailed for a few years—brutalism, postmodernism, minimalism, and the like—have come and gone.

We are largely dissatisfied with our efforts to build a new urbanism using the instruments of modernism. The scale is too big, it is too hard to introduce a distinctive (or quirky) detail of more human scale, and the traditional city built up in history seems better suited for the aspects of urban life that involve human contact, entertainment, distinctively urban pursuits. When artists and moviemakers picture the city built by modernism, it is to evoke the alienation and anonymity of city life, rather than those aspects of urbanism that bring people of different walks of life together in some common pursuit or in sociable interaction. Most current efforts to create a more interactive and attractive urbanism, to bring life back to the city, revert to traditional elements of design—a smaller scale, a degree of irregularity, a multiplicity of uses, the reuse of older buildings, and even traditional architectural elements in new buildings. The difficulties in producing an attractive urbanism constitute perhaps the greatest problem for modernism.

Most of the essays I have collected here on architecture, civic design, and urbanism were written before the recent burst of enthusiasm over some new directions in the history of modernist architecture. We are now in an age of new daring in forms and materials—the post-Bilbao effect, it has been called—that attracts wide public interest and excitement. But one suspects it will hold that interest only a little longer than did the striking forms of the World's Fairs of the past that these new and more personal elaborations of modernism resemble. World's Fair buildings were meant to be taken down after a year or two. These forays of late modernism into the city, while they can create a sensation, cannot create a city: whatever the character of any one of the greatly admired buildings of the last decade, we would not want another like it to be put up right next to it. This latest development of modernism transgresses at least one key dictum of modernism, "form follows function": in contrast, the architect often determines a form, and shoehorns the necessary functions into it. The forms do adhere to modernist dicta in that they are no longer classical or historical or reminiscent of one or another historic style. But the new iconic buildings also maintain another key dictum of modernism, "ornament is crime." The forms themselves become the ornament. Some remarkable buildings have indeed resulted, as they did from the same strategy in the early days of modernism: consider Utzon's Sydney Opera House, or Saarinen's TWA Terminal.

Whatever the virtue of these buildings, and some are indeed masterpieces, the earlier logic and rigor of modernism are cast aside. The city cannot be built of individual masterpieces, though certainly it should have its masterpieces. No model for building the city has emerged from the current excitement over star architects, as it did from the work and thought of the early masters of modernism. That task has been abandoned. Leading architects no longer write about the city, or about what it can and should be.[7]

These essays deal with aspects of the problems modernism presents: in public building, in building working-class housing—once a central mission of modernism—in creating monuments and memorials in an age of self-referential art, and the like. I have also included a group of essays on an old and various city, New York, which evokes the contradiction between modernism and the city, in this case the very archetypical city of modernity. New York for the most part eschews modernism in planning (aside from the public housing and middle-class housing projects built under state auspices). It has not leveled, as other cities have, large sections of the central city for a presumably better, more functional and efficient replacement. It is criticized by advanced architectural critics for its reluctance to embrace the latest variants of modernism in its building. Its housing projects tell us what was wrong with modernism, and its most successful gathering places tell us what was right with the city before modernism. Its central icons, themselves emblems of an earlier modernity, paradoxically predate modernism in architecture and design. I conclude with two essays on the state of two key professions, city planning and architecture.

Some of these essays date back fifteen years or more, and reflect responses to modernism in urban design and in architecture much earlier than that. They have appeared in various journals. The earlier ones have to some

[7] But note Moshe Safdie, *The City after the Automobile: An Architect's Vision* (New York: Basic Books, 1997).

degree been edited to delete references to contemporary events now forgotten. Others have been extended and rewritten. On the whole, they stand as they were written, recording the observations of an urbanist confronted by the revolutionary onslaught of modernism.

PART ONE

The Public Face of Architecture

CHAPTER ONE

Building for the Public: What Has Gone Wrong?

When we "build for the public"—our government buildings, our courthouses, our schools and colleges and universities, and we can extend the list to other public buildings—we imply that there is some legitimacy in the response of the public: whether it uses the building or not, whether it likes it or not, whether it feels it is an embellishment of the public life, worthy of admiration and pride, or not. There are, of course, practical needs a building must meet, and that play a role in all these judgments the public makes. Yet regardless of our ability or training to deal with professional aspects of architecture and design, our response to that most elusive quality of building and urban design, the aesthetic quality—do we find it beautiful or not, and do we find it suitably beautiful for the place and function for which it is designed?—cannot be ignored. It would be to act like moles to limit ourselves exclusively to practical considerations: the city, any city, reaches for more than that, and it is with that "more" that I deal in these comments.

So I consider the range of issues that come up in the criticism of architecture, a range elegantly and satisfactorily put in the words of Sir Henry Wotton: "Well-building hath three conditions: Commodity, Firmness, and Delight." Wotton was adapting Vitruvius, and I take the quotation from Geoffrey Scott's *The Architecture of Humanism*.[1] Commodity: it suits its purpose, it is a proper envelope for the activities that will take place in it. Firmness: it stands up without cracks or stains, pieces don't fall off, the parts fit together, it looks solid. And delight, the most elusive but also the most important of qualities.

John Ruskin, despite his disdain for Vitruvius, and his dislike of the Renaissance architecture that, with these introductory words of Wotton, Scott was defending, says very much the same thing:

We have three great branches of architectural virtue, and we require of any building,—

1. That it act well, and do the things it was intended to do in the best way.
2. That it speak well, and say the things it was intended to say in the best words.
3. That it look well, and please us by its presence whatever it has to do or say.[2]

Ruskin then acknowledges that there can be no general laws as to how buildings "speak." So he, too, is agreeing that it is commodity and firmness (how a building acts) and delight (how it looks) that are the chief criteria by which we judge architecture.

But, you will say, there is no accounting for taste, whether in art or in building. And so when a good number of us express our discontent with so much building

[1] Geoffrey Scott, *The Architecture of Humanism* (New York: Doubleday Anchor, 1954), p. 16.
[2] John Ruskin, *The Stones of Venice* (London: Everyman, 1907), 1:33.

for the public in recent years, the facile answer is, "But wait fifty years: we or our descendants will then find it powerful, or effective, or interesting, or charming, and we'll want to preserve it." I do not think that answer will serve: something has happened, and for most of our public building, we won't be eager to preserve it, and we won't find it powerful or beautiful or interesting: we'll be sorry it's there, and we'll wonder how it got there, and how we can improve it or replace it.

Does the widespread dissatisfaction with the public building of the last half century represent only the normal ebb and flow of public taste? Gibbon in the late eighteenth century wrote that the square of San Marco in Venice was "decorated with the worst architecture I ever saw."[3] John Ruskin, fifty years later, thought Bath was a "horrible" place.[4] I believe our present situation represents considerably more than a shift in taste or fashion, more than what we saw in the past with the turn against the restrained classical and Georgian in the Gothic revival of the mid-nineteenth century; or in the Beaux-Arts revival of the late nineteenth century that condemned the Gothic and Romanesque that were then popular. What we deal with now is not a battle of the styles, even though the arguments between the modernists and the postmodernists, the international style of the 1930s and whatever happened to challenge it in detail, is a battle of the styles within the larger style of modernism. But in comparison with those muscular conflicts of the past between author-

[3] John Rosenberg, *The Darkening Glass* (New York: Columbia University Press, 1961), p. 48.

[4] Michael Brooks, *John Ruskin and Victorian Architecture* (New Brunswick, N.J.: Rutgers University Press, 1987), p. 6.

itative views over how a building should look, we have today the merest skirmishes around a common norm that has effaced all historic styles. And a norm that leaves most of us discontented. How many of us would look forward with enthusiasm to the design of fifty new state capitols, or a national capitol today? We are, rather, grateful that we possess those we have, all completed before the rise of modernism effaced historical styles. The buildings that serve these present purposes may be, on the whole, no masterpieces, but few of us think we can do better today.

What is the basis for our discontent? Is it mere nostalgia? An ignorant (in the sense of uninformed about design) preference for what is common and familiar, perhaps vulgar, against what is sophisticated, refined, complex?

And whatever our discontent, do the conditions of modern life permit anything else? If they don't, we may have to stop there, whatever our discontent. There may be no alternative.

••

All our architecture is in one sense "public." Homes of the most modest scale are seen, and generally meant to be seen, and whether meant to be seen or not, form part of the urban fabric. And the public—the authorities, the laws and regulations, and our neighbors—plays a very large role in how we may build our own houses. Even the buildings of secret societies present a public face to the world, and often a quite magnificent public face, as we see in the buildings of Masonic societies.

It is our public buildings and spaces, our capitols and courthouses, our opera houses and theaters, our colleges and universities, our public squares and parks, with which we are most concerned: they all make a rather more substantial effort to impress, to shape public spaces, to declare their public function, to strengthen in those who view them a civic consciousness, a pride in government, city, public life, and major institutions.

Indeed, when it comes to private building, that is, the building of houses, there is really no great discontent over design. The building of houses seems to follow traditional designs, for the most part. Modernist innovation in house design has produced its masterpieces over the past eighty years, and continues to produce its annual crop of prize-winners, but has very little influence on the houses builders put up and most people buy and live in, or indeed on the houses that people who can afford it have architects design for them. Consider the enormous new houses the new wealthy now build, often to the outrage of their neighbors. But the outrage is over size, not style, for the style is generally a blown-up version of some traditional house. Oddly, it is only when the building of houses becomes *public* building—the public housing of the United States, the council housing of Britain—that we see the characteristic grumbling against modernism and the international style emerge.

The public at large, and even the sophisticated public, is in the position of knowing what it likes and what it doesn't like, but not being able to explain just why. Controversy concentrates around the new, which one would think would best represent present tastes and present needs. It is much more muted around the old: indeed, anything old today bears a presumption that it is better than anything that might replace it.

Architects are properly annoyed and even outraged when an ever more powerful preservationism and distrust of contemporary professional architectural taste and capacity denies them sites and opportunities, and restricts many to modernizing old buildings. What has happened, they ask in irritation, to that forward-looking spirit that characterized our Western societies until recently? We would not have thought twice in the Renaissance about tearing down the remains of Roman structures and using their very stones for new ones; or in the Baroque age of transforming every Gothic church in the new mode. In the sequence of historical revivals in the nineteenth century we found every new style (presumably based on an old) better than the one before it. And, until just a few years ago, we were quite ready to find the Victorian and Edwardian buildings of the last historic revivals repulsive and worthy of replacement by modern steel, concrete, and glass. As a result, we now have books titled *Lost New York* or *Lost Boston* or *Lost London*, regretting their loss and appealing not merely to the taste for the quaint and the archaic and the old-fashioned, but to a veritable and deeply felt sense of loss and tragedy in considering what we have destroyed.

Perhaps the strangest part of the whole story is that it was when architects and planners became most concerned with improving the lives of ordinary people, of citizens, with creating a better environment for all, that to present eyes they committed some of their most grievous errors. Today we do not much fault the architects and planners who built for kings and princes, for the great powers of church and state. Indeed, our democratic societies spend fortunes to maintain those extravagant buildings, squares, parks, that were designed not for the people, for ourselves, but for the private pleasure of kings and prelates, great nobles or merchant princes. So much, on the other hand, that has been built by major modernist architects explicitly for ourselves, for ordinary people, we now find unattractive and even worthy of destruction before their time, as in the case of the public housing of the United States or the council estates of Britain. Some of these have been dynamited, after lying vandalized and half-vacant; others seem candidates for destruction. How is it possible that great quantities of housing, following the models and prescriptions of the most distinguished architects, built to high standards, should have failed so miserably?

The phenomenon is general. In England, Prince Charles's complaints about modern building—office buildings planned around St. Paul's in London, the earlier proposed modernist addition to the National Gallery, the replacement of Edwardian buildings in the city of London with a building by a major modern architect, James Stirling—evoked wide response. Across our cities we find much that is new no improvement but rather a falling off from what is old. I live in Cambridge, Massachusetts, and one could begin there to assess what has gone wrong. For example, consider the sequence of buildings that have been built to house the Harvard museums. The original Fogg Museum of Art of 1925 is representative of its time. Its designer was Charles Coolidge, of Coolidge, Shepley, Bulfinch, and Abbott, which built much of brick Georgian revival Harvard, and the Fogg is a good example. A second Harvard museum for German art, built during and after World War I, evokes some south German or Austrian church. The last in the series is by the distinguished British architect, James Stirling. It has virtues: its interior provides a good deal of usable space, more for its size than its predecessors. But it is not a building to make the spirit soar. And this, recall, is a museum.

Or consider the buildings in which the Sociology Department has successively made its home. Again, we begin with a characteristic building of its time, Emerson Hall (Guy Lowell, 1900), quite similar in its red brick and limestone to the Fogg Museum. And we move to a massive, fifteen-story building by the architect Minoru Yamasaki, again no unknown: he was the designer of the World Trade Center in New York City, the two towers that were for a time the tallest buildings in the world. His building (1963) reflects one of those modest twists in the history of the international style—an effort to bring back a touch of something like decoration or ornament, to reduce somewhat the boring effect of the bare box. It is generally disliked. It doesn't have enough elevators, as seems true of all tall academic buildings. Its plaza seems pointless—swept by strong winds in winter, broiling in summer. It relates to nothing else at Harvard. It produces windstorms around its base because it is so high in an area where all the other buildings are low.

Or consider another sequence, the buildings that have housed the Graduate School of Design and its predecessors. The first, by a distinguished American Beaux-Arts architect, Richard Morris Hunt, was unfortunately torn down in the 1970s: it looked grand, and the people who lived and worked in it liked it, but it had little usable space behind its large entry hall. A more functional building, Robinson Hall (McKim, Mead, and White, 1904), replaced it. It matches the brick and limestone Emerson Hall, which forms the opposite side of the square on which it sits, and it is respectful to it: it is roughly the same shape and height, and of the same materials. But then a new structure was built, designed by the major contemporary Australian architect John Andrews, Gund Hall. It is a long expanse of concrete, its upper section, with narrow strips of window, overhanging the street and supported on thin concrete columns. Its rear is a giant glass staircase, running from the top of the building to its base, covering the drafting spaces of the students, and quite striking at night when students are at work. But its interior spaces seem cut up, unshaped, and left over, as they so often do in contemporary signature buildings, which express a single major idea—in this case, clearly the cascade of drafting rooms, covered by the great glass staircase. It was rebuilt at great expense, only a few years after it was erected, owing to some functional problems.

I am not stacking the deck in this little tour of a portion of my home grounds. Stirling, Yamasaki, and Andrews are no minor contemporary architects. One can stack it by going to the Cambridge courthouses, another sequence of buildings put up to house the same functions. The first building was perhaps the work of James Bulfinch, a well-known early nineteenth-century architect of Boston and Massachusetts. It is a modest and pleasing structure, of red brick, symmetrical, with a tower, suited to the small town Cambridge then was. The second is a rather grander structure, late nineteenth-century, with giant redbrick columns. The third, a building of the seventies, is simply a horror. It is of varied materials, tall, with no sense of dignity or grandeur. Its only virtue may be that its mean and low and hardly visible entry fulfills government requirements for access by the handicapped.

Across the river in Boston, one sees the same falling off of the modern against the old. There is the grand Boston Public Library of McKim, Mead, and White, and its new addition, of the same size, by Philip Johnson. Its exterior and interior are bare and functional. Perhaps the architects of the first had a more substantial budget for art and ornament, but the addition is certainly a falling off, in grace, in amenity, and in the response of the public, which loves the first, and makes use of the second. Or consider the old stone city hall, preserved for offices and a restaurant, and its replacement in concrete by Kallmann and McKinnell. The Old City Hall is no masterpiece. The new, striking when first built, seems now ungainly and odd. It sits on a plaza much too large for Boston, with its hot summers and cold winters. Subsequent efforts to make it of some use have not been successful.

Some of the things for which contemporary architects are criticized emerge from these contrasts. They don't relate themselves to what has gone before. When they claim they do, ordinary folk don't see the relationship. The architects of Emerson Hall, Robinson Hall, and the Fogg Museum created a square with their buildings. Each successive building related to the first building put up in this area, Sever Hall, by a truly distinguished American architect working in the 1870s, Henry Hobson Richardson. Even though the four buildings' construction spanned fifty years, each successor architect to Richardson seemed to make some acknowledgment—in the use of a common material, brick, or a common height, or siting the building so that it took into account the fact that other buildings were there—to what had gone before. The Cambridge courthouses, before the monstrosity of the newest, also related to each other, and this over a longer period of a hundred years. They, too, were all in brick and, even if of different scale, in their siting acknowledged another building's presence. Which is why a pleasant little park or square can now be placed between the two earlier courthouses. Nothing of any charm or interest will ever be placed around the new courthouse. Its design makes that impossible.

A second problem of our newer buildings emerges from this little tour: *scale*. New replacements are generally larger, much larger, than the older buildings, and scale presents difficulties. It is true that more students must be housed, more faculty, more research facilities, more judges, courts, and trials. The old buildings simply will not do because they are too small, and we would not want really—unless we are truly utopian—to cut down on the size of our universities and colleges, to restrict the number of our students, to limit access to the courts, or to reduce the size of our jails. All this is a product both of the increase of our populations—which may be seen as either desirable or unfortunate, but is a given fact—and of the greater access of more people today to the goods of society: its colleges and universities, its courts and public services, its libraries and museums. So all these institutions expand and must build on a scale that creates difficulties.

Huge buildings we admire were built in the past too. So there are other things besides scale that are problematic. One of them is that the features which used to structure scale for the eye, manage scale—systems of ornament and decoration—are no longer available to contemporary architects. So we are confronted by the huge height of buildings of repeated floors, the extended ranges of windows of unchanging size and type, the expanse of boring walls.

Scale is a problem. The most admired composition of buildings and spaces in the United States is the University of Virginia by Thomas Jefferson. Our third president was also a great architect and designer. He had many virtues. No one disputes the elegance and beauty of Jefferson's "academical village," with its two rows of modest structures, facing each other across a beautiful lawn, with one end closed by an exquisite domed building, the Rotunda, originally designed for a library. But no library of any size could now be fitted into it, or into many other domed buildings once built for libraries, whether the Radcliffe Camera at Oxford, the British Museum, or the Library of Congress. Why must it be so big, asked Prince Charles when he was shown the main office building of Canary Wharf in London. Alas, it can't be helped. Things must be bigger. Bigger may mean a greater opportunity for more grandeur and impact, a truly powerful statement of what it is that the building is trying to symbolize—government, learning, culture. But when combined with the dictates of modernism, it sets the architect a problem he finds it hard to meet.

Scale means that the attention to detail characterizing all great architecture must simply go by the board most of the time. The work is disaggregated and parceled out to many designers. In addition, the contemporary large building must to a great degree be shaped by contemporary practical needs, determined by structural engineers, air-conditioning and heating engineers, experts in electrical and electronic and communications facilities, and so forth. The architect is limited to the big picture in broad outline. When one considers, in the history of architecture, the degree of attention given by great figures in the past to the single facade of a church—the type of column, the decoration of a window, the placement and size of doorways—and when one reads how the details of these facades were disputed over decades and centuries, one realizes that modern building is a very different matter.

There are some architects today who believe, as Ruskin did, that they should be craftsmen and builders of their work as well as architects, and involved in every detail of their designs. The work of the theorist Christopher Alexander suggests that, and he has followers in Berkeley and elsewhere. But the architect who believes he must pay attention to every detail, or, even more, work with his own hands on his designs, must expect to live on his earnings as a teacher and writer and foundation grantee, rather than as an architect. As one contemporary admirer of Ruskin writes, "It is easy to understand why the entrepreneur-architects of Ruskin's day regarded him as `a malevolent of the worst description.' His visual criteria, if taken to heart, would have reduced them to spending a lifetime on two, perhaps three buildings; and while such a proceeding might have resulted in architecture comparable in aesthetic qualities with the medieval and early Renaissance buildings which had trained Ruskin's eye and established his tastes, the results, in terms of the architects' incomes, would have been disastrous."[5]

[5] John Unrau, *Looking at Architecture with Ruskin* (Toronto: University of Toronto Press, 1978), p. 138.

Another contemporary feature evident from our little tour is the range of new materials the architect has to choose from. All the early buildings I have referred to offered the architect few alternatives in terms of material to build with. It was brick or stone or wood. And if it was to be brick or stone or wood, the building wall naturally broke down into small units: courses of brick or stone, wooden siding or shingles, all a help in moderating large scale. The unbroken expanses of concrete of William James Hall and Gund Hall were not available, and neither were the glass and metal so typical of contemporary large buildings. The materials for building were given by the site and place, with few alternatives: in Cambridge it was generally brick, which was even used for sidewalks; in other places it might be local stone or wood. Can we deny ourselves the opportunities offered by new materials? I think not. If we were limited to hand-laid brick or cut stone, it would be impossible to build on the scale we need. Individually, we can withdraw. We can build new colleges on the scale of Jefferson's University of Virginia, for three hundred students and twenty faculty. But that won't answer the needs of the many thousands who clamor for entry.

We cannot imagine society's adopting a self-denying ordinance and rejecting access to steel and aluminum and bronze and titanium and glass and concrete and plastics, or whatever variants of these or other building materials are now available. This may mean that the buildings leak, or the windows pop out, or the concrete is marred by ugly rain stains, or that we find it harder than we expected to heat and cool and clean the building—and all these things have happened, because no new building material has undergone the long testing period of stone, brick, and wood. Nonetheless, both our desire to explore new possibilities and, even more, cost, must lead us to the use of new materials. But it certainly makes the life of the architect harder.

The most striking difference between the earlier buildings I have referred to and the newer ones is, of course, the absence of decorative detail. Whatever ornament and decoration might do for our large buildings using new materials, the fact is that our architects can no longer accept the legitimacy of ornamenting a building. "Ornament," John Ruskin insisted, was the essence of architecture. He was disputed on this by architects even in the mid-nineteenth century: no, the essence was (as it was called then) "proportion"—namely, arrangement of space. I think we would agree that Ruskin had a rather eccentric view of the relationship between architecture and ornament. But our contemporary view is at the opposite extreme. "Ornament is crime" and "less is more" are the guiding principles of modernist architecture, of the international style, and, despite a few weak efforts to modify them, they are still the prevailing practice. We may add a pyramid or dome or some other vaguely familiar form to the top of an office building, justifying it because it houses the air-conditioning or the huge blocks that limit the building's swaying in the wind. We will commission a sculptor to put an appropriately huge piece in the courtyard or lobby, or a weaver or ceramicist to make an enormous piece to cover the vast expanse of an office or hotel lobby wall. But the works of art will sit there, in the lobby or on the wall, like irrelevant intrusions, linked to the building only by the contemporaneity

of their creation, but by nothing that organically, struc-
turally, or aesthetically connects one with the other.[6]

Ornament, decoration, whether the modest arrangements around doors in Georgian style that Ruskin execrated, or the elaborate structural carving that he insisted
was an essential feature of building, is simply out. We
might have a modest arrangement of lines in the cast concrete or cut and polished stone that make up the curtain
walls of our buildings, as in William James Hall, but they
will generally look silly. If we cannot get sensual satisfaction from the materials themselves—the thin slabs of
stone or marble so commonly used to cover large buildings today, or the shiny metal—nothing else will be provided. Not only would it embarrass architects to design
decorative detail or call for it; they wouldn't know how
to do it, and there would be no craftsmen to provide it.
The workmen who once carved and sculpted what seem
like acres of decorated surface simply don't exist. They
have been replaced by a few artists or craftsmen, whose
cost is such that we can use them only for that odd piece
that we stick in front of or in the lobbies of our buildings
to show that we still believe in art (in any case, the government may require that a certain percentage of the cost
go for art), or for restoration.

We may wonder—we should wonder—why societies
that were once poorer, much poorer, than our own, could

----

[6] The problem of integrating modern art into modern buildings has, of
course, as is true of many of the points I make, been noted effectively before. Thus Venturi and his colleagues write in *Learning from Las Vegas* (Cambridge: MIT Press, 1977): "The integration of the arts in Modern architecture has always been called a good thing. But one does not paint *on*
Mies. . . . Sculpture was in or near but seldom on the building" (p. 7).

erect such elaborate structures that even maintaining them is beyond our capacities. Whatever the explanation, that is the fact. The replacement costs of our past great civic monuments would boggle the mind. The restoration and maintenance costs already do. One reason for this peculiar development that we would not decry must be that the cost of labor, of skilled and unskilled labor, has gone up relative to other costs. Our modern, democratic, industrialized societies no longer reduce workmen to subsistence, as the economic theorists of the Victorian age asserted was inevitable under the pressure of economic forces. Perhaps this is the final nail in the coffin of great architecture.

So much of all this is beyond the architect's control. He is not responsible for the greater scale at which buildings must be built. He is not responsible for the flow of new materials with which he must contend. He is not responsible for the decline or disappearance of craftsmen, or for their having achieved a level of income that makes their use too costly. And there is much else I have not discussed. He is not responsible for the automobile's ubiquity, as a result of which many of our public facilities must be located within acres of parking, so that the tight weave of older cities is torn up and cannot be replaced, and the entries of some of our major public complexes are turned into voids for automobile entry rather than portals for people. He is not responsible for what seems to be a social decision to simply spend comparatively less on building. This must be a factor, though there has been little discussion of it. The replacement costs of great nineteenth- and early twentieth-century buildings would be enormous. The restoration of the Statue of Liberty in the 1980s cost

$80 million—and recall we had available for sprucing up this great monument modern inventions, such as cranes and power tools and helicopters, that the original builders did not. The restoration of the entry building at Ellis Island—built by government for utilitarian purposes, the processing of immigrants—cost $140 million. What would its original cost in contemporary dollars have been? The restoration of Grand Central Station in New York City cost $400 million. What would it cost to build anew?

Dictators can decree enormous and costly structures: democratic leaders cannot, and responsible business leaders today, dependent on shareholders and banks, and threatened by takeover artists, cannot either. Whether it was that earlier stages of our society placed greater value on religious and public buildings; or were so arranged politically and socially that elite leaders could impose these enormous costs without restraints; or whether it was that the cost-benefit calculus which we use today for everything—the size of our defense establishment, or the relative benefit of roads and public transit, or jails and rehabilitation—simply wasn't available or wasn't considered suitable: for whatever reason, our attitudes to costs are different. When the Bishop of New York some years ago wanted to complete the Cathedral of St. John the Divine, built on traditional principles and designed to be the largest Gothic cathedral in the world, he was much attacked: why not spend the money on the poor and homeless? He found an ingenious response: he would take unemployed poor and minority youngsters from the neighborhood and train them to be stonecutters! (He had to import master stonecutters from England to start the process.) It was still considered an eccentric decision.

Because he cannot control so many features that determine our building today, the architect or architectural critic might be tempted to become a social reformer, as Ruskin did, or as Lewis Mumford did. Since it is society that decrees large scale, new materials, the decay of craftsmanship, modest costs for public uses, let us rebuild society. A great temptation: but in a democratic society the architect, even if he conceives himself as a prince, has no greater right or power to reform society than does anyone else, and less mandate than our political leaders.

But the architect does not get off the hook that easily if we try to understand contemporary failures in public building. The architect today, in addition to his responsibility for the functional aspect of building, aims at seeing himself as an artist, as he indeed always did. Perhaps he sees himself as an artist even more today because so much of the responsibility for construction is in the hands of other professionals. If he sees himself as an artist, he must be influenced by the contemporary understanding of what an artist is, that is, one who expresses an individual vision. This reflects what has happened to art generally. The modern sculptor or painter, even when he uses public funds on a public commission, does not want to compromise his individual vision, however incomprehensible it may be to others. If he is well enough known, he need not compromise it.

The architect as artist worked well enough when architects designed within traditions that limited and guided them. These traditions were expressed in the dominant style of the time. They imposed restraint; but they guaranteed that whatever came out would achieve large acceptance, because these traditions were also familiar to the elites who made decisions, and to the people who used buildings. These traditions simply don't exist anymore. For the serious architect every new major commission is a temptation to shape a new vision. He responds like the painter or sculptor, expressing himself, and is rather disdainful of those who don't understand the new vision, the new form, the new shape. And thus we have the disorder and confusion that recent work at Harvard exemplifies.

We can tolerate the varied forms of personal vision and expression of the painter or sculptor: we can look at his creations or pass them by. (Unless they obtrude upon us, whether we will or not, as in the case of some particularly objectionable contemporary public sculpture.) We cannot be as indifferent to the individual vision of the architect. It may conflict with the individual vision of the architect who put up the last building—of a different material, or scale. The architect with a strong commitment to his vision for the most part simply turns his back on the fact that there are other buildings there, and this contributes to making as disorderly and disorganized a city as we have ever seen.

••

So much has changed; but much also remains the same, and it is this that justifies some consideration and respect for the examples of the past, when we lived in societies more ordered by restraint. In the public life, many functions are still conducted at the same scale as a hundred years ago, indeed in antiquity. The trial still involves a relatively small number of actors, and we still limit the number of observers present. The classroom and auditorium are still what they were. The deliberative assembly has not increased in size to keep up with the numbers of citizens. The same chambers that served the state a hundred years ago can serve it today. Fifty or a hundred thousand could gather in Rome for their spectacles; and the same number gather today in our cities for ours, and very much, one would think, for the same reasons. Whatever the impact of distant viewing through television, there is an excitement in the actual presence of our fellow human beings that ensures we will always have an audience for games and contests, athletic as well as political.

The main reason we gather in public spaces is for commerce—to buy, to sell, to display, to bargain—and this was as true in the great cities we built in the past as it is today. This is a different use of public space from that required by the public business of the state, demanding different structures, serving different functions, but it has become the dominant form of public building today. The buildings we construct for our commercial and business functions shape the centers of our cities, whether Boston or Shanghai, and one suspects that business and commerce, private functions, simply play a much greater role in our lives than they once did. Where churches and city halls and capitols once dominated the skylines of our cities, office buildings now do. We can admire those earlier skylines only in engravings or photographs, or in a few preserved earlier cities.

We are commercial societies, and it is not surprising that we allow so much of the creation of our public space to be dominated by commercial interests. However, this need not lead to inferior public space, or space indifferent to public needs. Indeed, private interests on occasion build more extravagantly than the public builds for itself: the extravagance can be justified by the argument that it attracts more customers or clients or tenants. Further, the citizenry, through the increasingly complex system of public controls, through the numerous powers public authorities can employ to safeguard the environment, in effect plays a role in determining design. The public can bargain with the private interests to get the space that it seems unwilling to provide for itself by direct taxation. It can trade off permission to build higher for public arcades or theaters, as is done in New York City and elsewhere, and these means of getting public space do not necessarily lead to more poorly designed or less useful public space than do direct public measures. (They may contribute to a crowding and overbuilding that are detrimental, but the public has power to remedy this, too, for it is public zoning allowances that set the floor on the basis of which the private builder bargains with the public authorities for the right to build more.)

If we are unhappy with our public space, its quantity and its quality, we must look into ourselves for the remedy. The private builder builds with our permission. It is our own representatives who determine what facilities to provide for themselves and for us. However one struggles with the problem of public architecture, it is hard to escape the conclusion that the answer to improving it lies in the raising of public taste. However well kings or despots or robber barons or civic aristocracies may have done in the past, we don't have them anymore in our Western democratic societies. (And where they still exist, they in no way create marvels of public architecture.) Taste is the final arbiter, the taste not only of architects and their direct clients, of elected leaders, appointed officials, private corporations, but of the public in general, which can intervene today so easily at so many places in the process of planning and design.

To educate and raise taste seems like an unimaginably difficult task, and yet it has happened. Consider the example of the preservation movement. Would it be possible to tear down Pennsylvania Station in New York today? Hardly. We have financial benefits for remodeling historic landmarks that we did not have in 1963, which has permitted the restoration and reuse of huge nineteenth- and early twentieth-century railroad stations; we have more effective means of legal intervention, as was demonstrated in the successful suit to prevent a tower from being placed on top of Grand Central Station; and supporting both we have a public that appreciates architecture more, even if it can be bamboozled and confused by publicity and false authority. We have, as another example of the raising of taste, well-written architectural guides to almost every major city in the United States. Hard as it may be to believe, there were no such guidebooks to American cities forty years ago. It was as if only Europe had architecture, and we had only structures for temporary use that it was not worth recording and appreciating. Indeed, this aspect of the education of taste has worked so well that it is now a toss-up whether we do not appreciate the buildings of the past too much, making it difficult to adapt our cities to the present.

Admittedly it is easier to educate public taste to the virtues of the past—the buildings, after all, are already there, and the appreciations have already been written— than to educate it to make decisions for the future.

We are left with our greatest difficulty in public building. We can appreciate and preserve the buildings of the past. But how do we build for our public functions today? We have abandoned the language of classical architecture, of pediments and columns, which served to indicate great public functions in Western architecture for twenty-five hundred years. Occasionally forgotten or decried, this architectural language returned again and again, to serve as the symbol of our greatest aspirations in public life. We seem to have no replacement. The fainthearted and short-lived effort to remind us of those classical elements in "postmodernist" architecture was entirely unsatisfying, though it was sometimes entertaining. It built stage sets, which looked as if they would have no longer life than stage sets.

We can preserve the buildings of the past. We can't build them again. The language of the past can be admired and studied; its loss can be, and is, regretted; but too much has changed for it to serve us today. We are suspended between a language that cannot be used and a language—the language of modernism—that is unsatisfying for major public purposes, but for which we have no replacement.

I think the first steps toward a more satisfactory language have been taken. We have developed a proper respect for the achievements in public building of the past. We have become emboldened in criticizing the failures in public building of modernism. But whether contemporary architects can move toward and develop a more satisfactory language for public architecture is the great question.

We can find the words to describe the building we want. In one formulation—that of Daniel P. Moynihan, writing for a committee dealing with the mundane problem of providing federal office space forty-five years ago—"the policy shall be to provide . . . facilities in an architectural style and form which is distinguished and which will reflect the dignity, enterprise, vigor and stability of the American National Government." Grand words. But can we find the physical form that embodies them?

CHAPTER TWO

The Prince, the People, and the Architects

The Prince of Wales, in his speeches and book, *A Vision for Britain*, attacking modernist architects for buildings they have constructed in the postwar years in Britain, aroused an uproar among architects. One writer in the leading British architectural journal *Architectural Review* even found the source of the prince's taste in the architecture of Nazi Germany. He reproduced some pictures of new housing from a German publicity handout of 1940, and sure enough they show single-family, attached, homes with pitched roofs on their own little plots. Because the Nazis preferred single-family houses to apartment blocks, he finds a "precedent for the Prince." Of course we find the same preference in Pare Lorentz's famous movie, *The City*, made for the New York World's Fair in 1939, or in the books and articles of the reformers Clarence Stein and Lewis Mumford, advocating planned communities of low density for families. And these were no Nazis. But architects give the prince no quarter.

Another architectural critic in the *New Republic* took the prince to task for colonialism, racism, and imperialism because he likes classical architecture and would prefer to see more classical elements in contemporary building. In this storm of denunciation, the prince could find satisfaction only in the fact that the ordinary people seemed to agree with him, and that his critics were hysterical.

Which raises a paradox: How is it possible that modernist architecture, which began with deep social concerns, and one of whose themes was proper housing for workers to improve their lot, now requires an elitist defense, arguing that only properly qualified, professionally trained experts should discuss and criticize architecture? How did a socially concerned architecture come to be condemned, fifty years later, as soulless, bureaucratic, and inhuman—a critique that received wide acceptance among ordinary folk who enthusiastically and overwhelmingly applauded the prince's attacks on contemporary architecture?

It was in the thirties that modern ideas in architecture first began to filter back, with some influence, to the United States. Americans returning from Europe began to bring us news of the modern movement. Some of them were mostly interested in the new stripped-down, unornamented, "functional" aesthetic forms, but others were more interested in housing for workers. Catherine Bauer's *Modern Housing* had a great influence on concerned architects, on planners, and on the early public housing movement. She brought back pictures of the new housing being built in Europe by socialist or socially concerned governments. We looked at the pictures with admiration. Instead of the messy working-class districts we knew in American cities, with their crowded buildings built right up against the street line, with their mixture of housing and stores and pushcarts and signs, with their sidewalks crowded with pedestrians and horses—there were not many cars in poor areas then—we saw simple blocks of buildings, in modern styles, oriented to catch the sun, with ample space around each block.

Yet today these once-admired building models for workers from Germany and Holland and England would not find many admirers; without knowing when or under what regime they were built, most people would prefer those individual homes, shown in the Nazi publicity pamphlet. And many architects would agree. Moshe Safdie, in his book *Form and Purpose* (1982), shows pictures of Israeli apartment complexes on the hills around Jerusalem, built under a social democratic government. And he contrasts them unfavorably with Arab housing built without benefit of modernism, or government housing programs for the poor and low-income groups. In other words, the product of architectural concern for the working classes looks like pretty poor stuff to us today.

What seemed in the 1930s and early post–World War II decades to be responsive to social needs—and indeed *was* responsive to social needs as far as architects and planners and socially minded governments could discern them at the time—now seems to us inhumane, soulless, bureaucratic.

It is a very upsetting development, if we are concerned to have architects take more account of social considerations, that the housing produced at a time when architects were most socially minded now appears to us pretty poor stuff. Were we wrong then about what was good housing for the poor, and are we right now? And if our tastes have changed so radically, is it possible that they will change again, and that we were right then and are wrong now?

Consider a concrete example of how our tastes and judgments about housing for the poor have changed since the thirties. There is an aerial photograph, much reproduced in reformist books on housing and urbanism, of one of our first housing projects, the Williamsburg houses in Brooklyn, set in the midst of a sea of slums and tenements. We see from the air the endless grid of streets, lined with unbroken rows of tenements. We can see in the middle of each block, if we look closely, something rather fuzzy—the backyards behind the tenements of each block. In the middle of the photograph a dozen blocks have been cleared away, obliterating tenements and streets, and set on this white and empty site are lined up slabs of housing, placed at an angle to the street grid, as if to remind us that the original street grid was set down by soulless, market-minded surveyors. These new houses for the workers are presumably sited scientifically to catch the sun, or for some other good reason that caused their designers to ignore the original street grid. Around the buildings is an expanse of empty land, which will be dedicated to playgrounds and greenery. I recall, as a social-minded, and socialist, youth, looking at this picture, proud at what had been done, worried about how long it would take to clear away the surrounding sea of slums.

When that photograph was first published, the tenements represented the terrible past, the housing project the future. We all know what housing projects represent to us today. Those older buildings, if they have survived, are now often more desirable not only to poor people but to middle-class people too.

What explains this upsetting reversal of taste? Is it a matter of designers' idiosyncrasies, a fad, a fashion, which prefers the remaining tenements and brownstones of New York—properly remodeled, of course—to the housing that was built as part of a great social experiment? That social experiment incorporated, to the extent this could be done in the practical world of bureaucrats and financial limitations, the thinking of socially concerned architects and planners. Is it that we simply and irrationally love strong cornices, stoops, columns, heavy lintels, strongly marked sills, the occasional decoration that graced even the workers' housing of the early twentieth century?

If that explains the reversal of taste, it would be irresponsible of us to prefer the old. But it turns out that the old is *also* preferable to many of the people for whom the new subsidized public housing was built. Now we must avoid the mistake of explaining people's preferences for one kind of housing or another solely on the basis of differences in design. People with few choices don't decide on the basis of design. If we were to ask them, they might say the project is less safe, or has too many drug-addicted and delinquent families, or that they want to live near their mothers, or they might give some other reason that relates to the social composition of the project or the bureaucratic rules under which it operates. Or if they prefer the project—and many do—we might find out it's because it is comparatively so cheap as a result of its subsidies, and not because of its design and more spacious surroundings.

Design isn't everything. But design does play a role not only in the distaste of present-day designers and architects and planners for the results of the socially concerned architects and planners of the past, but in the preferences of the people with limited choices who reject or accept them today.

And so we have our problem: why is it that the sophisticated intelligence of socially minded architects and planners didn't produce satisfactory environments for those
with the least choice? Even worse: why is it, as my example suggests, that environments built by commercial
builders, trying to simply make a profit as best they could,
so often beat out architects' environments in terms of appeal to ordinary people? Now that is something one has
to ponder. It is all too easy to understand why the environments created by anonymous architects on Greek islands, in Italian hill towns, in Moroccan cities, are so
much more attractive to architects and designers today
than what either sophisticated modernists or postmodernists create. That problem is a familiar one, and we have
answers that are more or less satisfactory. The town grew
organically over time, in one traditional style, with one
major traditional building material; it enclosed a life defined by a traditional culture. What resulted impresses all
architects and designers, of whatever persuasion. In years
of leafing through architectural books and magazines, I
have never yet seen a picture of one of these Mediterranean urban environments that was used to illustrate a *bad*
environment. Every architect or designer loves them. It
is only reformers who are unsophisticated as designers,
generally native, who want to sweep them away because
of crowding, or dirt, or limited air, sun, and parking, and
replace them with the building blocks that have become
the uniform residence of people all over the world.

So we understand well enough why these environments have become so attractive to us. We know why, or
can guess why, even the modern displaced Arab, who does
know about other ways of building, who can use a variety

of materials, who has to build his housing fast rather than over centuries, and who may want to accommodate cars, seems to build a better environment, according to Moshe Safdie, than the Israeli government agencies, with their advanced Western-trained architects and designers, modern standards, up-to-dateness in all respects.

For an architect to lose out to the Arab—or any other traditional builder of the vernacular housing of a traditional culture—in the way of producing good housing is not so devastating: after all, we are up against all that traditional wisdom, developed over the ages. But to lose out to the *commercial* builder is another matter, and one that cannot make the sophisticated designer-architect very happy. And yet very often the commercial builder beats out the architect-designer.

The question is why—and I suspect the answers will teach us more than we can learn from the Mediterranean village or the other wonderful works of the vernacular builder.

Consider two examples of this competition between the commercial builder, with no higher ambition than to produce what will sell or rent, and the sophisticated architect-designer. The first comes from England, and it is the case of the town of Sunderland, a shipbuilding and coal-mining town, fallen on hard times, in which old housing was cleared away for new development in the period after World War II. England, we should recall, stood in the first few decades after the war at the forefront of planning internationally, and at the forefront of Europe in the provision of good housing for the working classes. It was a Mecca for all interested in good planning and in sensible replacement of housing stock. The case of

Sunderland has been described in a fascinating book by Norman Dennis, *People and Planning*.

The worst housing, of course, went first, and there seems to have been little opposition to clearing it; after all, all those who lost their housing were guaranteed new, well-subsidized, modern housing. By 1965, the worst of the slums had been cleared, but central government money was still available for going further, and planners selected the areas—by their standards—that should be leveled, with the people rehoused in new modern flats. By this time, the resistance was severe. Why? Consider the houses that were coming down, to be replaced by modern flats. They are typical of the row houses for workers of the dreary industrial towns of England. These "cottages," as they were called in Sunderland, were built for the working class by unnamed builders a hundred years ago. Many were rented, but most were by this time owned by their inhabitants. The houses sit directly on the sidewalk. There are no trees on the street. There is no front yard. We find an entry and a bow window on the first floor, and if there's a second, as some have, two more windows above. There is a tiny backyard with a brick outhouse. What could possess people to prefer these anonymous and styleless dwellings to new flats, heavily subsidized to boot? But if we look more closely, we see that one facade has been stuccoed, another left in brick. One entry has a flat top, another an arched one. Some windows have heavily marked lintels, top and bottom. Others have the lintels stuccoed over. At the end of one block, in a unit identical to the others, is the Gardener's Arms, a pub.

We can understand some of the reasons why people preferred to stay, and some of them have nothing to do with architects or designers. They had lived there a long time. They had their friends there. They had their local stores to shop in, their churches and chapels. All this would be hard to replace in the new areas where they were to be rehoused. They were close to the center of town, with plenty of buses. In the new outlying areas to which they would have to move, there were fewer buses, running infrequently. And a center still has advantages, however modest the town, for convenience, for liveliness. Many of those to be rehoused owned their own cottages, and could do with them what they liked, and arrange them to their taste. They were no longer crowded. But after all this, what is striking is that housing built with ostensibly no attention to the occupants' tastes and desires, thrown up to cover the most land and make the most money, using the materials and technology of the 1870s, was considered superior by many of those living in them to the new flats designed by the best planning authorities using good architects. Imagine what the cooking, bathing, and toileting facilities of such cottages were. The W.C.'s were typically out in the backyard, and the cottages had no bathtubs. Here was not the unfair competition of the Greek isles or the Italian hill towns—it was ordinary working-class, uninspired housing, and yet the residents preferred it.

Could they have been provided with something that gave them the advantages of the old houses they had, and which eliminated the very striking disadvantages? Very likely. But we have some evidence that a taste for a proper modern style on the part of the architects made a close replacement impossible. The local authorities were committed to flats:

In discussing with the relevant officers the reasons for choosing flats as a form of development in Sunderland the interviewer was told that "high-rise blocks are essential to the skyline of the town." Seven blocks of 16-storied flats were built at Gilley Law, on the outskirts of the town, as a result of an "aesthetic choice."[1]

One is stunned at the thought of sixteen-story apartment houses in Sunderland, where the top density of the area to be cleared (two-story houses) was only sixty-eight rooms per acre. Most of the rehousing was to be done in modest three-story flats. Yet the residents also opposed that.

So we can well understand why many of the people of Sunderland preferred to stay in their old houses and their old neighborhoods. They even argued that their disadvantages were advantages. The fact that the main window was right on the pavement, they said, meant more "privacy." "Passers-by don't get the chance to look in— they are past too quickly."

We understand that everyone prefers a place of his own, with his own front door and backyard. We also understand that when we build at the high densities of large cities, not everyone can have them. But consider a dense city, Manhattan. We find that even the commercially built housing of New York City had virtues that new housing could not provide.

The plan for Manhattan has been denounced by every sophisticated planner. As Lewis Mumford, and others, argued, the checkerboard plan was designed for easy mar-

---

[1] Norman Dennis, *People and Planning: The Sociology of Housing in Sunderland* (London: Faber and Faber, 1970), p. 214.

keting of properties. With streets and avenues coming at fixed intervals, each block was the same size, and each could be reduced to the same property modules for easy marketing. There were no odd-sized lots, and modules could be cumulated for larger property sizes. And so the peculiar Manhattan block, with its long and narrow street side, its short side on a wide avenue, broken into twenty-by-one-hundred-foot building lots. The plan required no sophistication—no diagonal streets, no adaptation to topography. And it turned out that utilizing it for commercial building required no sophistication either. The brownstone town house was invented for the upper middle classes, and put up by the thousands; the tenement and other apartment houses were invented for the working classes, and put up by the thousands. For grandeur, a few lots were put together for the town houses of Fifth Avenue, and later for huge apartment houses, a half block or block in size, on Park Avenue and on other avenues.

No one has ever had a good word for this nondesign, this simple adaptation to market needs—until we started destroying it. Then we discovered that the brownstones could provide good living quarters, even when they were broken up to house a half dozen or more families; that the tenements, once the severe overcrowding was remedied—that is generally the most serious problem in housing for the poor—also provided good living space. For a child growing up in these tenements, there was really no serious problem except crowding. The street side of the tenement provided life, variety, play spaces around stoops, even play spaces in the streets, before the traffic became heavy. Marbles could be rolled along the curbside. (I was always mystified at how kids could play mar-

PRINCE CHARLES AND MODERNISM 59

bles without a convenient curb along which to roll them.) On the other side of the tenement were the quiet backyards. They even had trees. Despite the crowding in the tenements, these backyards, completely surrounded by buildings that by law could not occupy the entire building space, and cut off on all sides from street and avenue, were quiet. These interior spaces are still surprisingly quiet in the midst of the noise of Manhattan—if, that is, people are not playing their TVs too loud.

Two kinds of structure have replaced them, insofar as they have been replaced for residential purposes rather than commercial and business purposes: we have public housing projects, built tall to reserve the largest amount of space possible for greenery and parking and to open up the apartments to more light and air; and more crowded unsubsidized apartment houses, built on a huge scale compared to the old brownstones and tenements, on large plots. The former reflect public decisions, partially unconstrained by market costs, while the latter represent market decisions under a variety of constraints that are more severe than those that limited the earlier buildings. Both, I would argue, have provided worse living quarters in some respects than their predecessors.

The story I have told is not one confined to New York City.

Herbert Gans, in his book *The Urban Villagers*, described the tenements of the West End of Boston, the area adjacent to Massachusetts General Hospital, before they were torn down to be replaced by modern apartment houses. The houses of the West End were quite similar to the tenement areas of New York, except that the buildings were somewhat lower and smaller. If we look at the pictures in *The Urban Villagers*, we find units not very different from Little Italy in New York, or the West Village tenements. Again, once the overcrowding of poverty was relieved, the people living there found their condition perfectly satisfactory—indeed, more than satisfactory. They fiercely resisted being driven out of their homes for new development for others.

Of course their satisfaction—like the satisfaction of the brownstone and tenement dwellers of New York—was not provided only or perhaps not even primarily by the design of their houses. One must take into account the fact that they had lived there a long time, and had their shopping places and churches and friends and relatives nearby. They also paid low rents for their older quarters. But I would insist that there were aspects of *design* in these apparently undesigned working-class areas that helped provide these satisfactions: they had a handful of neighbors on an entry, rather than twenty or thirty; they were closer to the ground, in three-, four-, and five-story buildings, and could watch their children at play or call to them; they had enclosed semiprivate open space—not in this case for them individually, of course, but still space in the backyards that provided a different and quiet experience—which their replacements, the towers-in-a-park design of public housing as well as the unsubsidized apartment towers, could not provide.

The point is not to praise the commercially minded builder, who is, of course, concerned with cutting costs to the bone and getting the best return on his money. It is, rather, to force us to ponder the comparison between thoughtlessness and sophistication in design at the point where it should most favor the sophisticated; to consider why private building for the incredibly poor workers of the past was preferred to the public building of our more prosperous societies for more prosperous people.

Values in design that are significant for human satisfaction seem to have been ignored by the sophisticated, who were cavalier about the characteristics and satisfactions of old neighborhoods. They were all too ready to wipe away what existed and start with a clean slate. Many preferred to, and objected to the costs of retaining some of the old and integrating it with the new. They were attached to forms, whether the high tower or the flats that look like factories or machines for living. It has been not architects but their critics—as well as resisting homeowners, tenants, and residents of old areas—who have limited mass clearance and have sparked as much rehabilitation as we have. It was not the architects who advocated rehabilitation, though to my mind rehabilitation offers designers wonderful opportunities.

Most significant, designers failed to explore just what it is people find attractive in areas and buildings for whose design characteristics not much, if anything, can be said. How often have we seen those pictures of endless Levittowns, little houses with scarcely grown trees spread out over the landscape, as horrible lessons to avoid? And how often have we contrasted them—to their disadvantage— with gleaming visions of great towers? Let us put aside for a moment the detailed economic arguments that justify density, and let us recognize that very often the overall cost of single-family homes packed closely, or apartments in low-rise buildings, would compare favorably with twenty-story apartment towers. I will not enter into the argument of comparative costs, which is in any case complicated, but studies have shown that the advantages are not always in one direction, and that often "an aesthetic choice"—to quote from the Sunderland investigation—a choice by either public authorities, designers, or commercial builders, dictates height.

So let us go back to the contrast without worrying for the moment about the economics. Levittown on one side; on the other, striking apartment towers, and they have recently been striking indeed—serpentine on the outskirts of Paris, inverted pyramids on the outskirts of Rome, or spiky concentrations of concrete on the hills of Jerusalem. Whatever criticism the architect or critic may have of the latter, they are at least "interesting." But let us look at the contrast ten or twenty years after they are completed. In Levittown the trees have grown, and various types of fences wall in back- and front yards. Some buildings sprout additions on top, some on the side; with the children gone, rooms are being remodeled from bedrooms to libraries, and so on. The apartment towers show no such opportunities for change. How could they, when their residents have so little power over their environment? The trees will grow, and the landscaping may improve—if there's money for it—but the buildings remain frozen, impervious to substantial change.

Am I saying the architect can't beat Levittown, and that there is nothing to his skill, his training, his taste, his occasional genius, that makes up for the ordinary crass effort to provide what people want in the most immediate sense at a price they can afford? No, I would not say that, but rather that the architect—although there are some remarkable and admirable exceptions—has not tried hard enough to find out what people liked, and like, whether in old slums or new developments, and to see what his skills could do to satisfy, build on, and improve upon that. I admit it is more fun to explore Greek islands and Italian hill towns than American slums and suburbs, but there is as much to learn in the latter as in the former.

Wherever social scientists examine these issues, they find a taste that architects on the whole do not find it interesting to satisfy, a taste for the low-rise, the small scale, the unit that gives some privacy, some control, some access to the ground, a small piece of land wholly under one's control. I am not, of course, describing a universal taste. But for people raising children—and indeed many others—it is a near universal taste, if people have a choice. Nor is there any reason to think that it is necessary or desirable that people be educated *against* that taste and develop a new taste for a larger or gargantuan scale. On occasion, conditions seem to make what most people want impossible, particularly in the very largest cities. New tastes are developed, and people find it is possible to adapt to tall blocks and greater density—many have, and many more will have to. Even when we adapt to such necessities, there is much to learn from how people live and use space. Nor am I convinced that the exigencies of finances or the requirements of ordinances and laws will make it impossible to provide environments people find more satisfactory.

The sociologist considering what people like and what they find satisfactory is likely to appear a real spoilsport to architects and designers, a rather glum soul who, first, tells us that they prefer their old buildings—any old buildings—to new ones, and, second, that even when you drive them out of their old buildings and they see the appeal of something new, it tends to be a homey, fussy, dowdy single-family house they prefer, rather than sparkling towers of interesting shapes or modernist structures of glass and aluminum. After all, architects and designers want to soar, to design and to build new and not yet imagined structures, and are we to confine and cabin them by what the ordinary man prefers and insists upon?

Well, to begin with, in a modern consumer society, the ordinary man will eventually get what he wants—unless it is being provided by central government, heavily subsidized, and being given to him whether he wants it or not, as in the case of council housing blocks in England or public housing in the United States. In both countries, we are now demolishing the tall blocks that were the admired model for family housing only thirty or forty years ago. But the architect and designer can still soar, because there are many more structures in the world than those required to house people and provide them with an urban environment. After all, historically the architect has soared only when he built for the rich, for the state, for the church. He still can—if these clients will let him— and in addition he now has a very substantial client who wants things big and striking, the corporation rearing its towers. Not that he should or could ignore what people want in working environments, or convening environments, or even worshiping environments, but everyone accepts the symbolic role of such structures, and one can break out without the need for an economical accommodation of needs.

And of course there are other ways of soaring, of building big, and once again one thinks of the Greek isles and Italian hill towns and Moroccan cities, in which a generally accepted approach to building, guiding development over a long period of time, has created environments to which people cling, and which delight the eyes and souls of architects and designers. But if we are to expect the accumulation of small-scale environments—and basically what I have been talking about is the virtue of the small scale—to cumulate into grand structures and environments, we probably need more changes in our society than I can envisage. Christopher Alexander and his associates have made a heroic effort to establish such a way of building for our day, in which more or less anonymous action produces large and substantial effects, and it is an effort that must arouse our sympathy and awe, even if we recognize its problems. Perhaps there is still a way for the architect to provide a process, a set of tools, a mechanism whereby individual action can cumulate to great harmonious wholes—without the architect's becoming, as so many modern form-makers have insisted, the dictator of an environment. But the only way of doing that, in the absence of dictators, is through a steady and dedicated concern with how people live, what they want, what they find desirable and attractive, and what they find troublesome and inconvenient. This knowledge must be gleaned before one builds, while one builds, after one builds. If the great scheme that says, Isn't it delightful to put everyone into a huge triangle, or an obelisk, or a sphere, has to collapse under this investigation, so be it. We can always have the drawings.

Little by little, is, I suspect, the answer, not only in building, but in public policy, where many great schemes have come crashing down.

Pondering his study of Sunderland, which he began
with the easy optimism that well-trained planners and
designers know, of course, best, Norman Dennis was
driven to another conclusion. He writes:

> As Edmund Burke said in another connection, the high
> level of satisfaction in areas like [the ones scheduled to
> be torn down] "is the result of a choice not of one day
> or one set of people. . . . It is made by the peculiar cir-
> cumstances, occasion, tempers, dispositions and moral,
> civil, and social habitudes of the people which disclose
> themselves only in a long period of time."[2]

Again, and finally from Burke: "If circumspection and
caution are part of wisdom, when we work only on inani-
mate matter, surely they become part of duty too, when
the subject of our demolition and construction is not
bricks and timber, but sentient being. The true law-
giver"—and I would add, the architect and designer too—
"ought to love and respect his kind, and to fear himself."[3]

It is this point of view, not lack of architectural exper-
tise, that connects the prince with the ordinary people
and divides him from his architect critics.

[2] Ibid., p. 298, quoting from Edmund Burke, "Reform of Representation
in the House of Commons," in *Works*, 6:47.
[3] Ibid., p. 366, quoting Edmund Burke, *Reflections on the Revolution in
France* (World Classics edition), pp. 186–87.

CHAPTER THREE

"Subverting the Context":
Olmsted's Parks and Serra's Sculpture

The age when we built great city parks, or parkways, or boulevards, is over, and has been for fifty years or more. If one has been raised in New York City or Boston, one knows how much these cities were embellished by the park and parkway designers and builders, and preeminently by Frederick Law Olmsted. Our efforts are devoted these days to retaining as much as we can of their achievements, rather than adding to them. But occasionally a new opportunity to add to our parks arises. The last major piece of "undeveloped" land on the island of Manhattan, the former railroad yards on the Hudson River between Fifty-ninth and Seventy-second Street, will, on the basis of plans worked out between Donald Trump, the developer, and community groups, provide opportunity for a park on the Hudson River. What will it be? What can it be? This was the challenge placed before student landscape architects in five major schools, and the subject of an exhibit of their answers in New York City a few years ago.

New York City and parks—the two would appear to be in as mortal competition as any two concepts one can try to juggle together. New York City is as remote from nature and the natural as any great city in the world. Its famous gridiron pattern was laid down relentlessly on what was once a rich natural environment, covering streams, leveling hills, filling valleys, straightening out a varied shoreline to serve shipping and industry and roadways. Some bits of open space were left in the gridiron plan for Manhattan, owing mostly to the odd lateral course of Broadway, running diagonally across the grid, which could not be easily changed, and which thereby left triangles as it crossed the major north-south avenues to become "parks" or "squares."

A great act of imagination and foresight reserved the central part of the island for Central Park; another great act of foresight created Prospect Park in Brooklyn. We in this country did not have a heritage of palace gardens and hunting parks of kings and great nobles to turn into green spaces for our cities. New York has no great tree-lined boulevards, with green strips, to open up the city, as we find in Continental cities, or old fortifications that can be turned into city sport-grounds and parks. Its few efforts in this direction, puny by Continental standards—Eastern Parkway in Brooklyn, the Grand Concourse in the Bronx—have fallen on hard times, as their bordering apartment houses, no matter how grand, are with difficulty prevented from becoming slums, or rehabilitated once they have become slums. Its truly large parks are some leftover spaces at the city's edges. We are grateful for them, but Van Cortlandt and Pelham Bay Park are scarcely the Bois de Boulogne, from the point of view of public investment, or symbolic meaning in the eyes of the city-dwellers.

New York City has been paved over to the point where hardly a bit of earth shows, where street trees, with whatever hope they are planted, often do not survive, in which the bushes even of Central Park—as a story some years ago told us—have to have their roots chained to some underground anchor to prevent vandals from pulling them up, in which green displays to brighten entries to public, apartment, and office buildings will have to be dispensed with in the fear they cannot survive the assaults of a polluted environment, and an uncaring, larcenous, or positively malicious citizenry. What can landscape architecture, the art of designing the fragments of open space available, of shaping plants and grass and bushes and trees and water, mean for this most relentlessly hard of cities?

Olmsted's Vision

I was born, and spent the first ten years of my life, on a tenement block in East Harlem, between Second and Third Avenues. Elevated trains then ran along both avenues, erected on iron structures. They made for intriguing photographs but a bad place to live. They were torn down in the thirties and forties, and the story was that the iron supports went to Japan to be shot back at us in World War II. There were no street trees, no green strips. That was the world I knew. But three and a half blocks to the west was Central Park. It is a part of the park, the far north, where one does not find meadows and playing fields, statues and formal elements, such as the Mall and the Bethesda Fountain and the Conservatory lake, which are all far to the south.

It is the park as Olmsted and Vaux must have envisaged it—the green relief from a crowded city, an evocation of unspoiled nature, with its trees, and springs, and boulders, and wandering lanes. It was, in a word, for someone growing up in East Harlem, wonderful, and I put the accent on "wonder." Of course Olmsted's nature was not nature in the raw, wilderness nature. Nor was it the site of Central Park as Olmsted found it. The boulders were moved to make appropriate romantic patterns evoking perhaps, in a modest way, the Catskills; the streams were shaped; the lakes were dug; the plants and trees were brought in, and I assume some were not native. The typical Olmstedian vision, the English park, with an expanse of green meadow bordered by great trees, is not easily maintained in our northeastern climate, as we are told by Anne Whiston Spirn in her fascinating book *The Granite Garden*. The rain and moisture are too irregular, the summer is too hot, and left to itself any meadow rapidly reverts to scrub, on its way to becoming forest, and the intermediate condition is not pretty.

Nevertheless, Central Park was a wonder. When one penetrated it, the skyline of the city disappeared. As a boy, frightened of getting lost in the park, I was told by my older brother that I should, when lost, climb to the highest rock and look for the great red lantern on the tall Fifth Avenue Hospital; that marked east, and I could orient myself by it to find my way out of the park. Olmsted's scheme was to ring the park with trees, so that the straight, man-made line of buildings that would in time encircle the park would be blotted out, and the park user could imagine himself in distant meadow and woodland.

It worked for me, and gave me an experience that the brick and concrete and iron city could not.

It is therefore understandable that whatever criticism the Olmstedian vision has attracted in recent years would not find favor in my eyes. And it has attracted much criticism, directly and by implication. One sees it criticized or ignored in the kinds of plans and constructions many landscape architects now favor, and in the way in which open space is managed in many new urban developments. Just such a criticism was made when the *New York Times* architecture critic, Herbert Muschamp, reviewed the proposals of the student landscape architects for the new park in Manhattan. "A Park Is Not Just Another Pretty Space," ran the title of his article. That was clearly designed to pique the interest of those, like myself, who thought that to be pretty was one of the desirable attributes, and perhaps a very important one, of urban parks. The new park will be the most important addition to usable open space in Manhattan in many years, if the project ever comes off. It will be south of Riverside Park, which runs north from Seventy-second Street on the Hudson River almost to the end of Manhattan Island. The site is now an expanse of abandoned railway yards, piers, a highway that must be rebuilt. Donald Trump planned to erect there, in headier days, the tallest building in the world, among other things. Community opposition, presumably aided by the collapse of the New York real estate market, led to a new plan that has been uniformly welcomed with admiration.

The plan consists, gratifyingly, of the extension of an old plan. It extends southward the Riverside Drive we know. There will be an unbroken serpentine row of

apartment buildings (and some office buildings) bordering the Drive on the land side, attempting to evoke the
line of apartment buildings of the 1920s that now border
the old Riverside Drive to the north, but unfortunately of
much greater height and banal design compared to the
older apartment buildings. The street plan is only common sense, which we have with pain rediscovered in recent years. We have had enough of urban superblocks
obliterating the urban street grid, thank you. So it is considered a breakthrough when a hundred-year-old design
for Riverside Drive and Park is simply continued southward into the new area made available by the decline of
rail freight traffic.

Landscape architecture students at five schools took
on, as a project, designing the new park that will occupy
the southern portion of the site. Herbert Muschamp chose
one of their proposals to illustrate his review of their
work. We see in the illustration a field of upright steel
beams, set on grass. In the background is a rusting metal
structure. This certainly illustrates the thesis of his title,
that is, that "a park is not just another pretty space." This
brutal image is chosen by Muschamp to reflect desirable
new directions for the design of open space for a city like
New York. He wrote that this display of student work
"shows great promise. The students have risen to the level
of the project's ambitious intentions. Overall, these designs are refreshingly free from formula: no modernoid
lunar landscapes with lollipop lightbulbs, no `Olmstoid'
caricatures of Frederick Law Olmsted's pioneering work
of a century ago."

In view of what I have said of my experience of Central
Park, it is understandable that I did not take lightly this

dismissal of Olmsted as a proper inspiration and influence for someone designing a park in New York today. I carry no brief for the other alternative, "modernoid lunar landscapes." But what did Muschamp mean by "Olmstoid"? The illustration he chose for his review, the gaunt upright steel beams and rusting iron, was not promising, and I decided to find out just what was happening among young practitioners of landscape architecture when they considered what was appropriate for that strange city, New York, and went to see the exhibit for myself.

It was indeed fascinating. I was reassured to learn that the Olmstedian vision is not dead. One student, from City College, writes in the description of her design: "This is a romantic design for Riverside South that harkens back to a green, Olmstedian vision of a Park as a place to commune with nature, to enjoy spectacular views and sunsets, to enjoy trees, green vistas, and quiet gardening. It is also a place, like Central Park's Bethesda Fountain, to enjoy the public theater of New York." I have no argument with that (though perhaps this student was trying to crowd too much on a twenty-one-acre plot). A few other designs are similar. But such proposals will not get any attention from Herbert Muschamp, or any other contemporary critic. Some of the students favor, and his illustration exemplifies this, a kind of industrial brutalism that reminds one of the history of the site and links one to the harsh city to the west. He particularly applauds those schemes that "propose to restore ecological balance by returning at least part of the site to its former condition as a salt marsh." He favors those that try to enlist advanced technology in the restoration or maintenance of ecological balance. Thus one scheme proposes a grove of forty windmills that would generate power to light the park at night. Another scheme combines the restoration of the salt marsh with eight windmills for energy. Some schemes recall the desolate industrial landscape bequeathed by the past, retaining some of its skeletal remains, or evoking it with chain-link fences. Some are, alternatively, highly formal. To quote one description: "An exploration of the temporal and cyclical forces of seasonal change . . . a central spiral amphitheater which generates many smaller spiralling forms." A few introduce social elements, though in different ways: one proposes a series of terraces made up of 322 ten-by-forty-foot garden plots allotted for a one-year period to individual citizens. By my count, perhaps three of twenty designs are in the Olmstedian tradition; as for the others, we find the ecological theme prominent (restoring the salt marsh), often combined with the technological. We find contemporary formalistic schemes. We find schemes emphasizing urban theater, and schemes giving the stark remains of the industrial past a large place.

I imagine the citizens of New York, even on the sophisticated West Side of New York, if given a chance, would vote for Olmsted. The students, on the whole, do not, and as a teacher I can understand that: they should explore, experiment, try even outlandish schemes. One student quotes from the fashionable French philosophers Gilles Deleuze and Felix Guattari one of those hermetic passages that current French philosophers delight in, as an introduction to his highly constructivist scheme of platforms, walkways, and ramps. He shows that in this respect students of landscape architecture are no different from students in literary criticism, sociology, philosophy, anthropology, and other fields, many of whom are now attracted by obscure and obscurantist theory. The passage that he places at the beginning of his scheme, and which we are to assume inspired or guided him, reads, "In short this limit is neither at the side of or beyond: it is a boundary between the two."

While the citizens, I would guess, would vote for Olmsted, the students would not, and one can understand that, as they search for the new, the different, the contemporary, something more suitable to our modern condition, and more suitable to the reality of New York City. But what do they find that is more suitable? Behind the surface characteristics of the non-Olmstedian schemes—ecological, industrial-archaeological, urban theatrical, formalistic—one detects two basic theoretical underpinnings. One is to extend some aspect of the existing city, and by extending it to assert that the pastoral, the shaped countryside, can no longer be part of the meaningful experience of urban man. The jagged or angular or spiral forms, the ramps and walkways, all represent the artificiality of urban life, its nervousness, its disorder, its remoteness from the organic, the tranquil, the quiet, and the peaceful. It would seem to these students something of a lie, I think, to design restorative spaces for the crowded, noisy, assaultive city. Something that extends the city, reminds one of the city, and is in some ways equally assaultive seems necessary. But, on the other hand, in extending the city in these various ways—with decaying industrial detritus, with angular forms, straight edges, a very sparse use of nature (except for the attempt to restore the original salt marsh, which is quite common)—they also want to simultaneously criticize and attack the existing city.

It is interesting to me that we can thus think of two ways of "contradicting" the city. One was Olmsted's way, which tries to remove its noise and crowding and sharp building forms, hides them behind a screen of trees, and presents to the eyes a tranquil meadow or lake, or streams and rocks recalling a wilder nature. The second is to take those elements of the city that we might all consider unpleasant and to abstract from them something that in some respect exaggerates them: the city's disorder, or the temporality of its forms, or its hardness, or its sharp and inorganic edges.

In other words, it is landscape architecture as social criticism. One can argue that Olmsted's landscape architecture is also social criticism, and make the superficially powerful point that Olmsted's social criticism is simply the past criticizing the present, the genteel criticizing the vulgar; and on the contrary, that the kind of social criticism we see in these student projects is the future criticizing the present, a future that may be a return to a primal nature, or a technology we cannot yet realize, or the harsh remains of the industrial technology of today, or a utopia we cannot quite imagine. This is a rather grimmer social criticism altogether. And if we find the present-day city inadequate, if we find that it does not take into account sufficiently the ordinary and the human, that it is a city in which it is hard to raise children, find an apartment, move around, educate one's children, deal with the bureaucracy, protect one's life and property, why not this harder criticism?

Serra's Vision

Perhaps the most striking case of this kind of criticism realized in an open space in New York City was Richard
Serra's *Tilted Arc*. The story in its outlines is well known.
An open space existed in Lower Manhattan. On two sides
it was bordered by federal buildings, a modern federal
courthouse and office building. The office building is an
anonymous and really ugly very large structure of the
1960s. The open space was already shaped. It had a fountain (which, as is true, for some reason, of almost all New
York City fountains, rarely spouted water—either there
was a water shortage or it needed repair, or something),
and it had a decorative pavement, spiraling out from the
round fountain to fill the space. Indeed, the pavement
might remind one of the elegant paving of Michelangelo's
Campidoglio in Rome. Serra was already famous when
he was commissioned to do the piece of sculpture that
would decorate the plaza, though one guesses the term
"decorate" would not have been approved by him, or the
term "embellishment," or any other term that might
evoke the beautiful, the pretty, the pleasant.

Serra is a minimalist sculptor, interested in working in
the city. He had already placed major works in Lower
Manhattan: in one case, a tower of three huge plates of
Cor-Ten steel, thirty-six by twelve feet; in another a huge
arc of Cor-Ten steel, two hundred feet long, twelve feet
high, placed in a circular space at the exit of the Holland
Tunnel. He had been approached for major commissions
at the Federal Triangle in Washington, for which the designers were the architects Robert Venturi and Denise
Scott-Brown, and for a space in front of the Pompidou

Center in Paris, but neither had been realized owing to conflicts with the architects.

In a group of interviews published in 1980, when the design for *Tilted Arc* was complete but before it was erected, we learn something of Serra's intentions when it comes to working in urban and public space. His first public work in New York was a steel circle sunk into an anonymous street in the Bronx. As we see from the picture in this volume of interviews, the street paving is broken, the sidewalks are broken and littered, chain-link fencing borders lots filled with debris, and the street is lined with cars, some clearly abandoned or stripped. As Serra describes it: "After looking for a site in the Bronx for three or four months, I found a dead-end street that had stairways going up to an adjacent street, which would enable a viewer to look down on the piece from various levels. 183rd was a leftover street in a broken-down neighborhood, unencumbered by buildings; it had no public or institutional character." One assumes this is one reason it attracted him, and indeed why he was looking for a site in the Bronx, a huge urban area whose buildings, substantial and even rather bourgeois, were being leveled at the time in the most astonishing orgy of destruction of urban facilities we have ever seen in this country's cities. "Except for wrecked cars," Serra says, "there were empty lots and open space."[1] Clearly Serra was attracted to urban grit: he was not interested in the conventionally beautiful or commemorative, or the decoration or embel-

---

[1] *Richard Serra: Interviews Etc. 1970–1980*, written and compiled in collaboration with Clara Weyergraf (Yonkers, N.Y.: The Hudson River Museum, 1980), pp. 164, 166.

lishment of public space. One would be hard put to say what the sunken circle of steel does for the street.

Serra's view of public authority and government, already suspicious and antagonistic, was undoubtedly not improved by his experience in trying to get permission to place a piece of sculpture in a Bronx street: "I went to the Parks Administration, who told me they would try to assist me with the project for any site in that area of the Bronx. Their assistance was that of pointing out where permits were available. Finally, the police gave me a permit and said, `Give us $250 and we'll let you put that thing in the ground.' "

The interviewer asked why he was interested in that kind of site, and Serra responded, "I wanted to build a work in a New York street and was told, `Manhattan is out. Try the Bronx.' It could also have gone into a park, but I felt that a park would designate the sculpture as something different from what I wanted. Usually you're offered spaces that have ideological connotations, from parks to corporate and public buildings, and their extensions such as lawns and plazas. It's difficult to subvert those contexts."[2] The term "subvert" immediately seizes one. What does Serra want to subvert? And why?

Serra points out that he had been offered "picture postcard sites" in Germany for a major piece called *Terminal*, sites "that suggested conventional public sculpture." The site he chose in Bochum in the Ruhr Valley is on "the main artery of the town, with streetcar and bus traffic." The picture shows a huge, dark tower, leaning over a streetcar going past, and threatening alarmingly to fall on

[2] Ibid., p. 166.

it. It is made of four huge plates of Cor-Ten steel forty-one feet high. All this is preliminary to what became the famous or notorious *Tilted Arc*.

The interviewer asks why Serra, in view of his attitudes, accepted a commission for a conventional site in front of a major public building. Serra explains: it is because "I've found a way to dislocate or alter the decorative function of the plaza and actively bring people into the sculpture's context. I plan to build a piece that's 120 feet long in a semi-circular plaza. It will cross the entire space, blocking the view from the street to the courthouse and vice-versa." The interviewer asks: "So your intention is, in fact, to block the conventional views of the Federal building, the adjacent courthouse." That is certainly the effect, but Serra denies this is the intention: No. The intention is to bring the viewer into the sculpture. "After the piece is created, the space will be understood primarily as a function of the sculpture."[3]

Serra's public sculpture was clearly intended to work in opposition to the space in which it was erected. Speaking of the huge *Terminal* sculpture in a central space in Bochum, he told the interviewer: "I think if a work is substantial . . . then it does not embellish, decorate, or point to specific buildings. . . . I think that sculpture . . . has the potential . . . to work in contradiction to the places and spaces where it is created. . . . I am interested in work where the artist is the maker of `anti-environment' which takes its own place or makes its own situation, or divides or declares its own area. . . . I am not interested in work which . . . satisfies urban design

[3] Ibid., p. 168.

principles. I have always found that to be . . . a need to reinforce a status quo of existing aesthetics. Most of the architecture that has been built is horrendous." His *Terminal* piece, he says, "reduces most of the architecture to its cardboard-model inventiveness."[4]

To find most architecture, revival or modernist, inadequate is a legitimate aesthetic response. Few will be found to say a good word for the huge Jacob Javits Federal Building before which *Tilted Arc* was erected, and the notion of an artist transforming a work meant to "embellish" or "decorate" into something serving to undermine or criticize might appeal to all of us who find the specific buildings around the public space awful. But Serra was engaged in more than verbal or written criticism in an evanescent newspaper: he was building something large and permanent; and a permanent critique, particularly with its accompanying discomfort for all the people working in the building and using the space, is another matter. He is attacking the awful by increasing the awfulness. To the misery of working in an ugly and poorly designed building, it was Serra's thought to add additional misery in the form of a sculpture that was ugly to most people (including the art critic of the *New York Times*), that obstructed the plaza, that offered no space to sit on, that blocked sun and view, and that made the plaza unusable even for those moments of freedom when the weather permitted office workers to eat their lunch outside.

But Serra was doing more than critiquing the architecture: he was equally critical of the society and political order that it represented. In the case of the Federal Trian-

[4] Ibid., pp. 128–29.

gle project in Washington designed by Venturi and Scott-Brown, and for which Serra had been commissioned to produce a large sculpture, Serra had an opportunity to present his views to the commissioners of the Pennsylvania Avenue Development Corporation, where he attacked the Venturi–Scott-Brown design. Its most intriguing feature is a pavement that reproduces the original L'Enfant proposal for the plan of Washington. Serra compared the proposal to Albert Speer's work for the Third Reich. The interviewer asks how the commissioners responded. "They were shocked. . . . They thought I was un-American. . . . [Politicians] . . . cannot listen to an argument that tells them the architecture of Washington is ugly, pompous, inhuman. . . . It may be that in building a sculpture a block and a half from the White House, and within the context of L'Enfant's plan, it would necessarily be coopted by the ideological connotations of the place. But I didn't see it at the time. I hoped to be able . . . to build something that would subvert the context."[5]

Serra's intention in subverting is perhaps more aesthetic than political—it is the architecture he is trying to subvert. But one cannot leave it at that. It is the society and the political system in which such architecture is built, and which it symbolizes, that are also to him worthy of subversion. "In Washington, D.C., the work was defeated because it did not attend to the notion of elaborating on the democratic ideologies that this country thinks are necessary in terms of the decorative functions of art, or the political function of art. They wanted me to put flagpoles on top of pylons. My retort to that was I couldn't

[5] Ibid., pp. 185–87.

imagine putting a swastica [*sic*], a flag, or a symbol on top of a Brancusi or a Rodin."[6]

It is an attitude that insists on the autonomy of art, and insists that any attempt to celebrate political values is suspect and not to be allowed. Neither the swastika, the red star, nor the American flag. One is left to conclude, all are equally suspect. Yet societies and political systems do celebrate themselves, and some are more worthy of celebration than others. Art, it is true, is autonomous. When one insists on this autonomy for public art, all political systems are viewed with equal suspicion, whether democratic or totalitarian, whether they represent the will of the people or that of a dictator. This is an understandable point of view, but it is not, I would argue, legitimate for public art, whose very point is to symbolize common values, common concerns, yes, a common political system, rather than a distinctive, personal artistic vision. From this point of view much public art today fails, but there is little of it that is as direct and aggressive an attack on the common values as Serra's.

What is most intriguing is that Serra believed the society would take this attack lying down like a pussycat. In Germany, where avant-garde art—if we can still call it that—has a higher reputation, that may happen. But we discover that even in Bochum, which accepted and erected *Terminal* at great cost, matters did not stop there. A Social Democratic city government had accepted it; the opposition Christian Democratic party made the acceptance and existence of this brooding forty-one-foot tower of heavy rusting steel a chief factor in its electoral cam-

[6] Ibid., p. 130.

paign. The CDU, Serra tells the interviewer, "have plas-
tered 100,000 posters in the Ruhr Valley denouncing the
work." To Serra, this is practically Fascism: "The same
kind of repression was evident in the 1930's."[7] Once
again, we find a confusion of political categories. The CDU
was making the sculpture an issue in a democratic political
campaign.

Public Art and the People

The attack on *Tilted Arc*, when it was erected in 1981, took
a different form from the CDU's campaign in Bochum: no
posters were distributed. But the antagonism it aroused
among a host of people was no less intense. In typical
American fashion, the battle was fought not only in public but through the courts—everything in the United
States becomes a subject of litigation, and a public work
of art is no exception. Many questions relevant to public
art were raised that I will not explore here: whether the
General Services Administration, which had commissioned the work, was breaking its contract with Serra in
trying to remove it; questions of copyright infringement,
of due process, of freedom of speech. It is quite surprising
to see the full panoply of the Bill of Rights brought into
play over a dispute as to whether a commissioned effort
to embellish and decorate a public space is an offense that
should be removed.

The art establishment rallied to the defense of *Tilted Arc*.
The long list of those who spoke in favor of it at a public
hearing is impressive: curators from leading museums,
professors of art history, art critics and art dealers, leading

[7] Ibid., p.129.

architects, painters, sculptors, composers. Those speaking against could not have been more different: judges, federal employees, union officials, area residents. The confrontation could be summed up as the world of art against the people. The National Endowment for the Arts, at the request of the administrator of the GSA, appointed a distinguished panel to advise him. The GSA expressed the willingness to relocate *Tilted Arc* if an alternative site could be found. The artist resisted this strongly: it was a site-specific work, for this space, for this plaza, for these buildings. In the end, after nine years of troubled existence, *Tilted Arc* was removed and the plaza restored. It now contains trees in concrete planters and benches.

It must be said that Richard Serra stuck to his guns to the end, with no attempt to mollify the almost universal opposition of those who worked in the buildings around *Tilted Arc*. Introducing one of the volumes that have appeared on the controversy, Serra writes:

> [S]ite-specific works emphasize the comparison between two separate languages and can therefore use the language of one to criticize the language of the other.
>
> It is the explicit intention of site-specific works to alter their context. . . . Works which are built within the contextual frame of governmental, corporate, educational, and religious institutions run the risk of being read as tokens of these institutions. . . . In such cases, it is necessary to work in opposition to the constraints of the context, so that the work cannot be read as an affirmation of questionable ideologies and political power. I am not interested in art as affirmation and complicity.[8]

---

[8] *The Destruction of Tilted Arc: Documents*, ed. Clara Weyergraf-Serra and Martha Buskirk (Cambridge: MIT Press, 1991), pp. 12–13.

One doubts that the opponents of *Tilted Arc* were concerned about affirmation. They simply wanted to enjoy the sun in the plaza, to have a place to eat their lunch, and not to be assaulted by a very large and ugly object whose purposes they could not divine. In the words of Carole Glueck, of the *New York Times*, who I assume is no philistine, it is an "awkward, bullying piece that may conceivably be the ugliest outdoor work of art in the city."[9]

Many of the defenders of *Tilted Arc* were even clearer and more direct about its functions. One defender asserted: "There is an opposition in the space of the plaza. The opposition reflects the true oppositions in our society which bureaucracies work to deny: therefore, it has a critical function. The *Tilted Arc* is, I must admit, subversive. . . . Its very tilt, and its rust, both represents and opposes the building before it." And another defender: "It is a confrontational, aggressive piece of art in a confrontational, aggressive town, in a part of the city where confrontations in court are practically the order of the day."[10]

Douglas Crimp, one of Serra's leading exponents (and the interviewer who elicited many of the quotations from Serra I have given), writes that identifying with a piece of sculpture serves only to make one's acceptance of capitalist society more tolerable. He contrasts the awful Bochum tower in the Ruhr Valley with George Segal's sculpture of Youngstown steelworkers: the latter is too pleasant, and as long as we live in capitalist society, Crimp

---

[9] Harriet F. Senie, *The Tilted Arc Controversy: Dangerous Precedent?* (Minneapolis: University of Minnesota Press, 2002), p. 26, quoting from *New York Times*, August 7, 1981.
[10] In *The Destruction of Tilted Arc*, pp. 94, 103.

seems to be telling us, we must be confronted with that which outrages us. He does not seem to realize that the outrage of steelworkers confronted with a Serra is more likely to be directed at the government that provides the sums needed for such a construction, at the art bureaucrats who commissioned it, at the artists who advised that Serra was the man to do it, than at capitalism and capitalists, who, after all, have had no visible overt role in the enterprise.

The demand of the Christian Democratic Union party leaders who attacked the Bochum sculpture, according to Crimp, was "that the sculpture reconcile the workers to their brutal conditions by giving them something with which they can positively identify." But "their identification is utterly false, . . . the worker's pride is only intended to make their slavery more tolerable." Crimp ignores the fact that the CDU raised its anti-Serra slogan in the context of a democratic election: party leaders thought their attack would make the CDU more acceptable to more voters, including workers. Crimp goes further: *Tilted Arc*, he tells us, is "situated in the very center of the mechanism of state power. . . . Serra's work does nothing other than present us with the truth of our social condition . . . a public that has been socialized to accept the atomization of individuals . . . cannot bear to be confronted by the reality of its situation."[11] And so on, with portentous references to Marx and in particular his essay *On the Jewish Question*. We find all this, and much else, in a

---

[11] Douglas Crimp, "Serra's Public Sculpture: Redefining Site Specificity," in *Richard Serra*, ed. Ernst-Gerhard Güse (New York: Rizzoli, 1987), pp. 34, 35, and elsewhere.

sumptuous volume put out by Rizzoli, and we must really wonder what these fulminations against capitalism to defend Serra are doing on those glossy pages.

What is so interesting in the Serra case is that Serra, in his antagonism to contemporary society and government, thinks of himself as in some way identified with the working class. He works in heavy steel plates; he uses foundries with real workers to roll and shape them; he himself, as one of his defenders tells us, "is exceptional in that he is a product of the working class."[12]

We see a strange evolution in theory here, one that reminds us of the fate of modern architecture, functional architecture. It begins in the effort to be honest, simple, economical, to reject false and elaborate ornament; and certainly one major intention in modern architecture is to build for the working class. But it ends in the furthest reaches of elitism, rejected by those for whom it was originally designed, who seem to prefer their modest little cottages with their crude architectural reminders of grander buildings to the simple honesty of functionalism. How remarkable it is that it was a prince who launched such a devastating critique of modernism and aroused such widespread popular approval for his attack. (We should recall also that this prince was concerned about the declining inner cities and had commended the community architects who worked with poor people in their neighborhoods, who respected their tastes, and who helped them improve their houses and their communities according to their lights.) In the end, the defense of a radical modernism became the work of an elite that the ordinary

[12] In *The Destruction of Tilted Arc*, p. 95.

person could not understand; and the attack on it was applauded by the common man.

I would hasten to say that this tells us nothing about the aesthetic merits or qualities of modern architecture and Richard Serra's sculpture. I know Serra has better and stronger defenders than Douglas Crimp, who seems to find its aesthetic merit in its function as an attack on capitalism (though no one else would notice it). But when it comes to architecture that must be lived in, and public sculpture that must be lived with, public taste is not irrelevant. One can argue that it is irretrievably debased by modern capitalism, and therefore the sculptor and the architect must withdraw into unbuilt projects, or find a surreptitious opportunity to spit in the face of the public. Undoubtedly public taste does not reach the height of the times aesthetically. But one notes that Calder, and Moore, and Picasso, and Oldenburg, and Dubuffet all manage to get their pieces put up without the kind of outrage that led to the destruction of Serra's *Tilted Arc*. It is possible for some artists to be ahead of and scarcely understood by the people, and still to be tolerated, and even appreciated. I would think we find the explanation for their success in the fact that they do not embrace the assaultive theory that Serra embraced—and, to come back to the beginning of this essay, that we saw embraced by so many of the contributors to the landscape designs for Riverside Park South.

One can understand and encourage the student or the adventurous landscape architect or the architect who embraces the most far-out and radical theory. But the important thing about the public artist's work is that it is not for him alone, or for an individual patron—it is for a public, it must be lived with, and while this need not check theory, it must to some degree check realization.

What the City Needs

What does the modern city need? What does New York, the densest of great cities, need? It does not need assault—there is enough of that in the life of the city, and the New Yorker does not have to be reminded of it. He does not need confrontation—there is also enough of that in the life of the city. He needs contrast, but not a contrast that makes the city, with its mixture of the harmonious and the jangling, the beautiful and the ugly, even more assaultive than it already is. He does not need to have its rare open spaces drafted for the purpose of teaching him about the city's problems, its poverty, homelessness, congestion, polluted air and water. We have many other ways of bringing all these matters to the city-dweller's attention. Conventional and unrevolutionary as it appears, we need what Olmsted and Vaux gave New York, release from the city's noise and turmoil and crowding and concrete.

One is reminded of Tony Hiss's delightful and insightful book, *The Experience of Place*. He begins with a walk into Prospect Park, another major work of Olmsted and Vaux, and he tries to get to the root of our pleasure in it and our satisfaction with it. He says many things that may seem far-out, basing himself on various psychologists and biologists and naturalists. One scientist, he writes, finds that human beings have a "deep, innate preference for a grass landscape." And he relates that preference, outlandish as the connection may seem, to the origins of man in some of the most extensive grasslands in the world, the savannas of East Africa. We like places with a wide outlook, for that provided security for us on the savannas of our distant origins. Other psychologists say, on the other hand, that we have an inborn preference for winding paths, for roads that provide some sense of mystery—what will happen next? Man as an animal is defined by a need for what piques curiosity as well as for survival. We also need, they say, legibility, "an environment that looks as if one could explore extensively without getting lost." "All those factors that modern research has shown to be part of the human response to landscapes," Hiss writes, "are present along the path to Prospect Park; the long meadow provides savanna, prospect, and legibility; the path itself affords mystery; the tunnel gives refuge; there is plenty of sky, natural light and information we can use to orient ourselves."[13] Great designers, such as Olmsted and Vaux, seemed to understand all this on the basis of experience.

Young students should reach out, try, experiment. Even if the theory that speaks to them is impenetrable to me, they should try to realize the hints and insights and possibilities they divine in it. But when they design and build for the public, one factor affecting what they design must be public response. Leafing through a record of work by students of landscape architecture at the University of Virginia, I find the following:

[S]econd year students took the challenge of designing a "green space" for Ballston, located in the Washington,

[13] Tony Hiss, *The Experience of Place* (New York: Alfred A. Knopf, 1990), pp. 37, 40–42.

D.C., metropolitan area. This park was designed to create a civic focus in an otherwise centerless development. The chosen site consisted of a one-acre lot located between two high-rise buildings, and on top of a parking garage.

Leaving all existing conditions intact, [one student] proposed a critique of the "instant city," a consequence of today's uncontrolled development. The design of the park acknowledges the systems particular to this place through the expression of collage. Imposing an artificial order on the collage, an idealized circular form occupied the center of the composition. The circle then breaks at the perimeter and spirals out to collide with the surrounding buildings, thus questioning this idealized realm.

I can't say how the design would work in practice, or whether the people of Ballston would recognize in it, or appreciate, a critique of their "instant city." But if the students empathize with the people of Ballston, living in a featureless environment, maybe what is necessary is not to critique it but to bring with their designs something they would not find in that graceless environment: perhaps humor, perhaps nostalgia, perhaps repose, perhaps even, if one is capable of it, something of beauty.

CHAPTER FOUR

Monuments in an Age without Heroes

It was not much noted, or indeed not noted at all, that the Million Man March of Louis Farrakhan on the Mall in Washington some years ago took place in front of what was described in the 1937 WPA guide to Washington as "the largest and most costly piece of statuary in Washington." This is the Grant Memorial, the major monument in Washington to the Civil War. It is 252 feet long. "Bronze groups of Union Cavalry and Artillery in action at either end of the long granite base are set off by couchant bronze lions around the central pedestal. On the pedestal is an equestrian bronze of General Grant, the second largest equestrian statue in the world, topped only 5 inches by the colossal effigy of Victor Emanuel in Rome. . . . The monument was unveiled in 1922, on the centenary of Grant's death." I am quoting from the guidebook of 1937, only fifteen years after the monument was unveiled.

The difference between 1922 and 1937 in how we approached the problems of monuments may be only fifteen years by the calendar; it is more like a century when we consider the two moments from the point of view of artistic tendencies and public and elite responses to them. In the universe of monuments, 1922 was still in the nineteenth century, 1937 already on the threshold of modernity. It was possibly already too late for the mass of realistic sculpture that makes up the Grant Memorial when it was completed in 1922. Modernism in art and architecture, in all its forms, was already in the ascendant in Europe. These attitudes were spreading to the United States in the 1930s. The distaste for the kind of monument represented by the Grant Memorial could already be read between the lines of the 1937 WPA guidebook. The WPA itself, which produced the huge guidebook to Washington from which I quote, has given its name to the last burst of figurative sculpture and painting in the United States, and to the last period in which public buildings accepted decoration and figurative art as an organic, legitimate, integrated part of their total impact. But the human figure was already on its way out, as we can see in the decoration of public buildings being constructed during the Depression. Human figures were already stripped down and flattened, a last way station on the road to their almost complete exclusion from the repertoire of major modern sculptors.

These last echoes of figurative art, the art that was once an unchallenged norm for public commemoration, were influenced by Art Deco, which was a purely artistic and decorative tendency, but they were equally influenced by the political movements of the time. In the United States, in WPA murals and the bas-reliefs decorating public buildings, we represented men and women engaged in useful pursuits; in Russia they celebrated heroic proletarians; in Nazi Germany it was muscular and healthy youth symbolizing a national revival. The buildings such figures graced were erected by very different political regimes, but whether they were built by the New Deal, Italian Fascism, Soviet Russia, or German National Socialism, there was, embarrassingly, a strong family resemblance among them. Muscled figures, male and female, marched across the front of public buildings with stripped-down columns or pilasters, in the capitals of very different regimes.

The traditions represented by the Grant Memorial were not completely exhausted when it was built. It was still possible to do better within these traditions, to build monuments that still speak to us, as the Grant Memorial does not. It is an odd experience to read the criticism of the time from the perspective of our own, when almost all figural and classical art is placed in the same passé and outmoded bag, and when memorials and monuments generally consist of blank stone or rusted metal about which not much can be said, though critics are hardly silent. Looking backward from our own age, we are surprised to see how much the critics of the age of figural art could read into the representations of the time, dismissing some, praising others.

At the other end of the Mall sits the much better regarded, then as now, Lincoln Memorial. It was, surprisingly, completed in the same year as the Grant Memorial, 1922. (We take a long time in this country getting to our heroes. In contrast, it took no time at all in Communist regimes, from East Germany to North Korea, to erect masses of monuments, undoubtedly because they didn't have to debate the matter, and we did.) Marian Anderson sang in front of this much better known and admired monument at the other end of the Mall in 1939, and Martin Luther King, Jr., gave his famous "I Have a Dream" speech in front of it at another mass gathering in 1963. Why Louis Farrakhan's Million Man March assembled in front of the now ignored monument to General and President U. S. Grant at the other end of the Mall I do not know. There seems to be much less going on in the Lincoln Memorial than in the Grant, but that is because we no longer can or bother to read the symbols. The Lincoln Memorial is filled with symbolism we no longer notice: the thirty-six columns represent the states in the Union at the time of Lincoln's death; the forty-eight stone festoons on the attic above the columns represent the number of states at the time of its construction; the figures in the murals represent, variously, justice, immortality, unity, fraternity, charity.

One characteristic binds the two monuments, whatever the difference in their quality and their fate in public regard. It was clear what they meant. Monuments were once replete with overt and direct meaning. A hero might rise in the center holding a document, if he were a man of peace, or sitting on a horse, if were a man of war. Around him, depending on the grandeur and expense of the monument, would be arrayed various figures drawn from a repertory with defined meanings. This figure might stand for the defeated enemy, that for the grateful country. The symbols of war or of peaceful achievement would be properly distributed around the site. Some figures might represent the virtues, others the vices, and the rivers or the winds, the seasons or the arts, the continents or the states or the cities could also be represented by figures, male or female. Inscriptions would grace the pedestals and further elaborate on the meaning of figures and scenes. The ordinary visitor might be ignorant of the intended meaning of the various figures and emblems and symbols and historical evocations, but that hardly affected one's enjoyment of and response to the monument. One could appreciate the craftsmanship in the decorations, respond to the soldiers, and admire the symbolic ladies in various stages of undress; children could climb on pedestals and figures and play in the pools; and the cognoscenti would be able to distinguish in quality and sophistication the work of one sculptor of the human figure from another.

As we know, much has changed. Long before the sophisticated critics of the present day began to discern in these monuments of the nineteenth and earlier twentieth centuries meanings that we presume were unintended by their sponsors and creators, we began to find this kind of monument, drawing from a received grammar of symbols with specific meanings, unsatisfactory, just as we turned against classical columns and pediments. Today, in the wake of Marxism, deconstruction, postmodernism, and other contemporary critical movements, it is all too easy to detect in these extravagant enterprises the symbols of imperialist arrogance, Western cultural hegemony, male chauvinism, homophobia, and on and on, so many meanings multiplied by contemporary theory that these monuments are helpless sitting ducks before modern critics.

Of course, even without our contemporary exponents of cultural studies reading new unintended and unconscious meanings into our monuments, they do change their meaning over time. We erect them for one purpose, and they begin to serve another. Eiffel's tower was designed to represent the frontier of the science and technology of the time, to speak to the world of France's preeminence in the arts of engineering by raising the tallest structure in the world. Today it stands for Paris and French elegance, its mathematically derived curves and arches speaking to us of grace and gaiety, and one can be sure the great engineer Eiffel had nothing like that in mind. The Statue of Liberty, originally named *Liberty Enlightening the World*, was intended by its French originators and creators to symbolize the friendship between France and the United States cemented in the American Revolution, and the beneficent rays of liberty reaching from the New World across the Atlantic, with the hope that it would in some way influence the authoritarianism of Louis Napoleon. By the time it was finally completed, more than twenty years after it was first proposed, Louis Napoleon was long gone, France was a republic, and the statue came to mean a welcome to immigrants, a notion scarcely in the mind of Laboulaye, who proposed it, or Bartholdi, who created it.

The successful monument incorporates symbolic meanings, without embarrassment, at its origin, and it can carry new meanings attributed to it over time without any necessary diminishment. The human figure, the obelisk, the pyramid, the column, ancient forms all, inevitably can carry many meanings, and continue to do so while aesthetic tastes, elite and popular, change. One did not need the new varieties of criticism of our own day to change our response to monuments and memorials in the past, to make earlier traditions appear overblown, pompous, extravagant. One could detect the transition even in 1922, when modernism in American arts and design was limited to a few advanced artists. The Lincoln Memorial already represented to some degree the simplification that modernism called for in building and design, even if it did not yet incorporate the antagonism of modernism to classical models and the direct representation of the human figure.

The reduction of meanings—intended meaning, communicated meaning, unambiguous meaning—in public sculpture and monuments has proceeded apace. In the wake of this change, we have moved from an age in which monuments were filled, overfilled, with meanings, in which they came accompanied with guidebooks to tell us what each element of decoration symbolized unambiguously (the details that could be spelled out in a monument as apparently simple as the Lincoln Memorial would amaze us), to one in which monuments and memorials stand mute, even if their creators and sympathetic critics insist they are telling us something. The mute monument is all around us, and the most successful monument of the last decades—the Vietnam Memorial, in its original form, before groups of human figures began to be added to it, to the dismay of its youthful designer and sophisticated critics—symbolizes this muteness. It does not tell us that these men died for their country, or for liberty or democracy, or that they died in vain. Indeed it says nothing except that they died. And in view of the ambiguity that surrounds the Vietnam War, this is probably all for the best. The fact that it asserts nothing, in contrast to the monuments of the past, undoubtedly helps make possible its universal popularity.

But that is only one factor in its popularity, and of course the monument is not really mute: it contains the names of those who died, perhaps the principal reason for its enormous success, and these do more to make it moving to its visitors than any possible inscription or piece of symbolic evocation could. And there is subtle art in its simple form, and even in its listing of names. Who was it who decided that the names should be listed in the order in which they died rather than in alphabetical order? If the decision had been the latter, we would have had a mass of Smiths and Joneses and other common names, and the alphabetic listing would have depreciated the sense of individual sorrow over each life lost.[1] Nevertheless, one must note that in contrast with the monuments of the past, there is very little, nothing but the names.

Perhaps there is no better example of the mute memorial than the artworks commissioned for the Holocaust Memorial Museum in Washington. Ellsworth Kelly provides ambiguous white forms. Sol LeWitt provides squares on walls. Richard Serra provides a large square steel plate on a stairway. One can pass all of these without noticing them, as most visitors do. Since they were created for the Holocaust Memorial Museum, one can perhaps think they stand for the muteness that the Holocaust induces in us, as one possible, and fully understandable, response. Except that what we see are clearly a Serra, an Ellsworth Kelly, a Sol LeWitt, akin to their other works and responsive to the context and the commission in no overt or easily observable way. Their muteness is the muteness of modern art, stripped of historical reference, and is divorced from any connection to the building in which they are placed and what it memorializes.

We should not be unfair to Serra, Kelly, LeWitt. I do not berate them for providing us with simply another ex-

---

[1] This was an even more severe problem with a proposal to list the names of the six million Jews who died in the Holocaust for the memorial since built in Berlin. Alas, it is not possible to know when each died, which we do know for the dead of Vietnam; and the enormous lists of common Jewish

ample of their trademark work instead of something that responds to the distinctive commission. And indeed, perhaps they did respond to the specific commission in a way that is clear to them and to sophisticated and sympathetic critics even if not to the uninstructed observer. The problem their works present in this context is that of modern art itself, not anything individual to them. If the objects were by the giants of the recent past, Henry Moore, or Alexander Calder, or Pablo Picasso, they would tell us as much, or as little. They would tell us, this is a Moore, this is a Calder, this is a Picasso. That communicates some meaning, but nothing connected to the intentions and hopes of those who commission works of art to serve a defined purpose.

What explains this development, this draining of overt meaning and communication from monuments? We still build them; we can do no other when it comes to great events, tragic or heroic, or great figures. While we now have a range of alternatives to the creation of memorials and monuments, great events, great men and women, still impose themselves on us and seem to call for something palpable that remains, that is designed to last for the ages. Such monuments still speak to us as against so-called living memorials: let us say, a fund to distribute help to the poor or scholarships to the needy or to do good in various other ways. Whatever the monument is, there is one thing it is not: it is not useful, in any obvious way. It symbolizes, it celebrates, it mourns. How have we come from the monument that means something, even

---

names would have made the enterprise ridiculous. The new Holocaust Memorial in Boston records six million random numbers on its glass columns.

if time changes that meaning in one or another respect, to the monument that by intention means nothing, that tells us simply, here is the artist and his work?

II

Two parallel developments have brought us to this point. One is the complex of changes in the larger culture, the confusion of our own times. We no longer know clearly who are our heroes, because none of them come to us without a crippling ambiguity. We no longer know whether we want to celebrate or mourn great events, or, if we are clear on that point, how to celebrate them, how to mourn them. The second is a more restricted development, that in art itself, but it has powerfully affected our ability to build monuments. The two have come together to bring us to the point where monuments, it seems, can no longer speak to us, and if they did, we would feel they were overdoing it, excessive in their emotion, grandiloquent in their claims, unsuited to an age of coolness and confusion.

Concerning the changes in the larger culture, there is little that I can add to what is obvious from contemporary disputes. How, for example, do we memorialize World War II? In Asia it ended with the atom bomb, but what did that mean? After the fierce debate over a proposed exhibit at the Air and Space Museum in Washington on the dropping of the bomb, we ended up again with muteness. All we could do was exhibit the plane that dropped the bomb, and then silence. Not another word: any would be too controversial. No simple celebration of victory—a word that already sounds old-fashioned and is hardly ever used today without quotation marks, actual or implied—is possible today, it seems. Charles Krauthammer noted that the official title for the celebration of the fiftieth anniversary of the end of the Great Pacific War, as the Japanese call it, was not VJ Day (Victory over Japan Day)—that would have been considered insensitive to the Japanese—but End of the War in the Pacific Day.

For the war in Europe, apparently, there is less controversy. We have managed to create a monument to World War II in Washington, though not without debate (See chapter 5). I was intrigued to note that in the burst of television documentaries on the fiftieth anniversary of the war's end, paralleling the images of the atom bomb for the end of the Pacific war, the major images to symbolize the end of the war in Europe were those of the horrors of the concentration and extermination camps exposed by the victorious Allied forces. No ambiguity there, one would think, but indeed there is, and not only in Germany, which is reduced to muteness by this monstrous scar in its past. Indeed, their giant monument to the murdered Jews of Europe, the Holocaust memorial in Berlin, is entirely mute—no words at all. Ours to World War II has too many words, in contrast, and too many symbols that no longer speak to us.

Or consider what our memorial to John F. Kennedy might look like. Or to Ronald Reagan. Perhaps it's all to the good that it takes us fifty years at least before we get to memorializing our heroes. (It took longer for Washington, Jefferson, Grant, Lincoln.) Even with Franklin D. Roosevelt, who raises fewer divisive questions than do our more recent presidents about just what it is we have to celebrate, it took fifty years and many designs to find something we could agree on, and we are not fully agreed yet on how he should have been shown. What about the ever-present cigarette in its elegant holder? Or the wheelchair? The cigarette was suppressed, but the disabled persons lobby insisted after the monument was completed that Roosevelt be clearly shown in a wheelchair, and a diminished Roosevelt in a wheelchair was added in a new entry to the monument. What was part of Roosevelt's image in his time was suppressed, and what he was careful never to have photographed was made visible.

We can attribute our ever-increasing difficulties in dealing unambiguously with heroes to many causes. The rise of the ever more intrusive mass media, vigorously exposing feet of clay, is clearly one. Another is the rise to prominence and some measure of power of new interest groups that view heroes from distinctive perspectives that were once not much evident in public life, and of which it was unnecessary to take account. Today the perspectives of one or another minority, or women, or the disabled, or environmentalists, and many others, must be reckoned with. And few heroes escape unscathed from the scrutiny of these groups.

The arts of publicity and entertainment and media exploitation can and to some extent do enlarge heroes, if only briefly, but they play a more significant role in diminishing them in the public eye. The popular media also compete directly with heroes and their monuments, providing something more accessible, less demanding, more amusing. Travel agents have noted recently that fewer tourists want to go to Washington; they seem to prefer Disneyland and Disney World, Las Vegas or Atlantic City. High school students no longer see Washington, Jefferson, and Lincoln on their classroom walls, and seem to be equally happy to skip seeing their memorials on their high school trips, as they replace Washington with more amusing sites. In Boston, the marked trail that guides the tourist through the city's many historic revolutionary sites—Faneuil Hall, Old North Church, the house of Paul Revere— found stiff competition for a while in a Bugs Bunny statue and a huge teddy bear that stood in front of the F.A.O. Schwarz toy store. It is with such statues that tourists want to pose to be photographed, rather than with the many worthies to whom statues have been erected. (I note that the John Harvard statue in Harvard Yard still draws as many tourists as ever for posing and photographing, but I think that is because it is considered camp—most don't think John Harvard was a historic figure.)

One sign of the times is that we also erect fewer monuments to our families and ourselves; I refer to gravestones, which are called monuments by those who make them, and the larger constructions that once graced nineteenth- and early twentieth-century cemeteries. Americans, as Richard Gill has documented,[2] increasingly favor cremation, rather than burial, and cremation requires no monument. (Even when Americans are buried, it is now commonly in memorial parks where the size and prominence of monuments are sharply limited.) Gill finds more in this phenomenon than a change in fashion or a response to cost. Our sense of a future to which we can look forward with some confidence is clouded. We have seen

---

[2] Richard T. Gill, "Whatever Happened to the American Way of Death?" *The Public Interest* (Spring 1996); and Richard T. Gill, *Posterity Lost: Progress, Ideology, and the Decline of the American Family* (Lanham, Md.: Rowman and Littlefield, 1997).

so many changes in our own time that we have no idea what the world will look like twenty-five or fifty years from now. This radical uncertainty undermines our interest in building something that might survive into this now unimaginable future. There was a time when interest rates and prices were relatively stable, when divorce rates were low, when the character of the work one did and the earnings one might anticipate in a profession were more secure, when even factory workers (for a time) had some security backed by unions, and when one could be sure the United States would remain the strongest and richest power in the world, and all this is gone.

In the past we found it possible to build for a distant future because we believed the future would be an extrapolation of the present, without violent and cataclysmic breaks. We don't believe that anymore, and our buildings change in response. Pennsylvania Station in New York City may have been built as solid as the Baths of Caracalla on which it was based. It was with great effort demolished after serving for only fifty years. Huge buildings become evanescent. They may lose half of their value before they are completed, may already be candidates for demolition at their completion because there is no economic return on their investment. And in any case they are commonly made of glass and steel and aluminum, rather than stone and masonry and brick, and look as if they could be taken apart by a screwdriver. So what place is there for monuments designed for the ages?

When the huge Ronald Reagan Building was being built in Washington—the grandest federal building that had been erected in Washington, intended to complete the Federal Triangle that has been rising since the 1920s, a building exceeded in size only by the Pentagon—there were rising complaints in Congress about its cost. It was not being built to meet an obvious need (though there is always need for more space for the federal government), and there was uncertainty over what it would be used for as it went up. Originally it was intended to be a World Trade Center, housing appropriate federal agencies. Senators Robert Dole and Daniel P. Moynihan, who was most committed to the building, proposed that it be named after Ronald Reagan, which may have helped persuade a reluctant Congress to appropriate the money to complete it. As one newspaper noted: "If you name a white elephant after Ronald Reagan, will conservatives in Congress buy it?" (They did.)

Senator Moynihan was unique among our national political leaders in expressing any interest at all in the physical form of our capital. (See chapter 6.) He was concerned with the rebuilding of Pennsylvania Avenue, the once tacky street along which presidents drive to their inauguration, from the time he came to Washington in a federal post in 1961, and helped create the Pennsylvania Avenue Development Commission. When he wrote the bill authorizing the building of what ultimately became the Ronald Reagan Building, he called for one of "monumental quality" that would "provide visual testimony to the dignity, enterprise and vigor of the federal government." It was once taken for granted that this was what important federal buildings should do, as one can see if one visits any federal courthouse built before World War II. It is hard to believe our nation is poorer than it was when it built those magnificent structures, clearly designed for the ages. But any building that tries to realize that ambition today—"to provide visual testimony to the dignity, enterprise and vigor of the federal government"—immediately comes under attack, as is the case with some of the more recent courthouses, which have been built under a program to attract top American architects to design them.

III

No time for monuments, one may conclude, and leave it at that. Our world undermines the attitudes of respect, reverence, awe that would support the building of monuments, that would appreciate them, use them. That might be enough to settle the matter.

But then, aside from what has happened to our culture, our society, to the world, there is what has happened to art. We need the artist to build our monuments: the sculptor, above all, but also the architect, the designer, the painter. The works of the preeminent artists of our time do not lend themselves to the functions of commemoration, memorialization, the communication of meanings, except for the meaning that the work has for the artist himself, or perhaps for the history of art itself. "Self-referential" has become the popular term for contemporary art and architecture, but the reference in question is available only to experts and specialists, and may make no sense and hold no interest for those who are not. Art, as we all know, has become obsessed with its means: the painter is concerned with paint, color, form, the canvas itself; the sculptor with his materials, stone, metal, wood; and now both are intrigued by newer materials such as plastics and neon lights and video and computerized images. Some of the most publicized artists of the day go on to even odder materials for art, such as meat spread over a human figure, or chocolate cakes mashed into mattresses. (The first was part of the permanent exhibit of the Walker Memorial in Minneapolis a while back; the second was featured in one Whitney Biennial show.) All this is as far a cry from Ozymandias as one can imagine.

It would be easy to caricature this development, and it is tempting to do so. No one has been a more pointed satirist of it than Tom Wolfe. If I had to vote, I would be on his side rather than on the side of the artists who have resolutely removed readily available sense and meaning from their work, the critics who have encouraged them, and the art historians who soberly record their achievements as something important and instruct hordes of art history students on their significance. The artists who use human figures, who try to tell the story of the events they memorialize, are clearly on the defensive today in the world of art—among art critics, in art history departments, in commissioning peer groups who select artists for major works. They are plaintive in defending themselves: they know they are on the losing side, for they are inevitably linked to past traditions in the face of the onslaught of the new.

James E. Young, in his fascinating book *The Texture of Memory: Holocaust Memorials and Meaning* (Yale, 1993), writes of Nathan Rapoport, the Polish Jewish sculptor who designed the Warsaw Ghetto Memorial. In defense of his work, which would remind us—with its human figures in despair and in triumph—of the Soviet style, or perhaps of the WPA style, Rapoport asked, "Could I have made a rock with a hole in it and said, `Voila! The hero-

ism of the Jewish people'?"[3] Undoubtedly nine out of ten
art critics today would answer, yes, better a Henry
Moore, the stone with a hole in it. That was the answer
of those who commissioned the art for the Holocaust
Museum, who were nothing if not sophisticated in matters of art.

Is this tendency to reduce meaning in art to meaning
for artists purely a matter of fad and fashion? One suspects there is something deeper motivating it. Those same
tendencies in modern society that hinder the unambiguous commemoration of great figures or great events make
it equally hard to resort to the artistic traditions of the
past without irony or mockery. I find it difficult to stand
resolutely against the massed voices of art critics and artists and commissioning bodies who would have to be hit
over the head to go back to human figures. Sometimes
they *are* hit over the head, by what they conceive of as
an ignorant public. And so the three soldiers by Frederick
Hart are added to Maya Lin's mute wall of names. And
the original winning proposal for the Korean War Memorial is taken over and radically modified by the addition
of a group of soldiers on patrol as its central image. The
journal of the American Institute of Architects, *Architecture*, disapproved of the changes in the Korean War Memorial. "Compromised Commemoration," was the title of
its critical editorial. The AIA is no body of radical architects and art critics. But it did not approve of how the
original winning proposal had been humanized, made
more accessible.

---

[3] James E. Young, *Texture of Memory: Holocaust Memorials and Meaning*
(New Haven: Yale University Press, 1994), p. 9.

The artist has been in rebellion against society for almost two centuries, and now the rebellion has extended to the point of victory, perhaps temporary victory, if not in society generally, then in the sphere of art itself. The art that represents the tradition of rebellion attracts more attention and more approval by far in the world of art than any work of art that represents acceptance of artistic traditions, of classic artistic materials, of the notion that one aim of art is to please a patron or a public. Art is gripped by the "tradition of the new," and the avant-garde of outrage and shock is institutionalized to the point where it is the artist of human representation and traditional design who can claim to be a rebel. A recent book on contemporary public sculpture begins with a sentence the author does not consider remarkable, but which I do: "The problems endemic to public art in a democracy begin with its definition. How can something be both public (democratic) and art (elitist)?" Harriet Senie, the writer, assumes that art by its nature must be elitist, and dismisses in so doing nine-tenths of the history of art.[4]

I have described a course in the making of monuments from meaning to muteness. Perhaps there was too much overt and intended meaning in the monuments of the nineteenth and earlier twentieth centuries. It would certainly appear so from our present perspective, which prefers the spare, the minimal, the stripped-down image, to the point indeed where what we have may be no representation of an image at all but simply a representation of the materials that were once used to make images. So we

---

[4] Harriet E. Senie, *Contemporary Public Sculpture: Tradition, Transformation, and Controversy* (New York: Oxford University Press), p. 3.

come to the mute, the nonspeaking monument. The public may not have been enthusiastic about this kind of monument or memorial at the beginning, but its taste, too, has been educated, and by now it tolerates this muteness. When the muteness is associated, as the Vietnam Memorial is, with a tragic and, in many minds, meaningless war, the public will actively respond to and appreciate it.

That is not the end of the line. There is the mocking monument, and the antimonument. The artist is no longer silent in the face of his commission; he undermines it or subverts it. The monument then is no longer silent; it becomes a critique of what it was intended to celebrate or memorialize. I prefer the subversion of humor to grimly serious subversion, in which the artist attacks his patrons and his audience and proposes himself as a critic of the society whose representatives have commissioned his work. The master of the mocking monument is Claes Oldenburg. On the dust jacket of Harriet Senie's *Contemporary Public Sculpture* is a picture of Philadelphia City Hall, with its crowning statue of Benjamin Franklin, and in front of it, huge and almost dwarfing the building, is an enormous black clothespin. One has to at least smile. I initially assumed the clothespin was not permanent.[5] If it were, the monument would lose its point and its humor. A giant clothespin (or any of the other objects of very ordinary life that Oldenburg blows up to monster size) is not intended for the ages.

The nonhumorous subversive monument is another matter. The artist begins to take himself too seriously, and

[5] Witold Rybczynski has told me, to my dismay, that it is indeed permanent.

may regard with contempt the needs, desires, and hopes of those who commission his art. So when Richard Serra was asked to provide a piece of sculpture for a square in New York City surrounded by a federal courthouse, a federal office building, and other public buildings, he put up *Tilted Arc*, a tilting wall of steel slashing diagonally across the square, which made uncomfortable or impossible the everyday use of the square by the workers in the surrounding buildings as a place to take one's lunch or enjoy the out-of-doors. This sculpture went beyond muteness to offensiveness, and some of Serra's comments suggest that this is what he intended. (The term "subversion" is common in current appreciations of advanced art, and here it would appear Serra hoped to "subvert the context." See chapter 3.)

The General Services Administration, which had commissioned and paid for the work on the advice of a distinguished panel, held hearings to determine whether the sculpture should be removed. The art world fought vigorously against the removal of this obstruction. It was the kind of clash that Harriet Senie had in mind in contrasting art as an elite activity and the public as the voice of democracy. Against the advice and impassioned resistance of scores of art critics, the wall was removed. This event is viewed by the art world as a triumph of philistinism, but such victories of uninformed public opinion are rare, and their rarity is a demonstration of the intimidating power of contemporary artistic opinion.

The antimonument, in which the artist specifically rebels against the monumental tradition, and may try to criticize ("deconstruct"?) the hopes and intentions of those who have commissioned the work, is the most characteristic monument of our time. A lead-plated thirty-nine-foot column in Hamburg was constructed as a monument to the Holocaust. It is designed to sink, a few feet at a time, into the earth until it disappears. People are supposed to write observations on it. But what will they write when there is nothing on the monument that explains what it is for? Another Holocaust monument in Austria is meant to recall a fountain given to the town by a Jew and destroyed by the Nazis. The monument is a re-creation of the original, but this time as its hollowed-out interior, dug into the ground. And there are other ingenious examples of the antimonument, particularly in Germany.[6] This makes sense: Germans have the hardest time, hard as it is for any of us, in figuring out how to memorialize the Holocaust, and equal difficulty in figuring out how to commemorate a spoiled history.

Just what the antimonument is against is often not easy to divine: it may be the monumental tradition itself; or the society and authorities who want to innocently celebrate or memorialize something; or popular attitudes to what is being celebrated or remembered. A huge mountain of shopping carts erected around and completely covering a Mozart statue in Salzburg was, one assumes, intended to subvert not Mozart but rather his commercialization. The citizens of Salzburg did not sense this distinction and demanded the immediate dismantling of the shopping-cart tower.

The antimonument is, of course, more than a German phenomenon, though some of the most startling exam-

---

[6] These examples of antimonuments are from James Young's invaluable *Texture of Memory*.

ples may be found there. At issue is the problem of modern art itself, whose mission of showing its contempt for bourgeois society now requires ever more outrageous acts and objects, or may be reduced to sputtering denunciatory slogans, which is a popular new approach to making art out of unlikely materials.

When it comes to the antimonument—the monument that the artist intends as a criticism in some sense of his commission, or the commissioning authorities, or some aspect of the larger community that has called for the work of art—it is quite proper for the commissioning authorities to say to the experts who have selected the artist, no, we don't think this will do. Undoubtedly we will have responses that are insensitive to the power of some contemporary images, to the range of meanings even a mute monument may carry. This was true of those who objected to the Vietnam War Memorial, to the black granite, to the absence of human figures, to the absence of any ennobling inscription. It turned out that the public, when it was built, disagreed. They found a great deal in it. It became the most popular monument in Washington.

It is also true that the public processes that must inevitably come into play when we build monuments in a democracy in time resulted in an addition to the monument in the form of a group of human figures representing the soldiers who fought in that ill-fated war. I don't think that bothers any of the many thousands who visit that memorial, despite the tut-tutting of the arts community. Nor do I find that addition objectionable. One may think of it, if one wishes to consider it in purely aesthetic terms, as balancing the wall, the way the Trylon and the Perisphere of the New York World's Fair of 1939 presented contrasting but balancing objects. I also think the next group of human figures that was added was too much, and any more—and varied interest groups keep on proposing yet additional clumps of human figures—would just be silly.

In the present age of discordance, there is really no way of settling these matters aesthetically. The authoritative voices in the world of art will almost uniformly prefer the new, even if mystifying or outrageous. Popular opinion will almost always be doubtful. These matters do get settled, but it is through politics, not aesthetic authority, which in the present situation is, I think, all for the best. We should not accept the authority of the arts community without demur, or accept the voice of the people as the voice of God. The two will inevitably come into conflict, and the conflicts will be settled in a messy way, as the arts community tangles with the public. Looking at the results of some of these conflicts—such as the removal of Serra's *Tilted Arc*, or the addition of the first group of soldiers to the Vietnam Memorial—I conclude that they are better ways of getting satisfactory public art than simply deferring to the authority of the dominant voices in the world of the arts.

CHAPTER FIVE

Modernism and Classicism on the National Mall

The National Mall in Washington, extending from the Capitol to the Lincoln Memorial, is in its design a unique national memorial space. One may find its like in the great royal gardens of France, but not in dense cities. First sketched in L'Enfant's original plan for Washington, it might then have reflected his memory of a still rural Champs-Elysées in Paris. But it was recast, after a century of disordered and conflicting changes and development, in 1902 by Daniel Burnham, Charles McKim, and Frederick Law Olmsted, Jr. They had been selected to form a Senate Park Commission, through the action of Senator James McMillan, and charged to create a plan for the park system of the District of Columbia. In their redesign, it was to become not a grand avenue but a quiet ceremonial space, extending from the Capitol, beyond the obelisk of the Washington Monument, where tideland was to be filled in to extend the Mall, and was to climax in a new proposed Lincoln Memorial. On its north and south sides were to be erected great new public buildings.

On the one hundredth anniversary of the presentation of the plan they proposed in 1902, the Mall as envisioned by these remarkably self-confident and competent designers was substantially complete, a rare example of a grand plan that was in time completed pretty much as proposed, surviving the vicissitudes of a hundred years of democratic government.

The Mall had become the great ceremonial space of the nation, host to vast assemblages, whether to call for civil rights when Martin Luther King, Jr., spoke there, or to mark the first few years of the AIDS epidemic when the extensive turf was covered by thousands of AIDS memorial quilts. But at a time when we demand ever more memorials, and in the most treasured space designed for them, memorials and museums crowd in on the Mall, burdening it and perhaps destroying the opportunity it provides for quiet reflection.

The most recent major intrusion, occasioning fierce conflicts over the character and future of the National Mall, is the huge World War II Memorial, completed in 2004. Many criticized its placement as a severe disruption of the Mall as originally intended by its 1902 designers. Their plan emphasized the vista from the Capitol to the Lincoln Memorial, interrupted only by the Washington Monument. The World War II Memorial was be sited on and around the oval pool just beyond the Washington Monument. Could any less prominent site, however, be appropriate for that great national crusade, particularly since the lesser and more ambiguous wars fought in Korea and Vietnam had already been given locations on the Mall? Equally criticized was its vaguely classical design, reversing more than a half century of modernism, in one or another of its variants, in building on the Mall.

It has been built, and for the moment controversy over it is stilled. A museum to the American Indian has also filled the last large space on the Mall available for a mu-

seum, but an African American museum is in planning
and will be squeezed into the Mall. A Latino museum
waits in line behind it. A monument to Martin Luther
King, Jr., already on the way, will be fitted in between
the Jefferson Memorial and the Washington Monument.
A large location opposite the Air and Space Museum has
already been selected for an Eisenhower Memorial. And
who can doubt that space will have to be found in time for
a memorial for Presidents John Adams and John Quincy
Adams, which is only the more urgent because they were
the only presidents among the first half dozen who were
not slaveholders, and because it may well include the first
woman to be memorialized on the Mall, Abigail Adams?

Public agencies have addressed the crowding of the
Mall, and proposed new spaces to be developed for major
memorials and museums. Still, the pressure to locate new
memorials and museums as close to the Mall as possible
is irrepressible.

Wherever our new memorials and museums are located, a central issue, joining the problem of crowding,
has become, as we see from the conflict over the World
War II Memorial, their design. The classicism that Burnham, McKim, and Olmsted took for granted when they
made their proposals for the Mall has long been super-
seded by modernism and its variants. What will these
new memorials look like, what can they look like, and
how effectively can they do their work as memorials?

The March of the Memorials

When the McMillan Commission of 1902 was doing its
work, there was only one great monument on the Mall,

the Washington Monument, and it had been completed and opened to the public only fifteen years earlier. Its vicissitudes—almost a century's passing between an initial proposal for such a monument and its completion, forty years in the building, political conflict and controversy through much of that period, endless difficulties in securing the money, radical revision of the original plan—foreshadowed the story of almost all the great monuments that have subsequently been erected on the Mall or in its precincts in fulfillment of the McMillan plan. But one particular moment in the history of these controversies marks a distinctive divide: it is the controversy over the Jefferson Memorial, which was to complete the original proposals of the McMillan Commission for Washington's monumental center.

They had proposed, balancing the Capitol and at the other end of the lengthened Mall of their plan, a monument to Lincoln, on filled land that was to be created beyond the Washington Monument. And it was built, very much as they intended, in a classical style, in remarkably short order, and was an enormous success. On the cross-axis defined by the White House to the north and the Washington Monument in its pivotal central location, they proposed another great monument to the south, balancing the White House. They did not suggest that it honor any specific figure, but there was only one person in the epic of American democracy who deserved to stand with Washington and Lincoln, and that was clearly the author of the Declaration of Independence, Thomas Jefferson.

It nevertheless took a Democratic president, Franklin Delano Roosevelt, perhaps contemplating the presence of two great memorials on the Mall to Republican presidents (there is the forgotten but enormous monument to Ulysses S. Grant at the foot of the Capitol), and none to Democrats, to restart the stalled process of a monument to Jefferson in January 1934, with a letter to the Commission of Fine Arts proposing it consider such a monument. John Russell Pope, the classicist American architect who was designing the enormous National Gallery of Art for the Mall at the same time, emerged as the architect for the memorial. What could it be, one would think in 1937, other than a classical monument, and preferably a domed structure, something like the centerpiece of Jefferson's great design for the University of Virginia? But modernism in art and architecture—somewhat belatedly, it is true—was rapidly gaining dominance among American critics and artists and architects. The National Gallery of Art had surprisingly escaped criticism while its design was being developed and modified. But the storm broke over the Jefferson Memorial.

Two streams have contributed, as we have noted earlier, to modernism in architecture, the social criticism that decried an architecture that ignored or disguised the realities of modern life and the needs of the working classes, and the aesthetic revolution that rejected all traditional historical styles in architecture. The two sources of modernism were not always in agreement, but they joined in the denunciation of Pope's design for the Jefferson Memorial. "With the country still in the midst of a serious depression," writes Pope's biographer, "the most vituperative criticism came from a group composed largely of advocates for the housing division of the Public Works Administration, including Catherine Bauer [later Catherine

Bauer Wurster], Carl Feiss, Talbot Hamlin, Joseph Hudnut, William Lescaze, and Lewis Mumford." Should such
a monument be built, it was asked, "in light of the fact
that two-thirds of the nation was inadequately clothed,
housed, and fed"? That is always a good argument against
building expensive monuments. But one suspects that
the rejection of all forms of historicism in architecture,
which is the chief mark of modernism, played a greater
role. "[A] torrent of letters opposing Pope's appointment
as architect for the memorial was presented at a House
hearing from a vast number of luminaries, including the
director of the Museum of Modern Art, Alfred A. Barr,
Jr." Frank Lloyd Wright, in a letter to President Roosevelt,
attacked the design as an "arrogant insult to the memory
of Thomas Jefferson." The faculty of the School of Architecture at Columbia University denounced it as "a lamen-
table misfit in time and place."[1]

It was "High Noon on the Mall," as Richard Guy Wilson
describes the conflict between traditionalism and modernism,[2] and the shoot-out came over the Jefferson Memorial. The Commission of Fine Arts, created to carry out
the McMillan plan, was no longer fully dominated by tra-
ditionalists. (Not that any strong proponents of modernism were yet members.) Gilmore Clarke, its chairman,
hoped that the design "would bring out some of the new
arts rather than transporting an ancient parti from Rome
to this site in the form of the Pantheon." William Lamb,

---

[1] Steven McLeod Bedford, *John Russell Pope: Architect of Empire* (New York: Rizzoli, 1998), pp. 220, 222.

[2] Richard Guy Wilson, "High Noon on the Mall: Modernism versus Traditionalism, 1910–1970," in *The Mall in Washington, 1791–1991*, ed. Richard
Longstreth (Washington, D.C.: National Gallery of Art, 1991), pp. 143–67.

whose firm had designed the Empire State Building, said, "I myself do not believe that the reproduction of imperial Rome in the shape of the Pantheon would represent in the slightest degree that simplicity, honesty of character that he [Jefferson] stood for." And another member of the commission: "I feel it is rather a dreary thing as it stands. . . . I regret that this has not been exposed to the full possibility of American design today."[3]

But then, one may ask seventy years later, and in the light of what has transpired with monuments and modernism since, if it had been a design expressing contemporary modernism, what would it have been like, and would we have preferred it to what was then built? One may doubt it. There is the rub: modernism and monuments do not marry well.

Modernism and the Monument

While this debate was going on, Lewis Mumford's *The Culture of Cities* was published, and there he put the matter quite starkly: "If it is a monument it is not modern, and if it is modern, it cannot be a monument." Mumford was certainly the most important American critic of urban form and design during the middle of the last century, between the 1930s and the 1960s. Before him the most prominent figures in urbanism were the promoters of the City Beautiful movement: Daniel Burnham, McKim, Mead, and White, Frederick Olmsted, Sr. and Jr., and the other figures who created the Columbian Exposition in

---

[3] Sue A. Kohler, *The Commission of Fine Arts: A Brief History, 1910–1990* (Washington, D.C.: The Commission of Fine Arts, 1990), pp. 71–72.

Chicago in 1893, and who in time served as members of the McMillan Commission. After Mumford there was Jane Jacobs, and the proponents of the various forms of postmodernism. For the advocates of the City Beautiful, the ideal city seemed to be in large measure monuments and vistas. For Jane Jacobs, committed to the lively and mixed city neighborhood, the monument just didn't exist. Mumford excoriated the advocates of the City Beautiful and was disdainful of Jane Jacobs's prescriptions.

What was the problem for Mumford? Why was there this fundamental contradiction between modernism and monuments?

Mumford writes, in a section of *The Culture of Cities* titled "The Death of the Monument," that monuments celebrate power and death, while modernism celebrates democracy and life. "One of the most important attributes of a vital urban civilization," he asserts, "is one that has rarely been achieved in past civilizations: the capacity for renewal. Against the fixed shell and the static monument, the new architecture"—he is talking about modernism—"places its faith in the powers of social adaptation and reproduction. The sign of the older order of architecture, in almost every culture, was the House of the Dead; in modern culture, it is the dwelling house, or House of the Living."

Architecture in the past was defined by its monuments to the dead: "The primitive burial mounds, the big stones of the Salisbury Plains or Brittany, the Pyramids and Sphinxes of Egypt, the grandiose gestures of a Sargon or Ozymandias, of a Louis XIV or a Peter the Great: these represent that respect for death which is essentially a fear of life."

He decries the cult of death, "thanks to [which], permanence comes in the structures of the city." Let me emphasize that word, permanence. But today,

> instead of being oriented toward death and fixity, we are oriented to the cycle of life, with its never-ending process of birth and growth and renewal and death. . . . the idea of fixity has been slow to resist change. . . . The truth is, however, that the notion of material survival by means of the monument no longer represents the impulses of our civilization, and in fact it defies our closest convictions. These Valhallas and Lincoln Memorials, these Victor Emmanuel Monuments and Vimy Ridge Memorials, these "Eternal Lights" that go out when the electric power station breaks down or the bulb blows out—how many buildings of the last century, that pretend to be august and monumental, have a touch of the modern spirit in them? They are all the hollow echoes of an expiring breath, . . . which either curb and confine the works of the living, like the New York Public Library, or are completely irrelevant to our beliefs and demands.

Then comes that comment I have already quoted: "If it is a monument it is not modern, and if it is modern, it cannot be a monument."

That reference to a number of monuments that would have been known, or might have been known, to his readers may confuse us and point up some problems with Mumford's dictum. Valhalla is an enormous monument in Bavaria, an almost perfect copy of the Parthenon, built in the nineteenth century to honor great Germans in the arts, literature, history. In style the Victor Emmanuel

monument in Rome is a huge wedding cake of extravagant classical and Baroque elements that no one has a
good word for today. But the Lincoln Memorial? Vimy
Ridge, one of the sober monuments to the dead of World
War I? The New York Public Library? All these monuments of intended permanence, drawn from the architectural library of the past, were equally anathema to Mumford. These days we would, and do, make distinctions
among them. I see a considerable difference between the
Lincoln Memorial and the Victor Emmanuel monument,
and not only a difference in the quality of the two men
who were being memorialized. And today I think many
would be taken aback by such a dismissive reference to
the New York Public Library, a building that does so much
for New York City, because of its design and function as
a major element in its urban fabric, and not only because
it is a great public library.

So, then, were there to be no monuments in Mumford's ideal city? Well, not quite:

> This is not to say that a hospital or power station or an
> air beacon [today we would call it a control tower] may
> not be treated as a monument to a person or an event;
> nor is it to deny that a contemporary structure might
> not easily last 200 years or even two thousand: that is
> not the point. What will make the hospital or the air
> beacon a good memorial is the fact that it has been well
> designed for the succor of those who are ill, or for the
> guidance of men piloting airplanes. . . .
>
> The death of the monument . . . has implications that
> go far beyond the conception of individual tombs, me-
> morials, or public buildings; it affects . . . the very tex-

ture of urban life. Why, for example, should each generation go on living in the quarters that were built by
its ancestors? These quarters . . . were planned for
other uses, other habits, other modes of living.[4]

Mumford was pointing to aspects of modernism, in architecture, in urbanism, and in design, that are still with
us, and continue to create enormous problems for monuments and memorials being planned and built today. I
would point to four aspects of modernism that contradict
by their nature the idea of the monument: functionalism;
lightness; impermanence; the penchant for new materials. All of these play a part in Mumford's—and modernism's—rejection of the monument.

What, after all, is the function of the monument? And
without a clear function, a program, what does the
modern architect do? The form of the monument is
not dictated by any mundane uses. It is true people have
to be directed to it, and through it, and out of it, and
comfort stations must be provided, and regarding these
needs there are certainly functional requirements. But
despite Mumford, a monument is not a hospital or a
school or a dwelling: it is meant to celebrate, to recall, to
honor. How does that connect with modernism's commitment to the functional, to the meeting of a need,
without doing anything more or anything less? And so
in modernism we have the undecorated window without
a frame that looks as if it had been punched out of a wall,
the modest and almost invisible entry, the flat roof, the
undecorated cornice.

[4] Lewis Mumford, *The Culture of Cities* (New York: Harcourt Brace, 1938);
all quotations are from pp. 433–40.

And then there is the leaning toward the light and impermanent, as against the heavy and the solid. One of the most talked about buildings of recent years was the "blur" building of Elizabeth Diller and Ricardo Scofidio— the building itself, whatever there is of it, disappears in a permanent mist. The perfect embodiment of the modernist spirit! A leading proposal for a memorial to the World Trade Center victims was two columns of light recalling the building. One of the idols and prophets of modernism, Buckminster Fuller, emphasized that progress lay in reducing the weight of objects. His most successful invention was a light but strong dome of metal rods that could be taken apart and moved, and when in use could be covered in fabric. Other contemporary expressions of the modern are buildings whose surfaces are ever-changing patterns of color or graphics, projected images. Buildings that can be dismantled or look as if they can be (Britain's Millennium Dome, for example) are among those favored by advanced architectural theorists; so are buildings that look as if they can shoot off into space, though as yet the mobile aerodynamic building is more theory than reality. All this favors new materials— fabric, plastics, illusions created by the manipulation of light. And what does this mean for a monument or memorial that is intended to be not for a time or a moment but timeless?

The Modern Artist Confronts the Monument

Modernism begins with an emphasis on the functional. It denies that it is part of the history of style, that it *is* a style, one among others. No, modernism asserts, its penchant for the functional, the impermanent, the changing, the new, simply reflects the reality of our culture and civilization, the steady and always shifting impacts of new technology and new needs. It reflects, too, a new social aim: we are no longer dominated by priests and princes; we abhor war and hope for eternal peace. Our societies aim toward a stable democracy and a widespread equality, and architecture should serve those new objectives. And so modern architecture's most prominent early achievements are in mass housing for the working classes and the poor and well-designed factories. Its objectives were better dwellings, schools, factories—not grander palaces and tombs. How, then, can the desire for celebration and memorialization be satisfied by modernism?

Despite its claim that it was the end of the history of architecture, however, modernism was also a style, time-bound, a rebellion against earlier styles, and as such it is part of the history of art and design, rather than the end of art and design. For architecture, modernism insisted on what we might call the ordinary. What else can one make of form following function, of the elimination of ornament, of less is more, of the apparent humble adaptation to needs, as contrasted with the imposition of extravagant grandeur? But if this was what modernism in architecture asserted, it was not at all what modernism in art meant. That, on the contrary, following in the romantic spirit of the nineteenth century, had become the celebration of the individual artist, following his own vision. The modern artist, it is true, was also a rebel against the past, against whatever was, but not in order to come closer to common needs and their satisfaction, but rather to create something new and startling and outrageous. The monument must draw not only on the architect but on the artist. The artist had become someone whose very being is antithetical to the notion of the monument in its aspect as a memorial that represents and reflects and is suited to a community. The modern artist has become a rebel against community. The modernist architect much less so: architects are inevitably more bound than artists are by the reality imposed by economic restraints and the common sense or taste of patrons, clients, users. But in his aspect as artist the advanced modernist architect also apes the posture of rejection of the given and the celebration of the new and rebellious.

For both modernist artists and architects, the monumental building, and the monument, posed a problem. The modernist American architect George Nelson put the problem well in 1944:

> The contemporary architect, cut off from symbols, ornament . . . and meaningful elaboration of structural forms . . . has desperately chased every functional requirement, every change in site or orientation, every technical improvement, to provide some basis for starting his work. Where the limitations were most rigorous, as for example in a factory, the designers were happiest and the results were most satisfying. But let a religious belief or a social ideal replace cubic foot costs or radiation losses, and nothing happened. There is not a single modern church in the entire country that is comparable to a first-rate cafeteria.[5]

---

[5] George Nelson writing in 1944, as quoted by Sarah Williams Goldhagen, *Louis Kahn's Situated Modernism* (New Haven: Yale University Press, 2001), p. 27.

This problem was most sharply posed when the leaders of modernism in Europe pondered the matter of monuments in World War II. As the war progressed, they realized that monuments would certainly be built after the war. If modernism rejected the monument, would not its role in the rebuilding of cities, in the expression of the public's desires, be sharply reduced? And so a debate began on how modernism could come to terms with monuments. A leading figure in guiding that debate was the distinguished architectural historian Siegfried Giedion, whose *Space, Time, and Architecture* (1941) and *Mechanization Takes Command* (1948) provided the most authoritative history of modernism. He was also secretary-general of the CIAM, the important major international organization of modern architects.

In 1943, during the war, Giedion, teaming up with the architect Josep Lluis Sert—who was in time to become chairman of architecture and dean at the Harvard Graduate School of Design—and the French modernist artist Fernand Léger, wrote "Nine Points on Monumentality." They took a more positive view toward monuments than Mumford had a few years before. They wrote: "Monuments are human landmarks which men have created as symbols for their ideals, for their aims, and for their actions. They are intended to outlive the period which originated them, and constitute a heritage for future generations. As such, they form a link between the past and the future." And further: "Monuments are the expression of man's highest cultural needs."

So they agreed monuments are needed. But the monuments of the recent past, they argue, "have become empty shells." Can modernism help? They acknowledge it has not yet been much help when it comes to monuments. But they explain: "Modern architecture, like modern painting and sculpture, had to start the hard way. It began by tackling the simple problems, the more utilitarian buildings like low-rent housing, schools, office buildings, hospitals, and similar structures." But as modern architecture takes up the task of city rebuilding, it has to grow up to the task of designing and incorporating monuments, and it can. They recognize that this is no easy task. They call for the collaboration of planners, architects, painters, and sculptors. They call for using modern materials and new techniques: "light metal structures, laminated wooden arches, panels of different textures, colors and sizes, light elements like ceilings that can be suspended from big trusses covering practically unlimited spans. Mobile elements can constantly vary the aspects of the buildings. These mobile elements, changing positions and casting different shadows when acted upon by wind or machinery, can be the source of new architectural effects. During night hours, color and forms can be projected on vast surfaces. . . . Monumental architecture will be something more than strictly functional."[6]

But is there not a contradiction between the earlier part of their manifesto—"[monuments] are intended to outlive the period which originated them, and constitute a heritage for future generations, they have to satisfy the eternal demand of the people for translation of their collective force into symbols"—and the means they favor when they describe what the modern monument will be?

[6] Siegfried Giedion, *Architecture, You and Me* (Cambridge: Harvard University Press, 1958), pp. 23–24.

There is another contradiction: they wish to employ modern architects and sculptors. These are ready to come out of the gallery and the museum and into the public sphere. Giedion refers to Brancusi, Hans Arp, Naum Gabo, Alberto Giacometti, Picasso.

The modern artist does not easily lend himself to satisfying "the eternal demand of the people for translation of their collective force into symbols." Artists have created their own unique symbols, symbols that identify them, that become their trademark. When we see a Brancusi, an Arp, a Giacometti, a Picasso, as part of a monument, what will we think? We will think, there is a Brancusi, an Arp, and so forth. Will we think of the collective effort they have been commissioned to celebrate, the tragedy they have been asked to commemorate, the hero to whom a monument for the ages is being raised? Not very likely.

The dilemma of modernism in dealing with the monument is that while it begins, at least in architecture, with the idea that it will accommodate the needs and uses of ordinary men and women, economically and directly, it has undergone an evolution and development in which the architect and artist become creators of the new and astonishing. They do not find it easy to celebrate the common ideals and emotions of a community. It is more likely that they celebrate themselves.

A few examples of this dilemma: in the Holocaust Museum, in Washington, D.C., as I noted in chapter 4, three leading modern artists were commissioned to produce works of art for the museum, works of art presumably in some way related to its theme. They were Richard Serra, Sol LeWitt, and Ellsworth Kelly. As one might expect, the three works are a Serra, a LeWitt, and a Kelly, easily identifiable as such. What they have to do with the Holocaust is not easy to divine.

At the west end of the museum is an outdoor sculpture, in two parts, labeled *Loss* and *Regeneration*, "in memory of the children who perished in the Holocaust." They are by Joel Shapiro. They are trademark generic modern sculpture, that is, beams of iron in various arrangements. How they are connected to the theme they memorialize remains a mystery.

A group of modern works of sculpture has now been placed in a sculpture garden. There are works by Henry Moore, Alexander Calder, Jean Arp, Frank Stella, and others. The cognoscenti would have recognized the artists. They could not possibly have recognized the distinctive point the works were trying to make, if any. The Stella, a riotous assemblage of colorful objects in various materials, was titled *Prince Friedrich von Homburg, Ein Schauspiel*. One assumes it was a joke. But perhaps not. Would we want any of them to design a monument?

The issue is, or one issue is, that we have a storehouse of forms and emblems from the historic past, and they evoke something. Obelisks, pyramids, columns, wreaths, steeples. . . . Sometimes they have become kitsch, and unusable. This is the case, undoubtedly, with the man on horseback. It isn't just that that is not the way people go into war or review troops anymore. The symbol simply doesn't jibe with contemporary life. Or the various nymphs or sylphs on many monuments representing the continents, the winds, the directions, the virtues, the vices, or what have you. They once meant something to us—they don't anymore. We can no longer read the language of classicism. Sometimes we're not sure whether the symbols still work or not. That is the problem with the World War II Memorial—a huge oval of columns, with wreaths on top, and with two triumphal arches at the short ends. It does seem like a throwback. But what could a truly modern World War II memorial have been?

There are many traditional forms and emblems that are not yet, I would think, exhausted and do serve to communicate something to people. And in any case the new forms of modern art and modernism either have their own kitschy meaning, like beams of iron agonizing with each other, or mean nothing at all. Perhaps the sophisticates can distinguish one construction of iron beams from another, one set of whorled metal sheets from another, so that one might mean triumph and another defeat, but most us can't and are left to say, "Huh?"

Alexander Calder's mobiles and stabiles are gentler constructions. One can see one on the west side of the Museum of American History on the Mall, an homage to Gwen Cafritz, a benefactor of Washington art. The homage is in the name alone: nothing obvious distinguishes it from other playful Calders. This will work to some extent. Would it work for a serious monument or memorial to note events or people that we do not consider a laughing matter?

When Modernism Succeeds

And yet memorials must be built—people demand them—by modern or at least contemporary architects and artists, and sometimes the dilemma is resolved and transcended, and we have a monument that is, despite Mumford, both modern and a monument. This is preeminently the case with the Vietnam Veterans Memorial in Washington. Not the least astonishing thing about it is that it was designed by a twenty-one-year-old student who had designed nothing that had been built before. It is worth studying why this modern monument succeeds when so many others fail.

I think there are three reasons why the Vietnam Veterans Memorial is able to transcend Mumford's dictum. One is that it is not a work by a trademarked modern artist. The artist's personality and style do not get in the way. Maya Lin was too young and unknown to have a trademarked and recognizable style. (Nor, of course, does every contemporary artist develop a trademarked style.) So we don't think of the artist when we visit it, even though many of the visitors must be aware of the remarkable story of its design.

A second is that it was a stroke of near genius to place the names of the dead on the monument by *date*, in the order in which they died. As I note in chapter 4, this meant we did not have the problem of lists of common names, which would have reduced the individual character of each sacrifice and each death. It meant, further, that those looking for a name would have to consult an alphabetical directory to find out where the name they sought was located, and then go searching along that long wall, descending deeper into the earth and ascending out of it. It offered what few monuments do, a degree of legitimate interaction (not the kind of interaction through a television or video that keeps breaking down): one has to look up the name in a directory and search for it along a wall—and then there is an additional form of interaction that may not have been in the mind of the designer, the tracing out of the letters with a finger, or the making of a paper tracing of the name. I note in a picture I have seen of the Kyoto earthquake memorial that the names of the victims there, too, are listed, and people are looking for them.

A third reason I would warrant for its success: its silence. Is there any other monument that refuses to say anything at all? There is not a single word aside from the names. Of course it suits the minimalism of modern art, which eschews inscriptions. But in this case the dumbness of modern art also suits the subject it is dealing with. It fits our ambivalence about the war—there is nothing to be said, and nothing is said. Neither that it was a victory or a defeat, nor that it was worth fighting and dying for or not, nor that it was heroic or its opposite.

But of course one cannot escape the skill or genius of the design itself. Minimal, as so much modern art is, without reference to anything else, it draws one into the declivity it creates, and evokes a mixed emotion suitable to the event it memorializes. All art, whether historicist, or classicist, or contemporary, has to depend on the skill or genius of the creator. It is only much, much harder when all historical reference, the storehouse of symbols and memories, is abandoned, and everything has to be created anew. That is the problem that modernism faces when it deals with monuments and memorials.

The Fate of the Classical

A good deal has changed since the shoot-out on the Mall in 1937 and 1938 over the Jefferson Memorial. Modernism in architecture triumphed but then lost some of its self-confidence. With a track record now of nearly a century, it can point to its masterpieces—but these are overwhelmed by a sea of dullness and more recently idiosyncrasy. It turned out that it was not so easy to speak to the spirit of man, to celebrate the great, to mourn catastrophe and disaster, without some help from the past. Even Pope is no longer universally execrated. Joseph Hudnut wrote in 1941 of his National Gallery of Art, "[S]urely the time cannot be far distant when we shall understand how inadequate is the death-mask of an ancient culture to express the heroic soul of America."[7] It was denounced as a "pink marble whorehouse" and a "costly mummy." Today, when we see what modernism has produced in the way of museums on the Mall, and they show a range of quality from the banal to somewhat successful, we are rather more tolerant. Indeed, when I. M. Pei was designing the East Building of the National Gallery of Art, we are told by J. Carter Brown, he "insisted that the Pope building not be touched. He loved the building, its great interior spaces, and its detailing."[8]

Most of us now find the Jefferson Memorial dignified and suitable to its purposes, and we may think even better of it when we ask ourselves what a contemporary design of the later 1930s might have been like, and whether it would have aged and survived as well.

Today we have additional major monuments to contemplate in this ongoing clash between traditionalism, of

[7] Bedford, *John Russell Pope*, p. 200.

[8] J. Carter Brown, "The Designing of the National Gallery of Art's East Building," in Longstreth, *The Mall in Washington*, p. 283.

some sort, and modernism, of some sort, in the Franklin D. Roosevelt Memorial, the Korean War Memorial, and preeminently the World War II Memorial. (And we will soon have other monuments to contemplate—the Martin Luther King, Jr., and the Eisenhower, and undoubtedly in time the memorial to presidents John and John Quincy Adams and perhaps Abigail Adams.)

The World War II Memorial marked a surprising and unexpected turn back to something akin to classicism. The shoot-out over the Jefferson Memorial was played out again, in a more moderated form. The controversial site, the oval pool to the west of the Washington Monument, almost dictated a symmetrical design, the kind that does not comport easily with modernism. No Maya Lin emerged from the anonymous competition for a design. Six of 407 proposals submitted were chosen for a second round of competition, all but one by established and well-known architects. Only one of the six, by students still in architecture school, suggested the tougher side of modernism. They proposed two bunkers of disparate form. All the designers were constrained by the requirement to provide a great deal of exhibition space, which could only be underground if it was not to disrupt the vista. After the first stage of the competition, the exhibit space requirement was dropped.[9]

Friedrich St. Florian, the winner, born in Austria, had come early in his career to the United States, as an ad-

[9] I lean here for the story of the World War II Memorial on the fine and full account by Nicolaus Mills, *Their Last Battle: The Fight for the National World War II Memorial* (New York: Basic Books, 2004).

mirer of American modernism, and in particular of Buckminster Fuller. Before he submitted his proposal for the
World War II Memorial, he had worked in a modernist
idiom. Indeed, with two collaborators he had come in second in the competition for the Pompidou Center in Paris.
Little in his past foreshadowed his winning design: an
oval of columnar forms ornamented with bronze wreaths
placed around an oval pool, with arches of triumph at
each of its two ends. Marble, bronze, wreaths, laurels, eagles. . . . These were not the typical materials and forms
of modernist architecture and design.

While the specific forms of St. Florian's design may be
far from a correct classical architecture in the judgment
of proponents of classical architecture, they were very familiar to architectural historians and critics. They recalled
the stripped-down classicism that was popular in the public architecture of the 1930s in the United States. Perhaps
we might call it the WPA style. But it was equally popular
in Nazi Germany and elsewhere. (Osbert Lancaster, in a
satiric picture-book history of architecture, shows on succeeding pages sketches of identical buildings in this style,
but one bears a swastika and is labeled "Third Empire"
style, the other a hammer and sickle and is labeled
"Marxist non-Aryan" style.)[10]

The editor of a leading architecture magazine called the
St. Florian design "painfully reminiscent of designs by
Nazi architect Albert Speer." One critical cartoon showed
Bill Mauldin–style disheveled GIs observing the monu-

---

[10] Osbert Lancaster, in *Here of All Places* (Boston: Houghton Mifflin,
1958), pp. 164–167. The illustrations are reproduced in Giedion, *Architecture, You and Me*, pp. 30–31.

ment skeptically. One says, "It looks like an officers club
. . . a German officers club."[11] One can imagine how painful all this must have been to St. Florian, who had paid
his dues to modernism and America. One wonders
whether he would have been chosen had the competition
not been anonymous. The connection of architectural
style to ideology and political regimes is not a simple matter. Roman imperial forms came to represent American
democracy. But some would undoubtedly argue that
their adoption actually represented a new American imperialism. I understand that the Chancellor of the newly
reunified Germany preferred a more modest version of
the chancellery that was to be built in the new capital of
Berlin, one resembling that stripped-down classical style,
but when he was shown a picture of a Nazi-era building
that looked remarkably like the sober design he preferred,
he reluctantly went for the fanciful modernist chancellery that has since been built.

The host of critics of St. Florian's design did not prevail, as we know. Some distinguished architectural critics
did defend it: Ada Louise Huxtable, Wytold Rybczynski,
Robert Campbell. In contrast, the controversy that had
erupted around Maya Lin's minimalist Vietnam Veterans
Memorial involved not sophisticated architectural critics
but only the aesthetically less sophisticated, some veterans themselves and supporters of the monument. There
was universal support for the design among architectural
critics. In contrast, the controversy over the World War
II Memorial was confined to architectural critics and

[11] See Mills, *The Last Battle*, p. 146, for the Speer reference; the cartoon
is reproduced in the illustrations for this book, following p. 108.

newspaper columnists. There does not seem to be any record of opposition to its design among veterans' groups, no hint of demurral or reservation—as there was in the case of the Vietnam Veterans Memorial—among the veterans themselves. The *Washington Post*, many of whose writers had been critical of the memorial, headlined its story on opening day, "National World War II Memorial Design's Critics Should Use Hearts, Not Eyes, Some Say." One visitor is quoted: "As long as it's a memorial, it could be a hole in the ground with a plaque on it and it wouldn't matter."

This visitor did not realize how prescient her remark was. One of the most admired memorials of recent years among sophisticates is just that. It marks the burning of condemned books by the Nazis on the plaza of Humboldt University in Berlin. Where the books were piled up and burned, one now finds a plexiglass window, through which one can view an underground room with empty bookshelves.

The contradictions multiply: the Vietnam Veterans Memorial was universally approved by sophisticated critics and condemned by those who claimed to speak for the people. Ross Perot, who had funded the competition, protested at the winning entry; Congressman Henry Hyde organized congressional opposition; President Ronald Reagan did not attend the dedication. But the memorial became immensely popular. Did the critics know something that the memorial's opponents, who claimed to speak for the people, did not?

The World War II Memorial saw the opposite constellation: resistance from architectural critics, but quiescent public officials and appreciative veterans quite ready to accept the design. Will public appreciation wither, and expert criticism be shown to be right? Will popular distaste or indifference develop for the World War II Memorial? There is one monument of great scale on the Mall that hardly anyone notices these days, the memorial to General and President U. S. Grant.

Memorials and monuments are difficult problems, and more difficult in the age of modernism than ever before, because modernism cannot help but celebrate the artist, his uniqueness, his originality, his striking gestures and indifference to traditional craftsmanship, his attitude of *épater le bourgeois*—if, that is, anything is capable of shocking the bourgeois these days. Monuments and memorials must draw upon the dominant artistic tendencies and artists of the day, and yet at the same time appeal to ordinary people whose taste and values the modern artist spurns.

It is too early to know whether the World War II Memorial represents an aberrational and anomalous jab in the direction of traditionalism and classicism, or a larger turn, a skepticism about modernism in which the modern represents just another possible style. But if, as in the case of the Jefferson Memorial, one asks, what might a contemporary World War II memorial have been like, one becomes a touch more sympathetic to the existing memorial, despite its faults. (Indeed, one wonders whether it might have been improved if it had leaned more toward the classical sobriety of Pope's National Gallery or Henry Bacon's Lincoln Memorial.) There seems to have been no distinguished modernist design that could have been accepted.

Wondering what a modernist design on the scale of the World War II Memorial could have been, one thinks of the largest contemporary monument that has recently been erected. It to be found in Berlin, and it is the monument to the murdered Jews of Europe. It consists of a field of thousands of rectangular catafalques—they are also called columns, or steles, but it is the catafalque they most closely resemble. These rectangular forms are closely spaced together, with just enough room separating them, three feet, for two people, perhaps, to squeeze past each other. The catafalques are of variable height, and look from above as if a giant scythe had swept over them, reducing some of them in some sections of the field to a foot or two or to the level of the ground of the monument, while others are ten feet tall. It was designed by the architect Peter Eisenman and the sculptor Richard Serra. Serra dropped out when the German sponsors asked for a reduction in the number of catafalques, and for trees along the side to soften the unforgiving field of concrete. He would not accept any modification in the design. Eisenman was more flexible, as architects are bound to be.

Does it work? One wonders whether and why people will be drawn into the labyrinth of paths it forms, and what they will do when they get there. In contrast, at the Vietnam Veterans Memorial, there is a reason to go down into the declivity, and there is something to do when one gets there—make a tracing, leave a memento. The critic Arthur Danto, visiting the recently completed monument, writes that "the memorial embodies nothing that belongs to what is conventionally understood to be the imagery of the Holocaust, it is radically abstract—a regimented complex of monoliths that refuse to name what they are intended to commemorate." Danto labels his reports "Mute Point." But, as he writes, "great memorials are not mute." [12] At least they should not be. That, however, is what modern art, in its most successful forms, the abstract and the minimalist, leans toward.

The task that Serra and Eisenman undertook was infinitely more difficult, in a far more challenging location, than St. Florian's. He was, after all, commemorating victory in a "good war," in the central ceremonial space of the victor. I do not think the Berlin Holocaust memorial succeeds in the enormously difficult task of memorializing the murdered Jews of Europe with a modernistic monument, and its muteness is a central problem. In contrast, the World War II memorial positively chatters, with inscriptions, sculptured plaques, stars, eagles, wreaths. . . . I have my doubts whether the forms drawn upon for the World War II Memorial still have the power to move.

The strongest argument in favor of monuments hewing to some degree to established traditions remains our fear as to what the alternative would be. Modernism has become individualistic, eccentric, "self-referential," to use the currently fashionable term. It is the expression of the "me," when what we want in our memorials is the expression of the "us." That is what makes us more friendly to the Jefferson Memorial today and reins us in in criticizing the World War II Memorial.

[12] *Nation*, October 17, 2005.

CHAPTER SIX

Daniel P. Moynihan and Federal Architecture

D aniel P. Moynihan, who served in the U.S. Senate from 1977 to 2001, probably had a greater influence on federal architecture than any other major public figure of the second half of the twentieth century. His retirement from the Senate in 2001 occasioned deep regret among architects, urbanists, and federal officials dealing with architecture and urban design in various departments of government. For decades, Moynihan was the one major influential elected official they could speak to and who could be expected to have an understanding and appreciation of what they were trying to tell him. He was unique among the members of the U.S. Congress in his high estimate of the role of architecture in government, and in his support for high achievement, both in the building of the past and in the current work of building for government. He would respond to calls about major buildings in danger, and exerted his influence to find new uses for them so they could survive. It is possible that he was the only member of the Senate who would have known that the massive and magnificent Customs House building on the tip of Manhattan, abandoned when the customs service moved into a new building in the World Trade Center, was designed by Cass Gilbert, the architect of the Woolworth Building and the Federal Courthouse in New York City, and he was one of the few who would have cared. (Indeed he did succeed in finding a new use for it, and in saving it.)

In his first year in the Senate, walking around Buffalo, as we are told by Robert A. Peck, who worked for him, "he spied the dilapidated Prudential building, one of the best-known . . . early skyscrapers by . . . Louis Sullivan. Moynihan told Buffalo's Mayor that if the city could see to it that the building was rehabilitated, people the world over would come to Buffalo to see it. (The Mayor is reported to have replied with an eight-letter bovine reference.)"[1] Moynihan may have been too extravagant in describing what a restored Prudential building could do for a declining Buffalo, but he did succeed in getting the building restored, and crucial in saving it was Moynihan's decision to put his own western New York office into it. When I visited it some years ago, I discovered that his staff maintained for his visits the excellent guide to Buffalo's architecture by Reyner Banham. They showed it to me, and it was remarkably well worn. The Senator, I was told, made use of it whenever he came to Buffalo.

We are very far from being able to clearly delineate the full range of his various roles affecting federal architecture, and the full scale of his influence. None of his official positions gave him any significant or formally recognized

[1] Robert A. Peck, "Daniel P. Moynihan and the Fall and Rise of Public Works," in *Daniel Patrick Moynihan: The Intellectual in Public Life*, ed. Robert Katzmann (Washington, D.C.: Woodrow Wilson Center Press; Baltimore: Johns Hopkins University Press, 1998), p. 87. Tim Russert, then working for Moynihan, reports that the mayor said, "Bullshit!" (remarks at the opening of the Moynihan exhibit at the Museum of the City of New York, March 29, 2004).

platform for intervention in such matters. We can scroll
through his various federal posts—assistant to Secretary
of Labor Arthur Goldberg in the Kennedy administration,
then Assistant Secretary of Labor (for research and statis-
tics), assistant to President Nixon for urban affairs, Ambassador to India, Ambassador for the United States to
the United Nations, four times elected Senator from New
York. They all involved him in major public issues in
which he played important public roles: the fate of blacks
in the United States and the role of the black family,
which he addressed when he was in the Department of
Labor; the problems of the cities, then afflicted by major
riots and disorder, when he served President Nixon; the
relation of the United States to the developing world,
when he was ambassador to India; the Cold War and its
reach into every corner of the globe, in particular the
Middle East and the Arab-Israeli conflict, when he was
ambassador to the United Nations; and a host of major
domestic and foreign issues, from saving Social Security
and reforming welfare to urban transportation and excessive secrecy in government when he was in the Senate.
But all along he maintained a strong interest in public
architecture and civic design.

This interest emerged at the very beginning of his service in Washington, though it was foreshadowed by his
experience in the late 1950s as assistant to Governor Av-
erill Harriman of New York. It was in that position and
directly thereafter, as he worked on a history of the Harriman administration at Syracuse University, that he began
publishing the articles in the journal *The Reporter* (then
edited by Irving Kristol) that first brought him to some
notice. One of them dealt with the epidemic of mortal

accidents on the highways, and the responsibility of automobile manufacturers and government to do something
by way of design to reduce the slaughter.[2] A second dealt
with the inevitable impact of the interstate highway program on cities.[3] Before Ralph Nader, Moynihan had
drawn attention to the role of automobile design in accidents, and he hoped to enter the Kennedy administration
in a position where he could do something about highway
building and auto safety, but the automobile industry was
powerful enough to veto any such appointment. Having
written a doctoral thesis on the International Labor Organization, he accepted somewhat reluctantly a position as
assistant to Labor Secretary Arthur Goldberg. It was from
that improbable position that Moynihan was able to
launch a statement—we might call it a manifesto—that
has played a remarkable role in improving federal architecture. To tell the tale in Moynihan's own words:

> There's a little story of how they [the Guiding Principles
> for Federal Architecture] came about. In the spring of
> 1961, the discussion of foreign policy in a Cabinet
> meeting paused for a moment, whereupon the next
> most important subject in government came up—office
> space. Indeed, we hadn't built any office space here in
> Washington since the federal triangle buildings of the
> 1920's and 1930's.
>
> The Labor Department, where I served as assistant to
> Secretary Goldberg, was scattered in 17 buildings

---

[2] Daniel P. Moynihan, "Epidemic on the Highways," *Reporter*, April 30,
1959.

[3] Daniel P. Moynihan, "New Roads and Urban Chaos," *Reporter*, April 14,
1960.

around the city. Then and there, President Kennedy set up something called the Ad Hoc Committee on Federal Office Space. Luther Hodges, Secretary of Commerce, was the co-chairman with Arthur Goldberg.

When we started, our report had a very detailed inventory—how much office space we needed for this department, that department, and so forth. As we set about this new building boom, we thought we'd put in some guidelines in there about what we thought these buildings should look like. So I wrote a little one-page guidelines for Federal architecture. One of the rules was that we should avoid an official style. We should seek to do what was the contemporary architecture of the time. There are great moments in architecture, there are lesser moments, but we wouldn't miss any.

The Seagram Building [designed by Mies van der Rohe] had just opened on Park Avenue in New York City. We would say, at any given moment, build whatever the Whiskey Trust is building. Over the years, you won't miss the best.

This is Moynihan's account. But then, how does something so casually produced become government policy?

Moynihan again: when President Kennedy got the report on federal office space, "[he] had a three-paragraph memorandum that said to the departments, all right, this is our program. Get with it. In his last sentence, he said that we will particularly attend to the proposal on Pennsylvania Avenue."[4]

---

[4] In *Vision + Voice: Design Excellence in Federal Architecture: Building a Legacy* (U.S. General Services Administration, December 2002). This publication,

The report of the Ad Hoc Committee on Federal Office Space had extended itself not only to the issue of the quality of federal architecture but also to the condition of Pennsylvania Avenue, then lined on its northern side by shabby and derelict buildings. Whether Pennsylvania Avenue was part of the original brief of the committee I do not know but doubt, just as the Guiding Principles for Federal Architecture was no part of the brief. But it is part of the art of government to know when one should go beyond what one has been asked to do. Moynihan went beyond in proposing his guidelines, and he may well have gone beyond in proposing the rebuilding of Pennsylvania Avenue, but that was an interest of the President's, and he gave his approval to both. Robert Peck tells the story, and I don't know any more authoritative account:

> History has it that President Kennedy noted the dilapidation of the private structures on the north side of the avenue on his inaugural ride to the White House. History does not explain how John Kennedy had failed to notice this condition during all the years he commuted as senator from the Capitol to his residence in Georgetown. In light of the fact that the Pennsylvania Avenue proposal appeared amid the banal-sounding "Report of the Ad Hoc Committee on Federal Office Space," as did the unsolicited Moynihan contribution of a set of

---

which comes from the Center for Design Excellence and the Arts, in the Office of the Chief Architect, Public Buildings Service, of the General Services Administration, is an appreciation of Moynihan's role in federal architecture, based on more than thirty interviews with architects, designers, officials of the GSA, curators, and others.

"Guiding Principles for Federal Architecture," some think that the whole thing, including the Kennedy apocrypha, was a Moynihan invention.[5]

Perhaps it was. But there was now presidential approval, for the Guiding Principles and for the rehabilitation of Pennsylvania Avenue. Does presidential approval, with nothing more (either in the way of an executive order, or some entry in the *Federal Register*, or legislation), make federal policy, and policy of such long-lasting effect that it is celebrated as having a major impact on federal architecture forty years after? Both the Pennsylvania Avenue references in the report—there was not yet a proposal or a project but only some hortatory paragraphs—and the Guiding Principles might have sunk without a trace in the wake of President Kennedy's assassination in 1963, but that was to count without Moynihan's energy and ingenuity, mere Assistant Secretary of Labor that he was at the time.

Moynihan reports:

One of the last instructions [Kennedy] left before departing for Dallas was that a coffee hour be arranged for the congressional leadership in order to display the model of the Pennsylvania Avenue plan and seek their support. Bill Walton [the artist who was a friend

[5] Peck, "Daniel P. Moynihan," p. 82. Peck served on Moynihan's staff when he was senator, but long after these events. His paper on Moynihan's role in public works was part of a tribute to Moynihan on his seventieth birthday, delivered in his presence, and one would think Moynihan would have corrected it if it was wrong. The story of the origins of both the Guiding Principles and the Pennsylvania Avenue proposal, as we know it, is from Moynihan. Historians in the future may be able to find a paper trail or add other recollections. But the matter is already forty-two years old.

of Mrs. Kennedy and the President], Charles Horsky,[6] and I were at lunch discussing this on November 22, 1963, when the White House operator called with the news that the president had been shot. We made our way to the White House; the final word came. We left with this task undone.

It took another twenty-five years. Jacqueline Kennedy made it possible. A day or so after the funeral, President Johnson invited Mrs. Kennedy to the Oval Office and asked what he could do for her. She asked for Pennsylvania Avenue. This became known, and made a claim on the Johnson administration. The enterprise acquired official if somewhat skeptical sanction, having been wholly informal under JFK. [Later in this account Moynihan notes that Harry C. McPherson, who was a friend of his, had "as counsel to the President saved the plan from extinction in 1964–5."] Richard M. Nixon, somewhat in contrast, was genuinely enthusiastic. . . . By the time he left office, the Pennsylvania Avenue Development Corporation had been established by act of Congress, and there has been no turning back.[7]

Moynihan was a master at attributing what he wanted to do to the presidents he served: it gave his efforts greater sanction. He here underplays his own role in pushing for Pennsylvania Avenue, from whatever position he held,

---

[6] Charles M. Atherton in *Vision + Voice*, p. 14, also has Arthur M. Schlesinger, Jr., there, but this, according to Mrs. Elizabeth Moynihan, is an error.

[7] Daniel P. Moynihan, foreword to Carol M. Highsmith and Ted Lamphair, *Pennsylvania Avenue: America's Main Street* (Washington D.C.: American Institute of Architects Press, 1988), pp. 10–11.

whether as a holdover in the Johnson administration or,
a few years later, as adviser on urban affairs to President
Nixon. As such, he could do things even Mrs. Onassis
couldn't. As David M. Childs reports: "Pat as Nixon's
urban adviser every day could go and take our plans [for
Pennsylvania Avenue] from the bottom of George
Schultz's [director of OMB under Nixon] desk and put
them on the top, which, of course, was the way to getting
things done in any administration."[8]

For Pennsylvania Avenue, it was clear, a specific plan
was required, and in time one was drawn up, fortunately—like all first plans—later very much revised in a
direction favored by all urbanists, and by Moynihan himself. (Moynihan had deferred to the architect Nathaniel
Owings, who drew up a somewhat Mussolini-like plan
for Pennsylvania Avenue calling for an enormous square
near the Treasury Building requiring the demolition of
Hotel Washington and other buildings. Moynihan, as we
will note later, did not impose his taste on architects of
reputation and talent.)

How were the very general points made in the Guiding
Principles for Federal Architecture kept alive, when in
fact no succeeding president (and one may even doubt
John F. Kennedy himself) was very much interested or
would think of giving it a place, no matter how far down,
on his agenda? Nor was Moynihan in much of a position
to nurture the Principles before entering the Senate in
1977. He did choose as his first Senate committee appointment the Committee on Environment and Public

[8] David M. Childs, in *Vision + Voice*, p. 15.

Works, which gave him some involvement in these matters, but he was a junior senator and the committee was
much more involved in the issues of the environment. It
was not until 1986, according to Robert Peck, when the
committee was reorganized following the Democratic re-
capture of the Senate, that Moynihan had real influence.
At that time, Moynihan chose to become chairman of the
Subcommittee on Water Resources, Transportation, and
Infrastructure of the Committee on Environment and
Public Works of the Senate. Unwieldy as the title of that
position was, it was one of great influence, particularly
over the city- and environment-shaping role of major
federally funded highways and public transportation.[9]

Moynihan was a master of the art of publicity, as well
as government. It would be an interesting enterprise to
trace how the idea of the Guiding Principles was kept
alive, even when there was no indication that they were
being followed anywhere in government buildings. The
Guiding Principles said three things. First, that public
buildings should be provided "in an architectural style
and form which is distinguished and which will reflect
the dignity, enterprise, vigor and stability of the American
National Government." Wonderful rhetoric, but not very
specific. Second, that an official style should be avoided:
clearly, no more Federal Triangles. Third, that the leading
architects of the day should be involved. "Design must
flow from the architectural profession to the Government
and not vice versa." Perhaps most important was its Moy-
nihanian rhetoric: "It should be our task to meet the test

---

[9] Peck, "Daniel P. Moynihan," pp. 69 ff.

of Pericles' evocation to the Athenians, which the President had commended to the Massachusetts legislature in his address of January 9, 1961: 'We do not imitate—we are a model to others.' "[10] Part of the art of advancing one's agenda is to quote the president, as if it is his views one is promoting, even when the president might not recall just what it was he said.

But the leading architects of the day were not bidding for government work, or being asked to do so, in the 1960s and 1970s. They had been called upon to design embassies around the world in the 1940s and 1950s, but that program was drawing to a close in the 1960s. We were entering a period of bland and uninspired federal architecture, whose aim for the most part was to emphasize efficiency and economy in providing office space, which is, after all, what most government buildings, regardless of their symbolic significance, consist of. Consider the important volume *The Federal Presence*, published in 1978, and inspired by the Task Force on Federal Architecture of the National Endowment for the Arts, with the hope that it would help improve government buildings. It concludes with the sad comment that federal architecture has declined:

> Today cultural historians, if they consider federal projects at all, find them unimportant. Critics of the building arts consign federal architecture to a second-class status and are virtually unconcerned with those federal policies that affect the use and appearance of public space. Likewise, public concern has been missing. The

[10] The Guiding Principles for Federal Architecture can be found, among other places, in *Vision + Voice*, pp. 4–5.

increasing preference for private over public life has been accompanied by an increase in the physical neglect of the public domain.[11]

If one looks at the illustrations of what were then the most recent government buildings in this volume, they clearly demonstrate the ordinariness of the architecture—their architects are not even named.[12] The Guiding Principles are not much in evidence in federal architecture at the time.

But they are there; there is some awareness of them: the credit for that accrues to Moynihan himself, and Moynihan had just entered the Senate when *The Federal Presence* was published.

Thus the Guiding Principles are surprisingly a presence in *The Federal Presence*. We see Moynihan quoted on page 540, from an article in the *AIA Journal* in June 1962. (One wonders how the journal would have known of him that early, before he had published a book, before he had gone to Harvard to head the Joint Center for Urban Studies.) On page 541, some powerful lines from Moynihan's introduction to Ada Louise Huxtable's *Will They Ever Finish Bruckner Boulevard?* (published in 1970) are quoted: "Twentieth-century America has seen a steady, persistent decline in the visual and emotional power of its public buildings, and this has been accompanied by a not less persistent decline in the authority of the public order." The authors of *The Federal Presence* are aware of the exis-

---

[11] Lois Craig and the staff of the Federal Architecture Project, *The Federal Presence: Architecture, Politics, and Symbols in United States Government Building* (Cambridge: MIT Press, 1978), p. 545.

[12] Ibid., pp. 539–44.

tence of the Guiding Principles themselves, which are quoted on page 542, without reference to their originator.

One wonders how the Guiding Principles were kept alive, but kept alive they were. David Childs, commenting on his first job, on the design for Pennsylvania Avenue in 1968, tells us that the Guiding Principles for Federal Architecture, "already then six years old, were still very much quoted. They'd gotten to the point where they were beginning to be understood, and they've only become more so as time has gone on. . . . His call to greatness resounded throughout a much larger community with such compelling conviction that those reverberations have lasted to today."[13] Childs is perhaps reading back into that time their present influence, but influential, as a kind of manifesto, they seemed to be.

In the GSA's oral history of the impact of the Guiding Principles on the fortieth anniversary of their formulation, architect after architect is aware of the Guiding Principles and happy they are there. They are one of the inspirations of the Design Excellence Program, which was developed by energetic and creative officials of the GSA in the late 1980s and early 1990s. These officials examined what was wrong with the way the federal government went about designing its buildings, changed the procedures to sweep away a host of requirements that deterred leading architects from considering federal work, experimented with different approaches to attract and guide the work of the best architects practicing in America. A key role in pioneering and developing a new approach was played by the Boston Federal Courthouse.

[13] Childs, in *Vision + Voice*, p. 125.

There, two very able judges, Douglas Woodlock and Stephen Breyer, the latter soon to be named a Supreme Court justice, became in effect, with the agreement of the General Services Administration, the clients for the building. They hoped it would become a model both as a federal courthouse and as a positive influence on the urban environment around it. Asking Bill Lacy to guide them in understanding the frontier architecture of the day, they devised a process in the building of courthouses that was further developed under the Design Excellence Program, and which has now resulted in dozens of impressive federal courthouses and other federal government buildings by leading architects.

In all this, it is my impression, Moynihan was an inspiration rather than a participant. He did not, as far as I know, play an active role in devising procedures, or in selecting architects, or in judging their work. He was no President Pompidou or Mitterand, determining that this design should be built rather than that. When it came to courthouses, I am not aware that he involved himself in the procedures that led to the building of the large new federal courthouse in New York City designed by Kohn Pedersen Fox (now the Moynihan Courthouse) or the Islip Courthouse of Richard Meier or any other courthouse in New York State. As a senator from New York he had a large role in appointing the federal judges, who then did variously involve themselves in the building of their new courthouses. He had a large role in getting the money appropriated for these expensive buildings. He worked tirelessly to get hundreds of millions of dollars of federal money for the new Pennsylvania Station in New York City that to be built in the grand post office adjacent to the site of the monumental building that was heed-lessly destroyed in the sixties.

But I detect a certain ambivalence in his attitude to modern architecture. His attitude seemed to be "Let the best architects be selected; yes, I will support and applaud them." But I believe that Moynihan, like so many of us, was no enthusiast of the breathless variety of innovative forms and materials and arrangements that are the trade-marks of leading contemporary architects.[14] In contrast, he rather enjoyed, indeed was enthusiastic about, the somewhat classical Ronald Reagan Building, the enor-mous structure that completes, to the degree it will ever be completed, the Federal Triangle. He placed in it the Woodrow Wilson International Center for Scholars (which he had helped create) and his own office after his retirement from the Senate. He would lead his visitors in an appreciative tour of the building, which his tireless political efforts had helped to create—even to the point of his accepting its being named after a Republican presi-dent. Nothing is easy in government, and part of his ap-preciation of the building was undoubtedly due to the fact

[14] A hint as to what his attitude might have been to frontier contempo-rary architecture may be gleaned from his comments when, as chairman of the board of the Hirshhorn Museum and Sculpture Garden on the Mall in Washington, he accepted as a gift from the Institute of Scrap Iron and Steel the sculpture *Isis* by Mark Di Suvero. Moynihan said on that occasion that he accepted this "splendid gift." And further: "I recall that on the occasion that Margaret Fuller declared, `I accept the universe,' Carlyle remarked that she had better." He went on, in what must be intended as parody: "*Isis* achieves an aesthetic transubstantiation of that which is at once elusive yet ineluctable in the modern sensibility. Transcending socialist realism with an unequaled abstractionist range, Mr. Di Suvero brings to the theme of recycling both the hard edge reality of the modern world and the transcen-dent fecundity of the universe itself." And so on. In William Safire, *Lend me Your Ears: Great Speeches in History* (New York: W. W. Norton, 1992), p. 208.

that he had managed to get it done at all, so it could fill a huge hole in the Federal Triangle and replace a "surpassingly ugly" parking lot. But I think leading architectural critics and modern architects would look askance at the design of this contemporary building and fault it for trying to fit too comfortably into the classically correct Federal Triangle.

Moynihan appreciated the richly classically detailed older Senate office buildings. When the newest Senate Office Building, stripped of all classical detailing, had its plastic sheeting removed as it was nearing completion, Moynihan proposed the following resolution: "Whereas the plastic cover has now been removed revealing, as feared, a building whose banality is exceeded only by its expense; and Whereas even in a democracy there are things it is well the people do not know about their government: Now, therefore, be it *Resolved*, That it is the sense of the Senate that the plastic cover be put back."[15]

When it came to older buildings, there was no ambivalence in Moynihan. Regardless of style, the great structures of the past should be defended, protected, adapted to new uses if necessary. Yes, to Cass Gilbert's Beaux-Arts Customs House. Yes, to Louis Sullivan's Prudential building. Yes, to Daniel Burnham's Union Station in Washington, restored as a rail station (among other things) after the misguided effort to turn it into a visitors' center. Yes, even to the neo-Gothic armory in Buffalo—burned down, but Moynihan insisted it should be rebuilt rather than replaced by an economical drill hall. One must regret that when the Pennsylvania Station in New York City

[15] Peck, "Daniel P. Moynihan," p. 89.

was being demolished in 1962–63, Moynihan was only assistant to the secretary of labor and his influence was limited to the writing and attaching to a report on government office space the Guiding Principles for Federal Architecture. But in doing so, he did more to raise the level of federal architecture than has any other major public figure of the last few decades.

PART TWO

The New York Case

CHAPTER SEVEN

What Happened in East Harlem

Unlikely as it appears at first glance, East Harlem in Manhattan is an area that has been in large measure shaped by modernistic theory in urban design and architecture. It reflects what the housing reformers in league with early modernists wanted, and it offers ground for reflection on how well their ideas for rebuilding the city have fared. As in the case of any move from theory to reality, the story is not a simple one and its lessons do not all point in the same direction.

East Harlem begins where the elegant East Side of Manhattan ends. Its southern boundary is the most sharply defined border between poverty and affluence, urban misery and urban elegance, to be found in New York City, or perhaps anywhere else. Ninety-sixth Street is the border. One block north we begin to find the old tenements, the idle clumps of men and boys, brown or black, the storefront churches, the housing projects, the cheap stores with loud signs that define a low-income, indeed poor, neighborhood. Below 96th Street are the expensive apartments and shops, well-dressed men and women engaged in business or shopping, art galleries, bookstores, grand churches, and nonprofit institutions in discreet town houses.

From a street map, it would be impossible to see these distinctions, except that the superblocks north of 96th Street, which wiped out and replaced the regular array of the peculiarly shaped Manhattan blocks, long and narrow, would give a hint that housing projects are located there. On the map, the same wide avenues, with the same names, sweep up from the East Side into contiguous East Harlem. The same long, narrow blocks created by the street plan laid down for Manhattan almost two hundred years ago are found north and south of 96th Street. (The plan called for few north-south avenues, and many east-west streets, because it was assumed the city would need many east-west streets to accommodate the cargo from vessels in the East and Hudson rivers!) East Side and East Harlem have the same Central Park to the west, the same East River to the east.

The one decisive physical break that separates the Upper East Side from East Harlem is the sudden emergence, between 96th and 97th Street, of the New York Central railroad tracks from their underground tunnel running north from Grand Central Terminal. Park Avenue, above the underground tracks, turns at 96th Street from an avenue with an elegant central green park strip, lined by grand apartment houses, into a divided street with a massive stone viaduct running down its middle, carrying the railroad lines north.

One would not be surprised if such a massive construction had divided East Harlem between an east and a west section, the way tracks so often divide cities, but it does not: East Harlem is not much different whether east or west of Park Avenue. The decisive physical form is the emergence of the railroad from underground; the buried track, with Park Avenue above it, defines the elegant East Side, the railroad bursting from underground, roaring through the city, defines East Harlem.

That is the way it is now, but in the past, despite the railroad, that division between the most upscale and the most depressed parts of the city was not so sharp. Along Fifth Avenue, it was expected that elegance would continue north of 96th Street, just as it was established below 96th Street. After all, Central Park was right there, edging Fifth Avenue, all the way up to 110th Street. Why should elegance end at 96th Street? And indeed, up through the 1930s, it was not expected that it should: Mount Sinai and the Fifth Avenue Hospital were built along the Park; the New York Academy of Medicine built its grand Byzanto-Romanesque building on 103rd Street; the Museum of the City of New York was built at 104th Street.

If elegance still reached above 96th Street on Fifth Avenue, on the eastern avenues poverty was at home below 96th Street as well as above: in the 1920s and 1930s there were still elevated transit lines running along Third Avenue and Second Avenue, and there was a general uniformity in the tenements that were built on the East Side, whether below or above 96th Street, to house the working classes and the poor. They were the same buildings, trying to fit as many apartments as possible into the standard twenty-by-one-hundred-foot New York plots that were carved out of the long narrow blocks. There was no air or light in the interior rooms, which often opened on air shafts, and the only adequate access to air and light was limited to the front rooms on the street (with the El roaring by if one was on the Avenue), and the back rooms over inner courtyards.

If we were to try to explain the great break at 96th Street through features of either the physical landscape that once existed, or major man-made intrusions, it would not work very well. Yet we have two worlds, with a sharper boundary between them than perhaps between any two neighborhoods of New York.

Looking at this great divide, one would expect sharp conflict over the use of land between the classes. Why should there be such a concentration of housing projects above 96th Street, so close to where the privileged and well-to-do live? Why should the projects be limited to the north of 96th Street—why not expand below that boundary? There are no housing projects below 96th Street on the East Side, even though the original slum-clearance objective that dictated where housing projects should go could not have differentiated, in physical terms, the tenements of Yorkville from the tenements of East Harlem. But East Harlem was defined as a slum, ripe for clearance and housing projects; Yorkville (the east side of the East Side) was not.

One answer we might think of today is that East Harlem was black and Puerto Rican, and Yorkville was German and central European and white. But that was not a distinction that defined the two areas when East Harlem, in the 1930s and 1940s, first became a leading candidate for massive clearance and public housing. East Harlem in the 1930s was largely an Italian area: it was the area that Fiorello LaGuardia had represented in Congress, and the area that until 1950 sent Vito Marcantonio as its representative to Congress. It was the largest Little Italy in the United States, far larger than the historic Italian settlement on the Lower East Side first known as Little Italy or the Italian Greenwich Village. The other large population group of East Harlem was Jewish. I was born on East 103rd Street, between Second and Third Avenues: one side of the street was mostly Jewish, the other mostly Italian. When we moved out in the depths of the Depression, it was not because social problems in East Harlem were driving us out, or because we thought of it as a slum, but because the Bronx offered more room for the limited amount of money we could afford.

And yet from the 1930s at least, East Harlem was defined as problem country. Langdon W. Post's *The Challenge of Housing* already defines it so in 1938. He was the first chairman of the New York City Housing Authority (NYCHA) when it was formed in 1934, and a great advocate of public housing. To him the challenge offered by East Harlem was simple: total clearance and rebuilding. This was long before the notions of maintaining urban context, or preserving urban form, or rehabilitating existing houses, or historic preservation, carried any weight. And his maps do show East Harlem as leading the borough in tuberculosis cases and infant mortality.

East Harlem has been regularly scheduled for whatever treatment government programs have had to offer—large-scale clearance for huge public housing projects when they were the preferred reform to enlightened minds; later, spot clearance, vest-pocket projects, rehabilitation projects, Model Cities social interventions, work-training programs—whatever was on offer poured into East Harlem in greater volume, with more resources than just about anywhere in the city.

In 1959, Woody Klein, a famous reporter of his day, moved into a tenement in East Harlem (on 101st Street, between Second and First Avenues), and wrote a series of articles for the *New York World-Telegram* on this tenement, located on what he labeled the "worst block" in New York City. (It is a common form in New York journalism; there have been a number of "worst blocks" over the years.) I was intrigued—it was only two blocks from the one we had lived on, which was no longer eligible for "worst-block candidacy" because all of it had been torn down for a superblock housing project, George Washington Houses. By New York City usage there was no longer a "block" on 103rd Street between Second and Third; indeed, there was no longer a 103rd Street between those two avenues.

Klein's series was expanded into a very interesting book, *Let in the Sun*. The title is from a speech delivered by New York City's greatest mayor, Fiorello H. LaGuardia, in 1944: "Tear down the old," he said. "Build up the new. Down with rotten, antiquated rat holes. Down with hovels. Down with disease. Down with crime. Down with firecraft. Let in the sun. Let in the sky. A new day is dawning. A new life. A new America!"

Fifteen years later, Woody Klein, having meticulously documented every effort made to improve matters, wrote, "[M]ore money and manpower have been spent trying to save the poor people and old buildings in this one block during the past two decades than any other piece of real estate in New York." He also writes of this "worst block," "it has been compared to the slums of Calcutta." In the 1970s, the comparison of New York to Calcutta was so common that it was adopted as a running title for a series of editorials on New York by the *New York Times*.

Woody Klein was describing conditions in a tenement house, in a block of tenement houses. Most of that block also does not now exist. The dominating form of East Harlem was rapidly becoming the huge housing project. In 1969, a *Plan for New York City* was published, in six massive volumes. It was the final product of a much-delayed effort to create a master plan for the city, fulfilling the hopes of the visionaries of the LaGuardia era who had created the City Planning Commission, and who had included in their numbers so many early pioneers of planning and public housing. But by 1969, when the plan finally appeared, master planning was no longer held in high repute, and seemed a weak and ineffective way of dealing with difficult urban problems. City planning had metamorphosed into a discipline that wrestled with a host of programs of various kinds, physical, social, economic, all attempting bravely to shape better neighborhoods and a better city.

Thirty-five years after Fiorello LaGuardia had become mayor, the plan describes the area he represented and in which he had continued to live: "Every problem of slum life plagues East Harlem. Endless blocks of overcrowded tenements, glass-strewn sidewalks, stripped and abandoned cars and boarded up stores spread across the district, interrupted here and there by the tall, impersonal towers of public housing projects."

The plan was somewhat dismissive of the enormous effort and investment that, an aerial map shows, had transformed the area: "Although there is more public housing in this district than in almost any other place of comparable size in the country, the population is still crowded into decaying tenements that lack light, air, and often the most basic conveniences of a home. Public housing projects housing close to 53,000 residents have been built since 1940. Yet they only scratch the surface of the district's housing problems." Some scratch: that 53,000 was one-third of the area's population at the time. Further, thirteen new schools had been built since World War II, there had been major improvements to ten more, and yet another four were being completed or in planning.

Public housing, it seemed, might not be the answer: "In some cases, however, public housing has created new problems. Land clearance . . . has meant painful disloca- tion . . . thousands of poor families cannot qualify for ad- mission, or cannot cope with the red tape of admitting procedures or can find no room in public housing. . . . In addition, many of the huge projects have proved difficult to maintain."

By 1969, doubts about public housing were already the new common wisdom. The age of the giant housing proj- ects that had replaced so much of East Harlem was draw- ing to a close, as maintenance costs and social problems seemed to overwhelm any good the new housing had brought. We were into a new age, of comprehensive so- cial planning to deal with the social problems of low-in- come areas. The Model Cities program had been launched, and two-thirds of East Harlem had been desig- nated as an area in need of comprehensive aid under that federal program. That, too, was to pass.

Up to the 1960s, it is hard to find the kind of conflict over public housing in East Harlem we might expect. No one asked why there was no public housing below 96th Street. Well, there were tenements, it is true, but they were rapidly being replaced by private investment, particularly along Second and Third Avenues, newly opened to light, air, and a degree of quiet by the demolition of their elevated railways. No one argued much about relocation; Manhattan's poor areas had lost much of their population in the 1920s and 1930s; immigration from abroad had been reduced to a trickle by restrictive immigration laws, the Depression, and war; and migration from the South and from Puerto Rico was not yet a flood. Many tenements were boarded up. So it was easy to build in these areas. Despite the housing shortage that fastened permanent rent control on New York City during World War II, one finds no significant reference to relocation problems until the late 1950s. When stories began to be published in the New York newspapers about problems of relocation, they dealt with the effects of slum clearance on small business. Public housing projects did not contain stores; even urban renewal projects, where there were fewer legal problems in determining site reuse, included small numbers of stores, compared to the many that had been uprooted in the demolished areas. In the clearance for Lincoln Center, 325 retail businesses were replaced by a mere 20!

But by the early 1960s, the complaints over relocation were omnipresent, mostly descending on the head of the all-powerful Robert Moses, chairman of the Mayor's Committee on Slum Clearance. The main thrust of the complaints over relocation were directed, however, at urban renewal projects, where low-income people were being replaced by higher-income people, or by new institutional uses, such as cultural centers and university buildings. There was little complaint that public housing projects were demolishing the neighborhoods of the poor. In general the public housing projects of New York, including those of East Harlem, were welcomed in the 1940s and 1950s. And why not? Good, new, subsidized housing was to be available to low-income people. The housing it replaced was often crowded and badly deteriorated; much of it had not been built to high standards to begin with. The argument for light, air, open space seemed overwhelming, as against any argument one could make for the densely built tenements, shoulder to shoulder, lining the streets and avenues, leaving no open space in front, and unused or unusable backyards behind. In addition, the new housing meant jobs for the construction trades, a central motivation in the legislation that made public housing possible, and of the local political forces that supported it.

By the mid-1950s, there was already objection, and by the 1960s the drumbeat of complaints about public housing, coming from intellectuals, was beginning to win over enlightened public opinion. The original planners and reformers who had fought for public housing, urging the model of European social housing, were now disappointed or on the defensive. Perhaps the most decisive blow in the offensive against what public housing had become was delivered by Jane Jacobs in 1961, with her *The Death and Life of Great American Cities*. In 1962, another classic work, Herbert Gans's *The Urban Villagers*, told the tragic story of the destruction of the West End of Boston, an area very much like East Harlem, for replacement by upscale housing.

What had gone wrong? Why had the obvious advantages I have just referred to ceased to make a good case for public housing? What had happened was a decisive change in what urbanists considered good urban form and texture.

The New York City Housing Authority was committed, following the best thinking of the 1920s and 1930s, to giant projects: major clearance of slums, the land wiped clean, and a new, regular, pattern stamped upon the cleared land. Its very first large project, in the 1930s, Williamsburg Houses, reflects this: the grid of streets was replaced by a superblock, and the houses were set at an angle to the street grid almost as a demonstration against the grid. The argument was that this siting was best for receiving sun. But since each apartment now faced directly to the outside, with much of the land retained for lawn and trees and playgrounds and walkways, it hardly mattered, for light, which way the buildings were placed, and one cannot help thinking that there was a strong ideological factor in this siting: Lewis Mumford had denounced the grid, indifferent to features of topography and landscape, as the soulless imposition on the land of a commercial capitalism, interested only in uniform plots for buying and selling. In Williamsburg, and in the other giant projects of the New York City Housing Authority, the grid was decisively rejected. The land acquired through the streets' closing could be used for parkland, open space, trees, playgrounds. The pictures of Williamsburg and other early projects look idyllic and pastoral.

It is true that, as public building for low-income tenants resumed after World War II, it was no longer possible to limit the buildings to four, five, or six stories. They got taller and taller. In the East Harlem project, George

Washington Houses, that replaced the area in which I was born and grew up, the height was fourteen stories—in others, even higher. The height was determined by a number of factors, but one of the most important was the commitment to open space: light and air and lawns and playgrounds would not be given up, and they weren't, even if land costs dictated high density. The George Washington Houses cover only 13 percent of the land!

When public housing, once sacrosanct, the realized vision of the good society, came under attack, the attack was, surprisingly, mostly from above, from architects and planners who were turning against the Corbusian vision of towers in a park. Now one could argue it was a far cry from the Corbusian vision to the realized achievement of public housing projects. Public housing projects were, after all, for low-income people, and their design provided few amenities. In the mid-1950s, in New York City, cars were uncommon possessions in poor areas, not much in the way of parking space was provided, and even if there was something like an expressway not far away (FDR Drive), it was not the way the residents of these towers normally got around, as proposed in Le Corbusier's futuristic drawings. The vision of the New York City housing project was affected by the pastoral as well as the futuristic root of modern city planning, even if the apartment towers soared to fourteen stories and more.

The turn against the large project was based on more than a philosophical or aesthetic disagreement with Le Corbusier. Inevitably, social problems did develop in housing projects. The first were designed for a society in which vast numbers of people qualified for public housing, because in the Depression almost everyone's income was low, and great numbers were unemployed. One critic has said that the early public housing projects were designed really for a "submerged middle class," rather than the truly low income and poor—by which he means those who might have been expected, because of poor skills, poor education, and broken families, to remain poor and low income for a very long time.

The pastoral quality of the landscape was matched by the values of the early residents: they were happy to take the air on the benches scattered through the project; they enjoyed the grass and the trees. They hoped to get to Levittown, and many eventually did. In the families of the time, the father worked or sought work, the mother was at home to take care of the children, and the playgrounds were used for the purposes for which they had been designed. Watchful and disciplining mothers were available to supervise the children. But with a reviving and prosperous economy, inevitably the income and social characteristics of project dwellers changed. The submerged middle class surfaced and many among them left the projects, and indeed were forced to do so as rising income made them ineligible to remain. The elements of community life that policed open space and inner corridors weakened.

"Up to the early years of the 1950's," Anthony Jackson writes in his book *A Place Called Home*, "public housing in New York had been considered a success. Crime within projects was virtually non-existent, their racial mix provided an appropriate melting pot, and even a banking study thought their financial operation sound."

The Italians of East Harlem initially welcomed the housing projects. Who could object to new housing, larger and cheaper than what they possessed? But that changed very rapidly when they saw what the projects meant. One thing they meant was more Puerto Ricans, for this group was the most eligible in income terms, while the Italians, if their buildings were taken, generally had to find new housing in Brooklyn or the Bronx, or outside New York City entirely. E. J. Dionne in 1972–73, as a senior at Harvard (he later became a political reporter for the *New York Times* and the *Washington Po;t*, and is now a leading columnist for the *Washington Post*), studied East Harlem for his senior thesis. By then the remaining Italian population violently opposed the projects, which they saw as the turning point in the destruction of their neighborhood. "The projects brought in Puerto Ricans and Blacks. Politicians are held responsible. . . . Vito Marcantonio is especially held at fault." Italians, as he writes, "were poor enough to live in substandard housing, but not poor enough to get into the housing projects."

In East Harlem, as in the West End of Boston as described by Herbert Gans, the Italians were not well enough organized or strong enough to stop the projects. They could elect Italians to represent them, but that, it seemed, was the limit of their power.

In 1961, in her *The Death and Life of Great American Cities*, Jane Jacobs described in almost apocalyptic terms the destruction of the area, arguing, even while the bulldozers were at work, that forces existed that could raise its level on the basis of local investment.

> Eventually, much as the generosity of a rich nation might well extend massive aid to a deprived and backward country, into this district poured massive "foreign

aid," according to decisions by absentee experts from the remote continent inhabited by housers and planners. The aid poured in for rehousing people—some three hundred million dollars worth [the current cost of the housing projects of East Harlem would be more like five times that]. The more that poured in, the worse became the troubles and turmoils of East Harlem, and still more did it become like a backward and deprived country. More than 1,300 businesses which had the misfortune to occupy sites marked for housing were wiped away, and an estimated four-fifths of their proprietors were ruined. More than 500 noncommercial storefront establishments were wiped away. Virtually all the unslummed population which had hung on was rooted out and dispersed to "better itself."

Lack of money has hardly been the problem in East Harlem. . . . The money poured into East Harlem alone from the public housing treasuries is about as much as was lost on the Edsel. In the case of a mistake like the Edsel, a point is reached when the expenditure is reappraised and halted. But in East Harlem, citizens today have to fight off still more money for repetitious mistakes that go unappraised by those who control the money floodgates.[1]

The forces pushing for public housing (the forms and laws changed, but the resulting projects were pretty much the same) were strong enough to overcome all

---

[1] Jane Jacobs, *The Death and Life of Great American Cities* (New York: Vintage, 1961), pp. 306–7. As quoted in Eugene Joseph Dionne, Jr., "Little Italy Lost: The Breakdown of Italian Hegemony in East Harlem" (Honors essay in Social Studies, Harvard University, 1973), pp. 73–74.

opposition through the 1970s. The greatest of these forces were the trade unions and the builders, allied with political liberals. One could always point to the overwhelming need for low-income housing. The NYCHA always had an enormous backlog of aspiring tenants. The percentage of move-outs was low (and some of those were force-outs), and the NYCHA had no problem keeping all its projects filled.

The chief criticism came from those who had had a vision of a more harmonious and fulfilling community than they saw, a community that they once hoped would be built under enlightened public authority. Catherine Bauer, who had brought the early message of European social housing to the United States—along with Lewis Mumford—wrote one of the earliest critiques of public housing. It appeared in an architectural journal, not in a journal devoted to social issues (though in those days architects were more likely than they are today to think of themselves as having social objectives). But the place of its appearance, as well as its content, marked it as a critique from the outside, elitist, if you will. True community, she decided, had not been achieved; indeed more of it was to be found in the surrounding slums and tenement areas than in the housing project itself, built under enlightened public authority, committed to the best physical standards in terms of housing itself and open space. She wrote in her article, "The Dreary Deadlock of Public Housing," in 1957 in *Architectural Forum*:

> The public housing project . . . continues to be laid out as a "community unit," as large as possible and entirely divorced from its neighborhood surroundings, even

though this only dramatizes the segregation of charity-case families. Standardization is emphasized rather than alleviated in project design, as a glorification of efficient production methods and an expression of the goal of "decent, safe, and sanitary" housing for all. But the bleak symbols of productive efficiency and "minimum standards" are hardly an adequate or satisfactory expression of the values associated with American home life. And all this, in addition, often embodied in the skyscraper, whose refined technology gladdens the heart of technocratic architectural sculptors but pushes its occupants into a highly organized, beehive type of community life for which most American families have no desire and little aptitude.

The open space that was once the pride of the housing project now came under attack. The most powerful attack, of course, was that of Jane Jacobs (who was an editor at *Architectural Forum* when it published Catherine Bauer's article). She celebrated the street over the superblock; the mixed array of housing and stores and even little factories and artisan shops—such as one might have found in her far West Village home on Hudson Street—over the large project devoted to housing alone; the closely built streets, without gaps, against the verdant expanse punctuated by freestanding towers; the mix of income groups created by the complexities of small-scale development as against the uniformity produced by bureaucratic rules, reserving subsidized housing for the most qualified.

This guerrilla attack grew in intensity. By 1962, in addition, some housing projects in other cities surprisingly

were in trouble, in that they could not fill all the apartments, for reasons that were mixed but among which
crime was perhaps the most important. The project, originally a refuge from slum life, began to be seen as an epitome of some its worst features: broken families, unruly
youth, unkempt grounds.

The East Harlem projects suffered from the same image
that was uniformly fastened on all public housing projects, but they didn't really qualify. First, the NYCHA was
perhaps the best-managed housing authority in the country. If an apartment became vacant, it was immediately
filled from the huge waiting list. It was not allowed to
remain vacant, and it was vacancy, often owing to bureaucratic inefficiency, that abetted destruction by vandals and drug addicts. Second, the NYCHA had its own
police force and often boasted that there was less crime
in projects than in the surrounding streets. Third, it maintained a much higher quality of tenantry than many others: fewer on welfare, more with jobs, fewer with social
problems. As the civil rights revolution swept over the
country in the late 1960s and 1970s, the NYCHA's severe
management style, which served to maintain order, was
challenged and had to change—but it still did much better than most. No housing projects of the NYCHA lay
half-empty and abandoned; none were dynamited, as
happened in St. Louis and Newark; none were thinned
out and turned into middle-class housing, as happened
in Boston.

The relatively lavish provision of open space in the
New York City housing projects nevertheless came under
criticism. It was argued that such space was used more by
drug dealers and criminals than by resident mothers and

children, required more resources to keep up than were available, and was a waste of city land. The space could have been used for stores and community centers and social institutions. In East Harlem, the open spaces were not in fact neglected: they are well maintained, the trees grown, the lawns lush; the playgrounds are not vandalized or abandoned; the benches are not broken or disused, as anyone who strolls around the Washington Houses can see.

And yet in recent years the critics of the superblock, open space, and the large housing projects have won: there will be no projects like the Washington Houses built again in the low-income areas of New York. What is there, stays there—half of East Harlem is occupied by these giant projects, and almost two-thirds of the population of East Harlem now lives in them. The theoretical, philosophical, and aesthetic case that has been made against the large project, combined with the real experience of its social problems and the problems of maintaining its spaces and buildings successfully for their intended function, has prevailed. This means that in East Harlem all the funds available for low-income housing now go to the rehabilitation and maintenance of the old-law tenements and other forms of housing eighty or a hundred years old.

The programs under which old housing can be rehabilitated for low-income people—city, state, and federal—are so numerous, the sources of funds so varied, the regulations determining who can live in what kind of housing so complex, that they have spawned a host of new nonprofit agencies. These have developed the skills to fulfill the varied requirements that the programs set, and to rehabilitate, rent, and maintain the rehabbed buildings. It has become a fascinating enterprise, drawing in reformers of the 1950s and 1960s, militants and activists of the 1960s and 1970s, church groups and voluntary organizations of all kinds. Wholesale housing for the poor has become very small-scale retail housing—one tenement at a time, gutted and rebuilt into a few apartments that can be fitted into the hundred-year-old shell. Hope Community was one of the groups operating in East Harlem. Its director is George Calvert, who first came to the area in the 1950s to work in the East Harlem Protestant Parish, a reform group, and who in time directed a rather substantial enterprise in an old police precinct building he had bought from the city. He and his wife lived in the George Washington project, raised their children there, and were eventually forced out because their income exceeded its limits.

Alongside the nonprofits, working with public funds, one will find the occasional tenement or brownstone that has been rehabilitated by private funds, without subsidy. This creeping gentrification is a portent of the future.

The housing that was decried by the housing reformers of the 1930s and 1940s as slums worthy only of destruction is today maintained and restored at great expense despite the obvious deficiencies that led to such great quantities' being destroyed. Whatever their present condition—and many are mere shells—every building now is treated almost as a holy icon, to be restored whatever the cost. It is a very strange ending to a story that began with the enthusiastic condemnation and destruction of these tenements. A half century later we have an equally enthusiastic movement for the preservation and restoration of those that have survived.

The urbanistic critics have won. New York City should not be a verdant expanse punctuated by housing towers. We have Central Park for the verdant expanse. New York was built up densely on a uniform grid, with every street front occupied continuously by housing, stores, institutions. It is quite typical in New York for a large church to be placed chock in the middle of a block, with tenements or apartment houses flush up against it on either side. Or for a police precinct house to be located the same way in the middle of a block. Or a school to be so located, managing without a playground. Or a branch library. What was to be gained, the urbanists argued, by isolating the institution (or the apartment house) in open space? It reduced the density, reduced the number of watching eyes, increased opportunities for crime. No, the old was better, Jane Jacobs argued, and in time the intelligentsia agreed with her. The advocates of public housing were left isolated, unfashionable, unable to expand further, and limited, if they wished to continue to build good housing for the poor, to the restoration of the old tenements.

It is true that in other cities, and in other parts of New York, housing projects had more severe problems than in East Harlem, but if we are to limit ourselves to East Harlem, we are bound to report that it was not overwhelming social problems that stopped the expansion of public housing; it was, rather, the change in mood that condemned all huge projects, their bureaucracy and rigidity, even when they worked pretty well.

Of course there were other factors besides the changing mood of urbanists, city theorists, and reforming architects and planners that condemned the large project and its lavish dedication of open space to social uses. Other developments of the 1960s and 1970s served to bring to an end the era of big housing projects. One was the community organization movement. Community activism always prefers the existent to the very different that is going to replace it. Relocation had been carried out in the 1950s with relatively little protection of the sitting tenants or storekeepers or owners. The abuses of relocation became the most powerful argument of community activism against new projects. In time there was such suspicion of the large project that even when it involved no relocation, the presumption was against it. Even as tenements were abandoned, or vandalized, it became more and more difficult to propose large-scale clearance to replace them with a radically different urban form. New projects had to ape the old tenements. Urban theorists combined forces with urban activists. The first preferred the lively slums: all they needed was upgrading. The second feared what would come if they were demolished: the bureaucratic project for which they would not be eligible, the expanse of green and housing with no room for small stores.

A particularly effective attack on the project came from the analysts of urban crime, in particular the most influential, Oscar Newman. His major investigations focused on interior common space, and how it could be better watched and protected, through the design of the building, but he was also concerned with open space outside the building. Whatever the actual crime rates showed, the crowded street, with its shops and social institutions and hangers-on and hangers-out—women sitting on crates on stoops, men lounging around a local store—seemed safer, certainly at night, than the project paths edged by bushes and trees. Enclose the space, the new philosophy argued; reduce its quantity; do not let it extend beyond the houses; make sure every part of it is overlooked. But that is just what the old tenement street provided, not by intention, but because it used every bit of space.

With the rise of the drug trade and of crack addiction, the problem of open space in low-income areas became even more threatening. Every open space, whether in a project or not, could, it seemed, become a drug market. Washington Square, edged by fine apartment houses and churches and the buildings and adapted town houses of New York University, was as difficult to keep free of drug dealers as the open spaces of housing projects. The proliferation of the homeless in the 1980s raised another problem for open space: it could become a camping ground for the homeless, and its use by families and children became problematic. Interestingly enough, the open spaces of the housing projects did not become campgrounds for the homeless. Was this because of the efficiency of the NYCHA police? or because the homeless themselves preferred the lively precincts of Tompkins Park, edged by tenements and stores, undergoing gentrification, to the uniformity of the project? or because panhandling was more productive in upper-income areas?

The battle over housing project open space in East Harlem was not one among its users, the project residents. It was really between two elites who fought over the heads of users and potential users: the NYCHA, with its commitment to the forms it had created, to its huge projects and its open space; and the urban theorists, who called for denser use, for the replacement of the high towers by a continuous street frontage, and for more varied use. They argued for this because of the pleasures of urbanism it provided, because it served to create a richer and livelier community life, because it might reduce crime through the very nature of density and mixed uses.

But today the two epochs in housing reform—the earlier epoch of the giant project and the current epoch of the piecemeal restoration and rehabilitation of individual buildings, or small groups of building, preserving the original grid and continuous street frontage—seem to live in harmony in East Harlem, with neither the projects threatening the tenements, nor the rehabilitated tenements threatening to invade the projects. More than harmony, one notes a symbiosis. The project has no stores, but Third Avenue, edging the project, is filled with stores, some operated by locals, a few by chains, most by immigrants, Latin American or Korean. As against other areas in the city, where the numerous storefronts of the older era of city building (in which each tenement might have two stores on the ground level) may lie vacant, the stores along Third Avenue and other avenues facing the projects in East Harlem are all occupied. The projects provide a clientele. Whatever the percentage of land devoted to open space, the huge towers do provide a very large number of customers. In addition, the building of the projects radically thinned out the available stores; the rest are occupied, and while they are in no way upscale, they thrive.

And perhaps, even though the sidewalk and the stoop are still the preferred spaces for sunning and sitting, the tenement dwellers, inhabitants of both the untouched and the newly rehabilitated buildings, occasionally stroll into the project to enjoy the grass and trees and benches.

••

The conflicts we read about over housing projects seem somewhat muted in East Harlem. The dense city impinges closely on the project, and the sharp contrast of dense city and pastoral project gives a special value to the greenery and open space the project provides.

This somewhat halcyon picture should not lead us to forget far more serious conflicts over housing projects in other cities, which have led to the destruction of both housing and open space together; or the problems of housing projects in other parts of New York City. The South Bronx shows a different story: the projects there are even more dominant, the destruction of the old privately built houses (in the case of the Bronx these are not old-law tenements but often well-built apartment houses of a later epoch) more complete, the possibility of retaining the symbiotic relationship one sees in East Harlem between large-scale and small much reduced.

East Harlem is favored by the adjacency of the East Side, which encourages the desire to hold on to housing, whether for living or possible future capital gain. The processes that led to massive abandonment and destruction in the Bronx could not take hold as completely in East Harlem.

As for the social geography, it would seem inevitable that in time the affluent, gentrified East Side will move northward (the expansion southward has already in large measure taken place), and the local residents in tenements, restored or unrestored, will be replaced. Indeed, a modest degree of gentrification can already be seen as one walks north from 96th Street—a tenement here or there (perhaps now labeled a brownstone) is restored to a higher standard and has middle-class occupants. If this development continues, one reason will be that, for all its problems, East Harlem still provides the vibrant and varied street life that gentrifiers look for.

Had the project housing that occupies almost half the land of East Harlem grown to cover 75 or 80 percent of it, there would have been no possibility of such a development. It would seem to be natural for the East Side to expand northward, but the political obstacles will be formidable. How does one replace a public housing project with housing, whether under private or public auspices or a mixture of both, for higher-income tenants? A modest housing project has stood in the shadow of Lincoln Center and the enormous new towers for the affluent built adjacent to it on the West Side for some sixty years. Whatever the case in St. Louis, Newark, or Boston, it is hard to imagine in New York the political circumstances under which such projects could be replaced by housing for higher-income groups.

The existing tenements in East Harlem do provide avenues for invading gentrifiers. The housing form and arrangement are attractive to them. But even as the tenements are being rehabilitated, they are being locked into arrangements in which the new apartments are permanently committed to the poor. So while it would stand to reason that some day the middle and upper middle classes will replace the poor and low-income groups who now occupy this expensive urban land in East Harlem, the political and financial arrangements that have created both the housing projects and the rehabilitated tenements seem to ensure that it won't happen. East Harlem, an area of housing for the working class at its birth, just north of the area that defines elegant New York, will most probably remain so for the indefinite future.

CHAPTER EIGHT

Amenity in New York City

Privately Owned Public Spaces

Among the great cities of the world, New York is perhaps
the one that does least in integrating nature into the
urban environment. Cities, we know, must be crowded
and noisy and dirty to some degree, but connected to our
idea of cities is also urbanity, graciously shaped civic
spaces, avenues, noble buildings, monuments, and aspects of nature—parks, street trees, ornamental flowers—
though necessarily reduced, shaped, and confined in the
city. Whatever the man-made environment, nature is a
necessary background or accent. Modernist architects
and designers shamefacedly agree that most of their
buildings will be improved when the planting goes in,
when the trees grew up, when the ivy softens some walls.
Islands of peace are necessary amid urban cacophony,
and such islands are improved by aspects of nature in the
city, trees, water, flowers. These are all part of our idea of
the ideal city.

But compared to London, Paris, Berlin, and add as
many more as you wish, New York City, and in particular
Manhattan, is mean in what it provides in open space
embellished by nature. Compare the few patches of open

space in Manhattan with the profusion of green squares in London. Or the measly efforts to create something like a boulevard on Park Avenue and upper Broadway with even the minor boulevards of Paris. "There are no trees in the city!" Le Corbusier cried out despairingly on his visit to New York City in 1935, as recorded in his book *When the Cathedrals Were White*. Le Corbusier's ideal city consisted of skyscrapers in a park, and Manhattan had come closest to realizing it, when it came to skyscrapers. But where was the park? Is there, indeed, a single full-grown tree in Manhattan below 59th Street? There must be, but one doesn't easily recall where.

There are virtues to this overwhelming density of building, this banning of what is seen as superfluous open space, as was best pointed out by William H. Whyte, an enthusiast of New York's density. New York's density of building turns downtown and Midtown into something like enormous courthouse squares, in which a short walk takes one to all one's appointments, and one is likely to meet in the streets friends from the most unlikely and distant stretches of one's acquaintanceship. And as Whyte pointed out, New Yorkers can manage to make something of chance encounters on crowded city streets: they seem to do well enough without the piazzas, squares, sidewalk cafés, and other urban amenities common in many of the world's great cities. Whyte was also a perceptive and original student of what could be done to introduce those islands of relative peace and quiet that even an enthusiast of New York's density seeks in the city. He was a consultant to the city planners and officials who in the 1960s and 1970s tried to expand the number of such spaces in Manhattan, to soften the unyielding canyons that its city form and high land values create.

New York was the pioneer in introducing zoning into American cities in 1916, to limit how much air and space buildings could engross from their neighbors. Pre-1916 Manhattan not only built right up to the line that separated sidewalk from property; it also built straight up into the air, as high as technology and economics permitted. The 1916 reform did not seize from the developer open space at ground level, but it could take back from him part of the sky. In so doing it created, through its regulations that required setbacks from the property line as the building rose, the ziggurat or wedding-cake skyscraper that distinguished the New York City skyline. In 1961, in the first major overhaul of the zoning requirements of 1916, New York City became the pioneer in introducing a variant in zoning that tried to pry open spaces from the developer of new buildings. If the developer provided a plaza for the public, the city in return would permit the building to go up higher and contain more rentable space.

This was a unique program, responding to the realities of the American city, the American legal system, American urban economics, and the distinctive form of Manhattan. One could have imagined a public program that would have retained through legislation and regulation space for public uses, one that would have taken some space for public use from the developer under eminent domain. That might well have been the way the creation of open space was managed in European cities—or even in New York in earlier days. After all, New York was able to exclude from the marketplace the enormous and eventually very expensive swath of Manhattan that became

Central Park, and to create other great parks in Manhattan (like Riverside Park), entirely from public funds. But for various reasons the relative power and affluence of public and private players in the city seems to have so changed by 1961 that the best the city could do was to offer "incentives" to the private developer to provide some space for public use. This was the mechanism devised to moderate the incredible density that is the hallmark of New York City.

The result has been a peppering of Manhattan over the subsequent decades with a multitude of small open spaces, "privately owned public spaces," to provide some degree of relief from the crowding, the scale, the intensity of Manhattan. That Manhattan has to some degree been improved because of this program is doubtless true. In the downtown financial district, in the Midtown area, one finds plazas, well or badly designed, buildings set back from the street a few feet more than their neighbors, arcades, alternative paths through buildings, with varying degrees of amenity in the way of places to sit, ornamental water, available refreshments, artworks, a patch of green, or some trees.

This major public effort to introduce some space, peace, pleasantness, and grace into crowded Manhattan has been recorded and analyzed in a remarkable book by Jerold S. Kayden, *Privately Owned Public Space: The New York Experience* (John Wiley and Sons, 2000). This is a monumental scholarly account of an important aspect of New York City; it takes its place in a galaxy of important recent books on New York City, most prominently the huge volumes by Robert Stern and his colleagues recording the major buildings of New York. Years ago, on visits to Paris, I wondered why New York seemed to be so deficient in detailed accounts of the city's buildings and streets and monuments. In Paris, I could consult with admiration an encyclopedia of the city's streets, to find out more about the building in which I was staying, its history and neighbors. There was no equivalent in New York. But we are now approaching for New York a scale of documentation and criticism of the city's form that we find in other great world cities. We also now have guidebooks to the architecture of our major cities that simply did not exist a few decades ago. This itself is an achievement in self-consciousness that cannot but be of help to our cities. Kayden's book is part of that expansion of self-consciousness.

Kayden records in detail how the reform that led to the privately owned public spaces program came about, and how it has worked, and he reports on every one of the 503 public spaces that have been created under the program. In each case he gives us a plan of the public space, its relationship to the building to which it is attached and the surrounding streets, a photograph (by Kayden himself), and a full evaluation of how the space works—Is it used? How is it used? What amenities are provided? If it doesn't work, why not? The recording and analysis of this effort has produced a unique guidebook to a very important aspect of the city.

These 503 public spaces (almost all of them are in Manhattan below 72nd Street), if one adds them all up, make up eighty-two acres, five times as much space as the site of the World Trade Center, or almost thirty city blocks. In return for this space, New York City has granted developers more than twenty million square feet of additional space, almost twice as much as all the office space in the destroyed World Trade Center.

As any walker in the city knows, many of these spaces do not work well. While they have enabled the developer to increase office space (and in some cases, residential space) in his building and have added to New York's density, to the number of people and vehicles that crowd the city's streets, the relief they have offered in return ranges from the almost nonexistent or invisible to very pleasant refuges of space and some green inserted into the fabric of the city. After evaluating each of them from the point of view of their design and usability and the degree to which they are actually used, Kayden summarizes: "Although the policy has yielded an impressive quantity of public space, it has failed to produce a similarly impressive quality of public space. At their best, the spaces marry aesthetics with functionality, creating superior physical and social environments, set intelligently within densely packed urban conditions, for residents, employees, and victors alike." But "at their worst, by design and operation, the spaces have been hostile to public use. Many spaces are nothing more than empty strips or expanses of untended surface, while others have been privatized by locked gates, missing amenities, and usurpation by adjacent commercial activities in contravention of the spirit or letter of applicable legal requirements." Kayden finds that 41 percent of the 503 spaces are of marginal use, but over time the city did find out how to do better. From 1975 onward, the standards governing the exchange of additional buildable space for open usable space were regularly tightened, with more and more detail as to what the developer was required to do to make the space at-

tractive, usable, and available. Leafing through this cata-
log of the open spaces, one is saddened by how many of
them are nothing more than a sidewalk widening breaking the uniform facade of the street, that is likely to be
unnoticed by the passerby or confusing him as to why it
is there. In scale, when we add up all the pieces, the program is large and respectable. In what it has done for the
city, it is modest.

The achievement is particularly modest, despite the
quantity of open space that has been added to Manhattan, when one considers it from the point of view of the
models and hopes that inspired it. Indeed, perhaps the
most striking part of the story is how many of the open
and public spaces of Manhattan that were provided without benefit of economic incentive, before the program,
are superior to the generality of those that were provided
because of it. Not every building developer before 1961—
or after 1961—looked at his project in purely economic
terms. Some wanted to add to the beauty of the city and
provide some public ornament, just as builders, public
and private, in every great city have tried over the years
to do. And so there were models before 1961 of major
urban developments that also embellished the city with
open space, with a touch of nature, with a gathering or
resting place. One such recent model was particularly evident in 1961—the plaza in front of the Seagram's Building, designed by Mies van der Rohe, on Park Avenue, and
completed shortly before the zoning reform of 1961.
Other recent examples of open public space provided by
commercial buildings, all in the absence of any zoning
incentive, also existed: Lever House, also on Park Avenue; the Chase Manhattan Bank Building plaza in Lower

Manhattan; the plazas in front of the new extensions to Rockefeller Center on Sixth Avenue; the Time-Life Building; and the Equitable Building. The most useful—and used—of these was the plaza in front of the Seagram's Building. We learn from Kayden that this was intended to be only ornamental, and that Mies was surprised to discover that people were sitting on his stone ledges, and eating their lunches there. But it illustrated the hunger of New Yorkers and visitors for open and usable space that broke the impenetrable and strict regularity of the street facade. It also, I believe, illustrated the power of classical principles of design—symmetry, balance, regularity. The Seagram's Plaza, as against so many of the spaces created in the wake of the 1961 reform, is unique in that it was truly planned, and not simply a leftover space provided for a buildable space bonus. It leads us to think of the motives that are best activated for the embellishment of the city. They cannot be purely or only economic. That was the mechanism of the 1961 reform that provided so many privately owned public spaces for the city. But if one considers the best-loved and most used of the spaces in the city that have been provided by the private builder, it is clear that other motives must be drawn upon to provide the most successful civic spaces.

One cannot help but think back to the private development that has done most to provide a public square for New York City, and that is, of course, Rockefeller Center. As Sean O'Casey wrote, "The newcomer to New York City, American or foreigner, doesn't spend a glance on St. John's of Morningside Heights, or St. Patrick's on Fifth Avenue . . . , but makes for Rockefeller Center, where he can get an eyeful worth seeing."[1] Rockefeller Center was a commercial development—it still is. But it was a commercial development that was also entwined with civic objectives: originally to provide a new opera house for the city, later to encompass at least a major theater. As John D. Rockefeller, Jr., wrote in 1929: "While the prime consideration in this enterprise must be its financial success, the importance of a unified and beautiful architectural whole must be constantly kept in mind, and attained, to the fullest extent possible compatible with an adequate return on the investment."[2]

There is much to think about when one considers the success of Rockefeller Center's open space—the sunken center, the viewing areas that surround it, the channel between the two low-rise buildings that leads to it, with its changing seasonal plantings. As one discovers in reading the history of Rockefeller Center, as in the excellent and full account by Carol Herselle Krinsky (*Rockefeller Center*, Oxford University Press, 1978), it was an idea or conception that did not spring into existence in a day or a moment, but was mulled over by many designers, under the pressure of changing circumstances, over a good number of years. Nor was its success as a public space guaranteed from its birth: just what would happen to the sunken open space in the center of the development and what was to be its use was not clear, and its unexpected and unplanned emergence as a skating rink, in this most unlikely of spots—which since its begin-

[1] In Carol Herselle Krinsky, *Rockefeller Center* (New York: Oxford University Press, 1978), p. 2.
[2] Ibid., p. 30.

ning has regularly gathered a throng of sightseers—was only one of a number of uses that were considered and tried out.

Great open spaces do not emerge, for the most part, at a stroke. They grow over time. But they require, I would argue, some initial strong design conception that can be adapted over time to change. I am impressed by how many of the successful and used open spaces of Manhattan also reflect a classic regularity, indeed a Beaux-Arts-like consciousness emphasizing symmetry and balance. Of course this is encouraged by the regular street pattern of Manhattan, but, despite this encouragement, think of how many recently created public spaces consciously break with this pattern to favor some irregularity or idiosyncrasy. Consider, in contrast, the open space in front of the New York Public Library, and Bryant Park behind it, and the steps and fountains in front of the Metropolitan Museum of Art. They are classic spaces, and they work. That the steps are regularly occupied by a good number of people tells us how needed such spaces are. But one can also imagine ways in which they could be much less welcoming than they are. Thus the replacement of a steep stairway to the Metropolitan Museum many years ago with wide stairs covering a larger expanse of space made the walk up to the museum slower but provided more welcoming sitting space. That was one key adaptation in the evolution of the steps as a public gathering place.

The plan of Manhattan, as against the plan of Washington and so many other cities, was hostile to open spaces, plazas, squares. There were none built in. Only the odd triangles created by the diagonal of Broadway, as it sliced through the grid, provided places where a small green square or park could be located, though even these could be completely covered by money-earning buildings, as in Times Square. Green open spaces were in time created, the larger ones through public action, and others through the action of civic-minded philanthropists and entrepreneurs. Almost all were bounded and limited by the street plan. Rockefeller Center was unique as a private enterprise in being able to acquire the three adjacent blocks that belonged to Columbia University, so it could shape a more generous plan, while still accommodating commercial needs. But its success is not only based on the space available to it; it is also based on the skill of the designers and architects who worked on it, and on the civic-minded generosity of its owners.

Another design opportunity, on a space that coincidentally is about the same size as the original three blocks of Rockefeller Center, now faces New York as the result of the abomination of September 11, 2001. The first proposals, revealed on July 16, 2002, were not impressive. As in the case of the original privately owned public space program, they took it for granted that in New York City amenity must be paid for by greater density. And subsequent proposals, including the plan by Daniel Liebeskind chosen by the political authorities that in theory will guide the rebuilding—but which has already been modified, to the point of abandonment—all accepted the same limitation. The original quantity of office space on the site must be restored.

One would have thought, in view of the large sums committed by the federal government to rebuilding, that in this case public authorities would have played a more decisive role and reduced density to permit greater design freedom. Does Manhattan need more density?

What seems necessary for the design of successful open spaces is both skill at shaping a design that accommodates human desires, needs, and aspirations, and a willingness and ability to forgo the maximum economic benefit that can be derived from a site. One route to better design that should not be dismissed is to review what has been successful in Manhattan and what has not. In doing so, one will become aware that there are elements in the classic tradition of design that are well suited to and usable in Manhattan.

Subway Art and the Subway as Art

In the first contract for the New York City subway system, signed in 1899, we may read: "The railway and its equipment . . . constitute a great public work. All parts of the structure where exposed to public sight shall therefore be designed, constructed and maintained with a view to the beauty of their appearance, as well as their efficiency."[3] What a grand ambition! And at least as far as that first subway line was concerned, running from City Hall and Brooklyn Bridge up to Grand Central, across 42nd Street to Times Square, and up Broadway, the ambition was evident. Its art did not reach anywhere near the level of the extravagant Moscow subway, but there was some attention to decorative details. The distinctive ceramic panels that identified the first stations were designed by George

[3] Lee Stookey, *Subway Ceramics: A History and Iconography*, 2nd ed. (Brattleboro, Vt.: Lee Stookey, 1994), p. 14.

Heins and Christopher Grant LaFarge. Modest as they were, the subways did not do as well subsequently.

That early ambition was in decline in later years, as the New York City subways, despite their enormous scale and crucial role in the city, became the most poorly maintained and ugliest of any great system. The last twenty years have shown great improvements, but mostly at the level of functioning—new cars that break down less often, new technical systems not visible to the rider. The one great change in the subway environment visible to the subway user in these years was the elimination of graffiti. This was a success of such magnitude that it deserves a full-scale analysis, which I have not seen. When I wrote an article on the New York City subway graffiti in *The Public Interest* during the height of the plague and reviewed the efforts to control it, I concluded sadly that there was no solution. More intensive policing wouldn't work because judges would not impose severe sentences when they also had to deal with robbers, muggers, and rapists; and requiring unpaid work on removal by the culprits didn't work either, I was told, and only taught the graffitists new and better techniques of making what they considered their "art" unerasable. It was easy enough, the police told me, to catch the graffitists. But then what? The only hope, it seemed to me then, was a change in the culture: the graffitists, one day, would lose interest and move on to something else.[4] I was wrong. The problem could surprisingly be controlled by immediate removal of all graffiti, which required taking any car with graffiti out

---

[4] Nathan Glazer, "On Subway Graffitti in New York," *The Public Interest* (Winter 1978).

of service and cleaning it off, a program devised by David Gunn. I would have thought this would be unimaginably expensive, but it was done; the removal process is maintained; the graffitists were discouraged and shifted their attention to other surfaces. They have been replaced by the window scratchers, but even the worst efforts of the latter do not totally obscure the windows, and at least they and their defenders (if they have any) can lay no claim to art: no window scratcher has become famous the way some graffitists did, and no one publishes books of their finest work, as occurred in the case of the subway graffitists. If we ever find a successful way of incapacitating the window scratchers, there will be no howls from the avant-garde.

The original subway line, one can see, was built in an optimistic age, and with great ambition. That ambition dropped off with later extensions, such as the Lexington Avenue line. They were barer, but still made quite a play of displaying and bordering the station names in colored ceramic tile. The wonderful ceramic plaques that defined the original stations—the beaver of Astor Place, the ship of Columbus Circle, the grand purple seal of the City College of New York at 137th Street—disappeared for the most part in later extensions and remodelings. But the subways never descended, as they were expanded, to narrowly limited functionality. Clifton Hood, in his history of the New York subways, *722 Miles*,[5] writes that the Independent lines, built by the city rather than private investors, in the 1920s and 1930s, were constructed with

---

[5] Clifton Hood, *722 Miles: The Building of the Subways and How They Transformed New York* (New York: Simon & Schuster, 1993).

a strict economy in mind. But one can see, despite the evident economy, that someone was thinking of the color patterns of the tiles in the stations and used them to help define for the subway rider where he was. The tiles in the local stops between express stops are all of one color family, but lighten or darken (depending which way one is going) as one approaches an express stop. One could hardly say this was art. In time, as taste in art changed so that an expanse of black or white, hardly modulated, could be considered art, these color schemes for subway tiles could perhaps have so qualified: someone, after all, had to have the original idea, had to choose the colors and the shades; ceramic tile producers had to match them. Even if it was not art, it was a fillip to the jaded subway rider if he recognized the scheme, and I know that as a completely unsophisticated youth and teenager I enjoyed the subtly changing colors as the train whizzed past the local stations, and felt a sense of arrival when it screeched to a stop at an express station with a completely different color, signaling a shift to a new color family. How minimal were the aesthetic satisfactions the subway rider had to look forward to!

The changes that have taken place in the subway system over the years have battered it badly, but the improvement is evident and now reaches beyond the barebones essentials of dependable functioning to art and environment. The Metropolitan Transportation Authority has been engaged for some years in sprucing up the stations and adding art to them.

The first thing one notes in the new program is that the works of art commissioned for the stations are enormously varied—in the materials used, in the styles represented, in the places where they are displayed. There is artwork in the classic ceramic tile of the old subways, in bronze, in glass, in enameled porcelain. They are in varied contemporary styles. Some are representational, some abstract, some symbolic, some evocative of the past, and in many cases one thinks it will be hard for the unsophisticated subway user to know what to make of the art, assuming he or she notices it. Some of the pieces are on station walls, some on stairways approaching station platforms, some on mezzanines. The helpful guide *Arts for Transit* tells where the works of art are, which can be seen by a rider getting off a train and waiting for the next one, and which will require one to exit to view them and pay another fare to return to the subway.

It has been decided there will be no uniform scheme of decoration and artwork, as in the first IRT (Interboro Rapid Transit) line, and in the Independent lines that were built by the city. That is understandable: three separate systems have been cobbled together to form one unified system, available throughout its expanse with one fare. Despite the existence of a common map, and a uniform scheme of numbering and lettering the lines, one can easily tell whether one is on the old original IRT, the BMT (Brooklyn-Manhattan Transit), or the IND. Whatever the virtues of a system of ceramic plaques to mark and identify specific stations in the original IRT, or a distinctive system of colored tiles to mark groups of stations in the original IND, the future path of the subways, it seems, is not toward greater uniformity or even maintaining the uniformity that history imposed on parts of the system. Each station will, it appears, do its own thing, and they may be very different things indeed. This is one significant difference from the early decorative schemes: they were devised at a time when there was less dispute as to what art was, and what was suitable for public spaces.

A number of East Side stations (the 4, 5, and 6 lines route, or what was known once as the Lexington Avenue line) have had artwork installed, and I made an odyssey down the line from 125th Street to 42nd Street to see what has been done. The 125th Street station has conical bronze reliefs on the mezzanine walls. They are by Houston Conwill and are named *Open Secret*. They look well enough, but it is not clear what they symbolize, if anything. The markings on them might be a street grid, or might be influenced by something like an African design motif. Viewing them, one immediately notes a large and perhaps key problem for the program of art in the subways. Substantial as the artworks are, they make no great impression contrasted with the very extensive subway walls on which they are placed. There is a problem of scale: the inserted works of art may appear puny set against the walls of an extended mezzanine or subway station.

Going down to the station platform at 125th Street, one immediately notes a second problem. The station platforms are dismal: the floors are encrusted with old black chewing gum, as in so many New York subway stations, to the point where the floors seem composed of an asphalt-like product that is the end result of chewing gum trod underfoot. The tile walls, with their remaining patches of old decoration, are broken and streaked with dirt, and one immediately thinks, despite the philistine character of the thought, might the MTA not have done better to put the money expended for art toward cleaning up the station? It is a thought that dominates as one proceeds from station to station. One finds the same ugly and depressing station floors at the 116th Street and 110th Street stops. One wants to cry out, clean up the stations first!

This is just what has been done at the 103rd Street station. It is a revelation and cannot but be a lift to its users. The entire station has been retiled, walls and floors, in a pattern using three different colors: light and dark orange, and a brown. The new tile floors seem clear, for the most part, of chewing gum. The large original decorative tile name of the station has been cleaned and restored, and is accentuated by a border of new buff tile. It was most appropriate for the major design element in the original station to be the station's name, unglamorous as 103rd Street is, compared to Wall Street, City Hall, Astor Place, Columbus Circle. The commissioned artwork here, above the platform entrances, consists of ceramic tile murals by Nitza Tufino, called *Neo-Boriken*. Boriquen, as we all should know, is an old name for Puerto Rico. In this case, the connection is with the dominantly Puerto Rican character of the neighborhood above, perhaps the first Puerto Rican neighborhood in the city. The murals are colorful, suited to the area, but as in the case of 125th Street, they are too small in relation to the size of the station, and not particularly obvious, located as they are above the stairways. They make no great or substantial show and fade in comparison with the colorfully retiled and clean station.

Ninety-Sixth Street, which is to have mosaic murals that are now being installed, is also being fully restored and will be beautiful. The floors are new large concrete squares, the walls white tile, and when I came through it, a good number of workmen were to be seen, completing the tile work on the walls, and, wonders of wonders, scraping chewing gum off the new floors with an instrument that seems specially designed for the purpose. It was so easy to do! If new flooring is smooth and hard and non-porous—ceramic tile, or terrazzo, or polished stone or concrete—as against whatever floor material, hardly visible in old stations, was used under the chewing gum, it would seem, from the 96th Street case, no great matter to keep the floor clear of gum. A clean and brightly colored floor may inhibit some chewers from dropping their gum; perhaps with subway crime now so low some of the police can be detailed to hand out summonses, and we may hope that someday we will have gum-free station floors.

Forty-second Street has always been a problem, with its too narrow platforms, its too low ceilings. But what has been done on the mezzanine is quite wonderful. It is now clean and bright and colorful. The columns are stainless steel, and in the middle of the floor is installed in various colors a huge compass, a most suitable decorative element for an underground concourse where one is likely to lose one's bearings. The contrast with the station below is striking. The artworks listed for 42nd Street are *Fast Track* and *Wheelheads*, mixed-media sculptures that one finally gets to see at the end of the long and dismal passage connecting the North-South line with the Shuttle. The passageway is hardly improved by some old scattered colored tile, dating from a decades-old effort to brighten it. There is nothing in particular wrong with the works of art when one finally reaches them: it is just that the passageway is so long, and the sculptures too small relative to it.

The problem, to my mind, is that the MTA is thinking of art *in* the subway, but one should think of the subway as a grand construction, *as* art. It is the difference between art attached to the subway, and the subway conceived of as making an overall aesthetic impression. We see the same problem when we consider the art on the bare walls of the huge new lobbies of postwar office buildings. Large sculptures or graphics or illustrations, in various media, are attached to the walls in an effort to dress them up, but contrast the result with the wonderful lobbies of such buildings as the Woolworth, the Chrysler, the Chanin, and scores of others in which the lobby, with its decorations and distinctive materials, becomes a work of art in itself. This unity between architecture and art is something we find very hard to achieve now, particularly in light of the modernist dictum that declares ornament crime. Too much art meant to embellish architecture now sticks out like an irrelevancy, hardly big enough to match the enormous walls, despite the fact that the piece may be the biggest work that the artist has ever designed. The piece seems quite unrelated to the walls and the space, even though both were designed at the same time and in presumably the same style.

This seems to me the main problem with the new program of introducing works of art in the subways. The Washington subway is a work of art, but it was built as one great project, adhering to a single impressive design for its stations, which was created by a single architect. It has no need for artworks: it is truly the subway as a work of art, modernist art, made out of the structure itself rather than attached to it. In New York we deal with a heritage of variousness. But the very cleaning and retiling

and reflooring, with the use of imaginative colors and fit-
tings—the process going on today, if all too slowly—does
much more for the subway station, I believe, than the
occasional piece of art mounted on a platform wall, over
a stairway, in a mezzanine. Aesthetic concerns can be integrated into this station-rebuilding process, and it is clear
they are, on the basis of such stations as 103rd Street,
96th Street, 42nd Street. What is really successful in these
stations—the bright new tiling, the new floor materials,
the restoration of station names in tile—bears no artists'
names. When it comes to the specific works of art, artist's
name attached, they are generally no match for the subways. Even the advertisements are generally bigger.

What really works in the new program are the large
functional elements, such as the new iron grilles and rail-
ings. Subway stations need large expanses of grille and
railing to separate various areas, and some of the new
designs (such as one at 23rd Street on the Sixth Avenue
Line by Valerie Sandon) are rather clear improvements
over the iron grilles of the past. But few of the new elements represent so unambiguous an improvement.

Riding the subways, one may chance on occasion to
see an advertisement for *River of Time*, a documentary on
the building of the New York subway, which is shown at
the Transit Museum in Brooklyn, located in an old abandoned subway station. It is illustrated by a picture of a
stunning station, the original City Hall station, vaulted in
Guastavino tile. It has been closed since 1945. That is the
true art of the subway, the subway as a work of art. Could
not the MTA think of a way of reopening that station,
finding a use for the space, so that people can be awed by

the ambition that once created such a setting for the trains that carried the ordinary people?

The "Old City"

The appearance of a large one-volume encyclopedia of New York City in 1996,[6] apparently the first ever, led one to think of one of Parkinson's laws: when the capital is complete, the empire is ready to fall. Or perhaps, more grandly, of Hegel's owl of Minerva, which takes flight at dusk. For accompanying and following on New York City's economic and social woes in the 1970s and 1980s was a spate of major scholarly works that were unparalleled and unavailable in the days of its glory, wherever we place it, and this is a phenomenon that certainly deserves some consideration.

No one can deny the facts of decline and of struggle to retain preeminence for thirty years after the economic crisis of the 1970s that brought the city close to bankruptcy. The city continues to suffer under a burden of social costs that imposes tremendous strains on its budget, and that require an array of taxes and a level of taxation unparalleled in any other American city. Since the late 1960s, an inexorable one-seventh or so of the city's population, one million people, were on welfare, a few hundred thousand less or more depending on economic conditions, but a figure far transcending the 300,000 on welfare at the beginning of the 1960s. There have been various signs of recovery, perhaps the most striking being

[6] *The Encyclopedia of New York City*, ed. Kenneth T. Jackson (New Haven: Yale University Press;New York: New-York Historical Society, 1995).

the radical reduction in crime and in the numbers on welfare to the levels of the 1960s under the mayoralty of Rudolph Giuliani (1993–2001), and maintained since.

It remains true that New York cannot manage to find
the resources for the most minimal infrastructural improvements that are essential to a world city. It has not
yet connected its airports to its center by public transportation, though all its world competitors have, and even cities
such as Philadelphia, St. Louis, and Cleveland can manage
the feat in the public-transit-poor United States. The best
that could be proposed by the Port of New York Authority,
which manages the New York City airports, was a measly
effort to connect Kennedy Airport to the city subway system by a special line, an improvement that owes much to
the heroic efforts of Senator Daniel P. Moynihan. But it
gets those arriving at Kennedy as far as Jamaica in deep
Queens, where they must transfer to the city subway system. New York's major public transportation systems have
shown no significant expansion for sixty years. The last
significant extension of the subway system was more than
sixty years ago. The ancient water mains regularly explode
into geysers. The last major connections of Manhattan to
the rest of the city and the U.S. mainland date to before
World War II, and one cannot imagine that there will be
any more. Manhattan connections to Brooklyn and
Queens are dependent on some major bridges—Brooklyn,
Manhattan, Williamsburg, Queensboro—all of which
were built before 1909, and the city is hard-pressed to
maintain these crucial links in good repair.

New York has lost most of its manufacturing jobs. One
could debate whether that is such a serious matter for a
world city that must fulfill so many other functions, in

finance, in information industries, in culture. New York's preeminence as a headquarters city for leading American corporations has also declined. All in all, it is clear that New York casts a smaller shadow on the American scene than it once did. It still maintains, better than other northeastern and midwestern cities, its population. But its population was 6 percent of the U.S. total in 1940 and is less than 3 percent today. "The old country," the *Economist* labeled the United States in a supplement. "The old city," one thinks of New York, when one arrives from sparkling airports overseas, accessible by new public transit or commodious and clean taxis, and encounters New York City taxis with their dirty trunks and their anticrime barriers confining the passenger to a mean backseat, and debris-strewn freeways into the city, and as one ponders which of a number of difficult ways of getting into Manhattan by taxi one should attempt.

In contrast to all these and other troubles, information on New York flourishes, novels on old New York become best-sellers, and interest in New York, on the part of its inhabitants and visitors, is undimmed or expanded far beyond such curiosity in the past. An intriguing phenomenon. There was no encyclopedia of New York City during the decades considered by many its last good ones, the 1940s and 1950s and 1960s. There was no guidebook to its architecture. The first *AIA Guide to New York City* ("AIA" stands for the American Institute of Architects) dates only to 1967. It was a mere 464 pages; the fourth edition (2000), has grown to 1,056 pages, and not because of so many new buildings, but because so many more of the old buildings are considered of interest. Indeed, in the days of New York City's glory there were no guidebooks at all to the city, though many books on New York were written, particularly by European visitors: it was then the emblem of modernity. In the 1950s, while I was working as an editor at Doubleday-Anchor Books, I pondered the unavailability of guidebooks to New York, and to American cities in general. The large WPA guidebook to New York City—a prewar product of that creative period during the Depression when artists and writers were employed on arts projects by the federal government as a form of work relief—was out of print. In any case, a product of 1937, it was out of date. Old New Yorkers will recall that the only "guidebooks" to New York in those days were fat little pamphlets of newsprint, with lists of streets and a map for each borough, bound in red paper, and these would include a brief listing of sights. These crude guides were often used by taxicab drivers. (Cab drivers no longer carry them or their equivalents, even if they are available, not because they know where to go but because they will generally not take you to any but the most obvious locations in Manhattan in any case.) They were sold in candy stores, not in bookstores, and were used by deliverymen rather than visitors. It was embarrassing to the patriotic New Yorker when he compared them to what was available to guide the visitor in other world cities.

Matters are very different today. Any New York City bookstore (and any Cambridge, Massachusetts, bookstore, for that matter) will now have a wall of New York City guidebooks of staggering variety—architectural guides, art guides, shopping guides, ethnic guides, "lifestyle" guides (or should we call them "identity-group" guides?), and so forth. But beyond guidebooks there is scholarship of an astonishing range and depth. The archi-

tect Robert A. M. Stern has been engaged, with coau-
thors, in chronicling the architecture of New York City in
a series of large volumes of impressive scholarship. We
have had *New York 1900*, with Gregory Gilmartin and
John Massengale (Rizzoli, 1983), *New York 1930*, with
Gregory Gilmartin and Thomas Mellins (Rizzoli, 1987),
and the series has climaxed—but apparently this is not
the end—with the publication of *New York 1960*, with co-
authors David Fishman and Thomas Mellins (Monacelli
Press, 1995). At 1,374 double-columned pages, this single
volume of the three-volume survey outbulks the *Encyclopedia of New York City*. Each book in the series covers ap-
proximately thirty years of New York City building, before and after the date in the title. I would have thought,
after *New York 1930*, which reaches a monumental peak
in the great Art Deco skyscrapers of the city, there was
not much more to do, but my perusal of *New York 1960*
makes it clear that I was wrong, and while this volume
has to document many unfortunate buildings of the postwar period, one wonders whether any other city could
match the array and variety of the thirty years it chroni-
cles. Since this massive volume, Stern and his associates
have gone back to an earlier period partially covered in
New York 1900 and added 1,164 pages: *New York 1880*
(Monacelli Press, 1999).

One of the most surprising aspects of these volumes is
that there is no indication of any institutional support,
whether foundation, endowment, corporate, or municipal. Does the market alone support them? If so, it is a
remarkable story, and one well worth exploring for what
it tells us about current interest in New York City. I note,
too, that the richly detailed and fascinating *Historical Atlas*

of New York City, by Eric Homberger (Henry Holt, 1994), the only one I am aware of, has also been published without any reference to institutional support. And other New York books continue to come from the presses on aspects of New York City history that have until recently remained dark, as far as the scholarly world is concerned. So we have major recent studies of the history of prostitution in the city (Timothy J. Gilfoyle, *City of Eros: New York City, Prostitution, and the Commercialization of Sex, 1790–1920* [W. W. Norton, 1992]), and homosexual life in the city (George Chauncey, *Gay New York: Urban Culture and the Making of Gay Male World, 1890–1970* [Basic Books, 1994]). Key neighborhoods are being explored in depth: *Greenwich Village: Culture and Counterculture*, edited by Rick Beard and Leslie Cohen Berlowitz (New Brunswick, N.J.: Rutgers University Press in association with the Museum of the City of New York, 1993); *Inventing Times Square: Commerce and Culture at the Crossroads of the World*, edited by William Taylor (Russell Sage Foundation, 1991); *Morningside Heights: A History of Its Architecture and Development*, by Andrew S. Dolkart (New York: Columbia University Press, 1998). Of course books on Harlem multiply: *Harlem, Lost and Found: An Architectural and Social History*, by Michael Adams (New York: Monicelli Press, 2005), is a recent example. There is a major new history, *Gotham: A History of New York City to 1898*, by Edwin G. Burroughs and Mike Wallace (New York: Oxford University Press, 1999); a volume on the physical shaping of New York City, *The Landscape of Modernity*, edited by David Ward and Olivier Zunz (Russell Sage Foundation, 1992), and a volume contrasting the shaping of New York with that of Boston (*Invented Cities* by Mona Domosh [Yale,

1996]). This is the merest sampling of recent books on New York City. All in all, there is more than the most devoted lover of New York can keep up with.

This flood of scholarly work has been fully tapped in *The Encyclopedia of New York City*, edited by the urban historian of Columbia University, Kenneth T. Jackson. This book did receive institutional and foundation support. Major support, we are informed before the title page, came from the National Endowment for the Humanities, McGraw-Hill (though it did not publish the book), and Frederick, Daniel, and Elihu Rose, part of that civic-minded elite that does so much to maintain the city's cultural and educational institutions at a time when the city itself can, it seems, do so little for them. (Thus the expensive restoration of the grand reading room of the New York Public Library and the newly built planetarium at the Museum of Natural History also bear the names of various members of the Rose family.) A host of other individuals, foundations, and corporations are mentioned as supporters. The cultural life of the city is dependent on them.

What should an encyclopedia of a world city contain? The city touches on almost everything, and almost everything touches on it. New York City, in respect to commercial and business life, and artistic and cultural life, is the capital of the United States. The "culture capital of the world," one volume calls it: *New York: Culture Capital of the World: 1940–1965*, edited by Leonard Wallock (Rizzoli, 1988). Another dubs it "the capital of the American century" (Martin Shefter, *Capital of the American Century* [Russell Sage Foundation, 1993]). Drawing the line that separates the city from the nation is not easy. What corporations should be included? Most major corporations have been headquartered for part of their lives in New York City, even if their activities had little to do with the city. That is where the banks and the money were. Almost all important cultural figures can be said to have some New York connection, if only because their agents or publishers or galleries, or the theaters and concert halls in which they performed, or their works were presented, were there.

The editors carefully explain the principles that have guided inclusion and exclusion: "The people included in the encyclopedia are those whom the editors judged to have left a permanent mark on the city's history and culture. Most subjects of biographical entries lived in the city for much of their lives, although some were influential visitors (such as Lafayette, Lincoln and Dickens) and one never so much as set foot in the city (the Duke of York, for whom the city is named)." They admit that for "prominent figures in the world of film, music, and sports," links with the city may be "tenuous." So one finds: Béla Bartók lived in New York for only the last five years of his life. Fred Astaire? He was born in Omaha and died in Los Angeles, but he did live and dance in New York from 1917 to 1932, and New York does appear glowingly in some of his movies. Josephine Baker? Born in St. Louis, she became famous in a Broadway musical in 1924, and then almost immediately moved to Paris. Thomas Hart Benton, the great regionalist painter? Surprisingly, he worked in New York from 1912 to 1935. Richard Wright had only ten years in New York City, Enrico Fermi only five. Well, the encyclopedia gives us the data and the dates on the basis of which we can make our own judgment as to whether this person or that should have been included.

The encyclopedia also exercises a restraint on inclusion that may be questioned. Piet Mondrian, despite *Broadway Boogie Woogie* and other New York-inspired works, is not included, nor is Dylan Thomas, despite notorious visits.

One does detect some biases. The encyclopedia seems to favor figures connected with Columbia University, even if their work dealt only tangentially or not all with New York City. Thus there is an entry for Richard Hofstadter, but not for Arthur Schlesinger, Jr. Some works of reference limit the problem of selection by excluding all the living. Not so this encyclopedia. If one is a black leader, actual or aspiring, it seems one can make it into the encyclopedia remarkably young: Al Sharpton was born in 1954, Calvin Butts in 1949.

Matters are easier when it comes to neighborhoods. Hundreds are recorded and get briefer or longer entries (probably the longest is for Harlem). Every ethnic group gets an entry, from Albanians to Yemenis. Almost all the institutions of higher education, and a good number of the high schools and private schools, get entries, and all the rest are listed in charts, which are one of the best features of the encyclopedia. And there are some truly creative decisions, such as a list (five three-columned pages long!) of "Songs and Compositions Inspired by New York City (selective list)," which includes subdivisions for songs on the Statue of Liberty, Manhattan, Wall Street, Greenwich Village, Fifth Avenue, and other parts of the city that have stimulated the creativity of songwriters.

There are other features of the encyclopedia that must be applauded: every entry is signed by the writer, and all the contributors are listed with their affiliations and qualifications. There are seventeen three-columned pages of them, and one is amazed at the number of New York City experts in various arcane fields that can be mustered. Every person named in the encyclopedia on whom there is not an entry is listed in an enormous index (Dylan Thomas is to be found there, and one is referred to a page on which one finds the White Horse Tavern, where reference is made to his New York connection). The pictures, reproductions of prints, paintings, and photographs, are numerous, very well chosen, and very well reproduced.

One thinks back on Parkinson's law of declining empires, Hegel's owl of Minerva. What is the meaning of all this scholarly attention to New York, this outpouring of guidebooks, the arrival of the first encyclopedia? The first thing one must note is that if the United States is now, in certain respects, "the old country," New York, if we consider its place in the United States, is indeed "the old city." I think the interest in New York is sparked and maintained by the fact that it is a city shaped and in large measure completed before the age of the automobile. It is dense; its center is not pockmarked by parking lots; its streets are edged by unbroken lines of buildings and crowded with pedestrians; its architecture, even though the city has thoughtlessly destroyed so many grand structures (think of Pennsylvania Station, modeled after the Baths of Caracalla, and perhaps as strongly built), contains more examples of the buildings of the past 150 years than any other American city, and some of these, such as the cast-iron buildings of Soho, form large and unique neighborhoods of the past. Many of its great bridges are structures of the nineteenth rather than the twentieth century. Its icons—the Statue of Liberty, the skyscraper forest of Lower Manhattan, the Empire State Building, and the Chrysler Building—all took their shape before one-third of the last century had unrolled, and before modernism became mandatory for new building. (The Empire State Building graces the spine of the *Encyclopedia*'s dust jacket, the Statue of Liberty the front of it.)

New York is still, compared to Los Angeles, Houston, Atlanta, San Diego, cities that are newer and grow faster, the old city. And in an age when things change so fast, that exerts some fascination. The typical and most desirable settings for American domestic life—the suburb, the small town, the small city, some shaped by the automobile, some easily adapted to it—offer easier and better living. While New York can do more, much more, than it does, in improving livability, it will never compete with other cities of the United States, or indeed some world cities such as Paris and London, in livability, at least as that is defined by the generality of men and women. But it competes in other respects, and one of them is its built form, which one can consider a relic of the past. In an age when this form will never be seen again, it exerts its own fascination.

And so an enormous casino goes up in Las Vegas, "New York, New York," and its facade consists of a grouping of New York city landmarks and skyscrapers. We will continue to build skyscrapers and freeways—the centers of Atlanta, Dallas, Houston, our new cities, are nothing but. But we will never again build the kind of city exemplified by New York. We will never again build the kind of skyscrapers that are featured in the Las Vegas facade. They are, of course, not economic. Their soaring, tapering shapes do not provide the large floor spaces now needed; their masonry is too expensive compared to steel and glass and aluminum; they are ill-adapted to the age of high tech. But because they were once built, and fortunately have not all been torn down, they contribute to the uniqueness of New York, and to the interest in it, at both a scholarly and a popular level.

Of course New York is not—not yet—a museum city. It remains the only large American central city outside the South and West that has not undergone a radical decline in population. It attracts nearly 100,000 immigrants a year—an astonishing figure, in view of how hard it is to live in New York, the low wages available in its declining manufacturing and growing service sectors in which most immigrants find work, and the costs of living in the city. New York has major economic functions, and they are crucial to the maintenance of its health. It is these economic functions that provide the taxes that maintain the necessary city services, even at the minimal level to which New Yorkers have become accustomed, and that support the enormous and inefficient school system and the hugely expensive social services. Their costs quite dwarf what New York City spends on its police, firefighters, sanitary services, and street maintenance, not to speak of such luxuries as libraries and parks, which played so large a role in the city of the past, the city of my youth. They are now radically reduced, in their hours of operation and their maintenance, and their costs have declined to almost invisible fractions of the city's fifty-billion-dollar budget.

New York's health will depend on more, considerably more, than its interest to increasing numbers of scholars, or to visitors who support a vigorous and important tourist sector. The problems posed by its huge social service sector, its expensive public schools, its heavy burden of taxation, its capacity to attract and retain business and commerce, and in particular its ability to maintain its role as a center of world finance—these are the key matters that one must address when one considers New York. (And I should note, among other indications of the rising tide of attention paid to New York, the new *City Journal* of the Manhattan Institute, which addresses vigorously all these and other concerns.)

I have referred to New York as a "world city," and by that I mean not its size (now surpassed by many in the developing world), or its role in world politics: New York City is, politically, the capital of nothing, not even its state. If it is a world city, it is primarily because of its economic role on a national and world scale. Turning to the article "Economy," in the *Encyclopedia*, one reads, in Matthew Drennan's authoritative account:

> The 1980's saw New York City surpassed by Los Angeles as the country's leading manufacturing center. Only fifty-five of the five hundred largest industrial corporations had their headquarters in the city by 1992. In 1993 the economic activities associated with the port during the nineteenth century (the production, transport, and wholesale of goods) accounted for less than 15 percent of the city's employment, while those associated with the corporate headquarters com-

plex accounted for 28 percent. . . . By the mid 1990's
New York City was a post-industrial city. . . . London,
Los Angeles, Tokyo, and Hong Kong emerged as the
greatest challengers to its position as a national and international economic force.

This is the key issue, undoubtedly. But alongside this,
New York must pay attention to other elements that
make it a world city. It can claim to be, after all, "the culture capital of the world," as it is dubbed in the title of
one of the books I have referred to above. Here its role,
even as it has suffered decline in some respects, has surprisingly been enhanced in the past fifty years. I recall,
growing up in East Harlem in the 1930s, often going to
the Metropolitan Museum of Art, only a few blocks to the
west. It was free, then, and it was empty. It now charges
a high admission fee, is jammed with visitors, and has
doubled in size. It now also forms part of a "museum
mile," none of whose elements—the Guggenheim, the
Jewish Museum, the Smithsonian's Cooper-Hewitt, the
Neue Gallerie—existed in my youth. All this, and much
more, in the maintenance and expansion of New York's
museums, educational institutions, libraries, cultural
facilities, New York owes more to its public-spirited and
wealthy private citizens than to its government or the
government of the nation. New York continues to renew
itself even as large parts of its economy go under, its population of the poor remains enormous, its government is
barely capable of managing the maintenance or improvement of major facilities and infrastructure. Is New
York simply entering a Byzantine phase, where it becomes a city of interest to tourists who come to see the

monuments of the past, to scholars who document the minutest elements of its history, to collectors who pore over the material remains of the great city? (There is, of course, quite a boom in old photographs of New York, many of buildings now gone.) Not yet, I think. New York is a world city that has uniquely made itself and renews itself, often in surprising ways, with little or no help from the federal government, unlike its competitors among world cities, such as Paris and London. The old city would do well to take advantage of its age, and its great monuments, but that is not all it has going for it. After all, for what other American city would one undertake an encyclopedia, and in what city would one find the benefactors to make it possible?

CHAPTER NINE

Planning for New York City: Is It Possible?

A few years ago a six-hour television series on the origin and possible future (and end) of civilization, *Legacy*, concluded with two images. One is the unmistakable skyline of Manhattan at night, viewed from Queens, approached by great, illuminated bridges. The other is a crumbling ziggurat in a sea of salt and desolation, the ruins of a city of the very first civilization described in the program, ancient Mesopotamia. New York City, of course, is still alive, but it is placed at the end of this rapid progress through history for two reasons. One is that New York has served for eighty years or more as the defining image of the future. The second is that if someone wanted to warn us, as the creator of *Legacy* does, that certain trends may be threatening the survival of civilization, New York City will serve for that too.

The image of New York, and Manhattan in particular, with its incredible skyline, its great bridges, its crowded skyscrapers, does suggest some of the ways in which we might feel, uneasily, we have gone too far: in creating cities of enormous scale, in distancing ourselves from nature, in developing technologies and social organizations of such complexity as to be beyond rational control, in tolerating the rise of social aberrations and social problems that may destroy civil society.

New York, with Manhattan at its center, does seem to depart further from the ordinary, the familiar, the natural, than any other great city—further than its competitors in the United States, further perhaps than its competitors in the new, rapidly developing international economy. We may in time see Shanghai replacing New York as the epitome of modernity, for it indeed already surpasses New York in some respects—note the Maglev, the incredibly fast train from from its advanced airport—but for the moment it is still New York that paradoxically stands for the city of the future, as envisioned through most of the last century. Whether in Las Vegas or in the various mass market products (games and futuristic movies) in which the city of the future, whether doomed or not, is evoked, it is New York and its icons—the Empire State Building, the Chrysler Building, the Statue of Liberty, the great bridges—that will serve best, even though these most recognizable icons predate the rise of high modernism in architecture and design. And in general it is true that its buildings rise higher (even though the tallest building in the world is now in Kuala Lumpur, and will soon be in Shanghai), its engineering adaptations to its site are more complex, and its indifference to the ordinary and humble amenities, as most people understand them, of home, garden, shopping, transportation, are greater than in any other American city. Of New York, it is commonly said, "It's a great place to visit, but I wouldn't want to live there," striking evidence of a reputation for unlivability.[1] Many things contribute to this reputation: its

---

[1] *Fortune*, rating American cities from the point of view of their attractiveness as a place for business, said of New York some years ago: "The Big Apple is superlative in many ways, including cost: It is America's most expensive place to do business. Tax rates are highest, and so are office lease

high costs, its crowding, its noise, its subways, its cramped
housing, its taxes, its homeless, however unfair many of
these comparisons may be. (Its crimes and its homeless
may be no more numerous proportionally than in some
other cities, but its crowding, and the fact that relatively
few of its residents and visitors are protected from observing these conditions or being affected by them by being
ensconced in automobiles—in New York one must per-
force use the streets and the public transport facilities
more than in other American cities—does mean that both
are visually evident, more immediately, to more people.)

Contributing to all these problems of livability is the
physical site of the city. New York's problems are not
the direct result of the configuration of land and water
on which it has been built, but this configuration does
push it in certain directions, toward density, height,
crowding. These do exacerbate the conditions that reduce
the quality of life. New York's problem is how to make
the great decisions that permit a better quality of life, despite these given physical circumstances. Such decisions
have been taken in the past, as when Central Park was
reserved in narrow Manhattan; they can, one would
think, be taken again.

To begin at the beginning: Manhattan, the site of the
original settlement from which New York City grew, still
the dwelling place of 20 percent of its inhabitants, and

---

rates. It ranked poorly on most other cost measures as well as on crime
and pro-business attitude." New York's record on crime has since improved
greatly. A fuller statement might well have referred to problems in transportation and housing; in both categories, according to *Fortune*, New York
rates worse than *Fortune*'s top ten–all of which (except for Pittsburgh and
Kansas City) are newer Sunbelt cities.

providing the jobs for most of them (not to mention great numbers who come to work in Manhattan from the surrounding urban and suburban and exurban areas), is an island. Not only is it an island: it is bounded on the west by the lordly Hudson, not easily bridged or tunneled under; on the east by the East River, of a smaller scale but nevertheless one that dwarfs the Seine, the Thames, the Tiber, the Sumida, or any other river dividing a great city. To bridge it required one of the great engineering achievements of the late nineteenth century, the Brooklyn Bridge (the Hudson was not bridged until fifty years later, though tunnels had pierced under it earlier). Only to the north, with the Harlem River, do we find a waterway on a somewhat urban scale, with many bridges and tunnels connecting Manhattan to the Bronx and the mainland. The constraints to expansion are severe, despite the large boroughs of Brooklyn and Queens, set on their own extensive island, and the presence of Staten Island. But compared to the wide spaces available to a once expanding Philadelphia, Chicago, Detroit, among the older cities, to a Houston or Dallas or Atlanta or Los Angeles among the newer ones, New York City is pinched by geography. Among the older cities, only San Francisco and Boston are more constrained.

Of course all cities have their own physical constraints, but what remains remarkable about New York City among the great cities is that it is not easy to access from the country it serves as its primate city. Much of the history of New York can be written in terms of the problems of connecting the city to the continent across the Hudson. New York did become the chief port in the country when our heavy traffic was borne by water, and New York City had the advantages of both the great harbor, providing protected access to the numerous docks of a city surrounded by water, and the connection to the West by water through the Erie Canal, which first gave primacy to the port of New York. But the rise of the railroads was a challenge to the city, a challenge met by remarkably energetic entrepreneurs, who built wonders in the way of tunnels, bridges, and terminals (though most railroads stopped on the western shore of the Hudson, and their freight could reach the city only by water). They marked their achievements by erecting two of the greatest monumental railway stations in the world, one of which, in an act of vandalism that will indict forever the government of the city of New York, we have destroyed, to no visible or comprehensible advantage at all.

Perhaps New York did a good job of handling the challenge posed by connection to the rest of the country in the railway age. The challenge of connection in the age of the automobile, truck, containership, and airplane was more difficult. For a while, a political accident—there is no other way to consider the career of Robert Moses— permitted a good deal of adaptation to the new age, despite the physical constraints of the city's form. But that age, much decried for the costs that accompanied the effort to make New York accessible by car and truck, came to an end forty years ago. To ascribe New York City's adaptation to the automobile age (to the degree that it has occurred) primarily to the remarkable power accumulated by Robert Moses, and wielded by him for thirty or more years, may be somewhat of an exaggeration. Yet what is striking about the transportation facilities of New York City is how many of them were provided in relatively distant ages, such as the age of Moses, and how few in recent decades.

A political invention, the Port of New York Authority, could not in the end maintain the primacy of New York City as a port. Containerports required expanses of space adjacent to docks that New York City could not provide. The port moved off to New Jersey, where the mainland offered more space and direct access by rail and truck to the rest of the country. Competition from other ports, to the south and on the West Coast, reduced the role of the Port of New York.

In the age of air transportation, New York is still sharply constrained by its site: LaGuardia, Kennedy, and Newark airports must be reached through crowded tunnels or bridges, and the businessman entering or leaving New York, or the shipper of air freight, must always ponder what route will best get him to the airport.

The physical site has its most direct impact on quality of life in New York City by way of its effects on transportation, within the city, and between the city and the surrounding country. And yet no effect is direct, or unmediated by human intervention, an intervention that might have made things better or worse. Difficult surface transport in an automobile age reduces the quality of life in many ways: time lost in traffic jams, increased air pollution produced by slow speeds or lengthy immobility, delays in delivery of goods, noise produced by horns and sudden stops and bursts of speed to take advantage of temporary openings in the traffic stream. But what alternative, one asks, is there when jobs are concentrated in the southern third of Manhattan, and millions must be moved daily into and out of a relatively small space?

One notes some of the possible alternatives when one contrasts New York with other cities. One of the most remarkable facts about quality of life in New York, as it relates to transportation, is that for sixty-five years almost nothing has been done to introduce major new public transit facilities. If one looks at a map of New York City in 1939, such as that published by *Fortune* in a special issue on New York in connection with the World's Fair of that year, one thing that is truly startling is that no major new connection between Manhattan and the rest of the city or the mainland has been built in the two-thirds of a century since, except for one derisory tunnel to nowhere, the 63rd Street Tunnel.[2]

Would new connections help? Or would they simply add to the congestion? That depends on context: if they were simply a way of dumping more automobile traffic into Manhattan and nothing more, the addition would obviously not help; if the connections were new and improved tunnels for the subways, accompanying other improvements to make them more attractive to commuters, that would be a different matter. There are no one-mode solutions to any problem, including the problem of transportation.

So we must consider, in addition to the physical form of the city, other elements that make transportation difficult: the political and economic factors, and there are many, as a result of which the process of physical expansion of the transportation links between Manhattan and

---

[2] Jim Dwyer, a journalist specializing in New York City transit, observed correctly some years ago, "Since 1940, New York City is the only major metropolis in the world to have decreased its mass transit tracks."

the rest of New York and New Jersey came to a halt sixty-five years ago. All the major crossings over and under the Hudson, the East River, the Harlem River, by rail or automotive vehicle, for people or goods, were then complete. This fact properly reminds us of a heroic age of physical expansion, between the opening of the Brooklyn Bridge and the opening of the Triboro Bridge, when all the great bridges were built, a feat we can only marvel at. Today we can barely, in a much larger and richer city (by some measures), maintain the great East River crossings—yet they were all built in only a few decades.

Not only were the major automotive and freight connections between Manhattan and the surrounding parts of the city and New Jersey completed sixty-five years ago; so was the major system for the moving of people, the subways. The last major line opened was the Sixth Avenue subway, sixty-five years ago. The additions and extensions to the system since then, while adding up to enormous sums for longer station platforms, new tracks, new cars, some new connections within the built-up system, have been very minor, and amount to only a few new stations. Nowhere has the system been extended beyond the political limits of the City of New York, even though there are obvious extensions required at every point where the lines reach the edge of the city, since the growth of population beyond those edges has been enormous in those sixty-five years. Because the system's lines stop where they do, troublesome transfers from one mode of transportation to another are required, encouraging the complete avoidance of the subway. One is struck by the fact that in other old cities of equivalent size—New York's world competitors (London, Paris,

Tokyo), two with underground systems older than New York's—the underground lines have been extended to accommodate suburbanization.

New York manages with a transportation structure built and designed for a very different city and metropolitan area, one in which the amount of office space in the center was a fraction of what exists today, in which the numbers commuting from outside the city were a fraction of the numbers commuting from those distances today. The system manages with remarkably little in the way of accommodation to these great changes, but it manages at a cost in crowding, discomfort, and inconvenience that can in part, it is true, be explained by the peculiar constraints of New York's site but in larger measure reflects failures of public management. It is striking, as a reflection of this failure, that the East Side of Manhattan is still served by only one subway line, reported to be the busiest single line in the world. A second line has been proposed, urged, provided for in financing, begun, and stopped, over a period now of sixty-five years, since the single Lexington Avenue line took on the additional burdens caused by the demolition of elevated lines on Second and Third Avenues in the 1930s and 1940s. The line is once again near construction, but one wonders how much of it will ever be completed.

Transportation is, of course, affected by the island's long, narrow form, with the best connections to the north, and with all modes of transportation aiming at its lower third, where the jobs and chief public facilities are. But one can imagine adaptations to the site that would have limited the enormous crowding in the southern third of Manhattan. Of course these accommodations have in part occurred. The expansion of commercial, manufacturing, and office space and housing in New Jersey, Long Island, and Westchester are all accommodations to crowding and costs in southern Manhattan. These accommodations reflect the operation of the market; they have very little to do with any public intervention that might have taken into account costs of crowding.

••

Was there a place for planning, is there still a place for planning, in the development of New York City? "Planning" is, of course, a dirty word these days, but we should distinguish central economic planning, which turned out to be such a disaster in Eastern Europe, from those public decisions that affect the quality of life in a great city. Call those something other than planning if you will; but the fact is that no private decision could have reserved the central part of Manhattan for a great park, could have built the parks and Riverside Drive on the Hudson River, or built the great system of arterial roadways that still make it possible for New York City to operate, with whatever difficulty. The question is, what better public decisions might have been taken, may still be taken, and on what scale? These decisions are, in fact, taken all the time. They are taken when the zoning regulations are revised, and they are taken when developments that must breach the zoning regulations are approved; they are taken (or more likely, not taken) when a major artery of transportation must be replaced. So public decisions are regularly taken. Could they have been taken so as to enable the built physical form of the city, whatever the constraints imposed by the physical geography, to make New York a more livable city?

The huge growth of the center since World War II has been accompanied by the withering of major subordinate business centers in the Bronx and Brooklyn. These spread the jobs and commercial and amusement facilities, reduced the demand for transportation to the center, and evened out the use of various parts of the system. They certainly contributed to the quality of life. Was this withering itself in part to be attributed to the huge growth of the center, permitted by New York's expansive zoning envelope? One senses a connection, though other factors, in particular the attraction of the suburbs, the weakening, in numbers and income, of the population base for subordinate centers, and the growth of crime in the 1960s and 1970s, contributed to the decline of the subordinate business centers.

Of course one can ask whether it would have been desirable to limit growth in the center, whether that growth would simply have gone away outside the city rather than been channeled into the strengthening of subordinate business centers. But the fact is, that question, in any realistic sense, was not seriously discussed at all.

It has been discussed and considered in the world cities that are our major competitors—London, Paris, Tokyo—and in various ways growth in the center has been constrained sharply, with no great apparent loss in vitality owing to this fact, and a considerable gain in quality of life (at least in London and Paris—Tokyo is in a different situation). In contrast, in New York City, since the end of the period of the great public developments I have referred to in transportation, it has been assumed that all the city can do is accommodate private interests making their own calculations in the absence of major public guidance. One of the key questions that one must ask in talking about quality of life in New York City is, Was planning necessary? Is it necessary today? In the days of Mayor LaGuardia, when Lewis Mumford was our chief urban critic, and later, when the federal government, in the 1960s, was persuaded to support urban planning and paid for the training of planners, the answer was "Of course." In New York City, however, it became impossible to produce a plan of large vision. The plan for New York City that finally emerged in 1969 was not a plan on any large scale, but a description of the neighborhoods of New York and of the various interventions taking place in each—a work of value, but leaving in abeyance (or abandonment) the question of whether a plan was desirable.

It is striking that what we consider one of the great achievements of planning (really, zoning) in New York City—the exchange of the right to build higher and denser for street-level open space (plazas), for walk-through galerias, and for theaters—only increased the density. And what we consider another great achievement of planning, concessions in zoning to encourage building on the West Side of Midtown, only increased yet further the density of the center. These were indeed public interventions, but all on the side of increasing density in the center, simply accentuating the costs that come with increased density. Encouraged to build densely because of physical form, we accentuated the density through public action. Was there no argument to be made for reducing density?

I believe there was. There were, of course, certain advantages to the course we took—the cost of office space in Manhattan is much less than in our major world competitors, London, Tokyo, Paris. New York City is unique in the height to which it is built, in the center, in Manhattan, but also in Brooklyn and the Bronx, and that density does give the city qualities that other cities of lesser density do not have. These qualities have been celebrated by William H. Whyte and others: excitement, variety, ease of personal contacts in the dense center, maintenance of all kinds of specialty facilities. (Even *Fortune*, in a gloomy assessment of New York's virtues for business adds, "But in certain industries—media, the arts, investment banking—it remains top of the heap.") These effects of density may be considered a contribution to "quality of life," though most Americans, particularly as they enter those stages of life in which they are raising children, discount the virtues that density makes possible: they create the kind of city such people would rather visit than live in. One also notes that great cities like Paris and London are not built to great heights, that their business districts spread over a larger section of the city, and yet liveliness and diversity and the pleasures of the street manage to exist, even when the street line is built up to five or seven stories, rather than a dozen or more.

Is it not possible that we have gone too far? Lewis Mumford once wrote that New York City was saved from transportation strangulation by the Depression, which stopped for a while the building of new skyscrapers. We have now been through a number of cycles in which the building of office space has dwarfed the towers of New York as they existed in 1929, and all during these cycles we have done little to restrict this growth, or to add to the capacity of transportation channels to bring more people into the city, or facilitate their moving about the city. (The effect of an increase in office workers on crowding has been somewhat mitigated by the sharp decline in manufacturing in the center, and by the replacement of old commercial and manufacturing space by housing, which reduces commuting pressure.) I think we have gone too far. We see costs to the quality of life when the new office buildings engross midblock sites, wiping out older, smaller buildings, which provide space for modest business establishments. A map of New York City's transit shows all the main lines concentrating on Lower and Midtown Manhattan. A comparable map of London, Paris, or Tokyo would show a somewhat less centralized pattern. There controls over height have spread the business district over a larger area and thus reduce pressure on transportation.

Was such a development possible in New York City? Developers, it seems, hold the city to ransom, threatening, "If I can't build high here, and only here in the center, I won't build anywhere." In a time of troubles one would not care to take the risk and lose the development altogether. And it is true that issues of crime and security, as well as convenience, made it hard to distribute major new developments outside of southern Manhattan: attempts to place more development in the Brooklyn hub are not yet successful. (One would hesitate to promise anything for another old transportation knot, the South Bronx hub.) Yet it remains true that New York took the easy way out, allowing a concentration in the center that has been remarkable and unique, but which only accentuates the costs imposed by New York's geographical form.

Had there been efforts to maintain the attractiveness of areas outside the present dense center, New York would be a better and more livable city. One recalls a time when a major university, New York University, could consider building a large new campus far from the center, in the West Bronx overlooking the Harlem River, and did indeed build a fine campus there designed by McKim, Mead, and White. In the same period, a complex of museums was built as far north in Manhattan as 155th Street; somewhat later Columbia Presbyterian Hospital was built to the north of that, and Yeshiva University even further north. A complex of major academic institutions grew up between 116th and 122nd streets—Columbia University and Barnard College, the Union Theological Seminary and the Jewish Theological Seminary, the Julliard School and Teachers College. On the East Side, the New York Academy of Medicine and the Museum of the City of New York were built on 103rd and 104th streets. All the builders of these institutions expected that the city would continue to grow northward, and it did, and they would in no way be hampered by their distance from the center at the time they were building. All found themselves marooned in a city that seemed to be shrinking toward its center, and found it difficult or impossible to maintain urban amenity in the areas they had chosen.

In recent decades we have watched in dismay as many of these outlying institutions, representing confidence in the city and the areas in which they were located, have shrunk or been transformed, or have escaped to the center where a greater degree of safety and patronage may be expected. So the Bronx NYU campus was abandoned—who now remembers or visits the "Hall of Fame" that was located, and still exists, there?—the Indian Museum moved into the Customs House at the tip of Manhattan, and Julliard built a new school at Lincoln Center. The pressures on institutions to relocate to the center, somewhat moderated by the decline of crime in the past ten or fifteen years, are very strong. A plan was proposed to move the Museum of the City of New York into the restored Tweed Courthouse adjacent to City Hall; museum officials were clearly dismayed when that plan was scotched by Mayor Bloomberg's decision to relocate the headquarters of the remodeled Board of Education in that building—yet another example of withdrawal to the center, since its previous headquarters had been in Brooklyn.

While it is reasonable to inquire whether public policy could have facilitated or encouraged a city in which development was spread over a larger area, perhaps the costs of crime and social disorder in the last third of the twentieth century, leading to the pressure to seek the safety of the center, were too great to be affected by public policy. Perhaps there was no way of escaping the enormous concentration of all major development, business and cultural, in southern Manhattan and the weakening of the business centers in northern Manhattan, Brooklyn, and the Bronx.

••

Public policy offered no resistance to the giantism and concentration that New York's crowded site encouraged. When one examines the housing patterns of the city, one sees once again the predominance of large and tall buildings, in forms that have definitely affected quality of life. It is true that much of New York still lives in apartments in buildings of relatively modest height, five or six stories, and a larger proportion than one might think lives, like the rest of the United States, in individually owned single-family or two-family homes. But the pattern for apartment houses to remain relatively small was once quite common. It meant a building with a few dozen tenants, often built with an interior court. Even the narrow tenements provided a quiet zone in the unbuilt-on open center of the blocks that they ringed. In Manhattan, and to some extent in other boroughs, these have in large measure been replaced by giant structures, with hundreds of tenants, without interior courts, and with each room of each apartment facing outward, maximizing exposure to noise in all rooms. This has become the typical pattern of housing for the poor, the middle classes, and the well-to-do—though ironically the poor have more open space around these giant structures in public housing projects than the middle and upper middle classes do. The latter are dependent on housing put up by the private sector, which will fill the entire lot available for the largest possible apartment house. There is, as a benefit, often more light, but the tall building for apartment living creates difficulties for families with children, who now have to manage a new transportation mode, the elevator, subjecting them to new hazards. Public housing, which began with modestly scaled buildings, went higher and higher, and since these were clearly dwellings for families, the costs in terms of quality of life were serious.

The cost of land, we were told, dictated such heights. Yet much in amenity that smaller-scaled structures provided was sacrificed: easier access to the street and playground; fewer families on each entry, who, knowing each other, could more easily police public access; more varied play spaces. New York, it seems, simply had a taste for giantism and height—in its office buildings, its factories (where else did one find skyscraper clothing factories?), its housing, its public buildings. The physical limitations of the site gave the first push to this; public policy offered no resistance and even encouraged it.

••

Giantism is also evident in other public facilities. The New York elementary school is built to house a thousand or more students. The New York high school is built for three or four thousand, and often houses many more. There was never a good reason for schools of such size. Private schools, which reflected perhaps better what parents wanted, never reached such sizes and did quite as well on their smaller scale. There are no economies of scale in schools, and yet schools of great size have been built in New York decade after decade. Of course there was a convenience to it: the number of struggles over site and design could be reduced; there were illusions that there could be savings in management. The lengthy, anonymous corridor of the double-loaded apartment slab, the typical building form of the last three or four decades for housing, whether for the well-to-do, the middle class, or the working class, was matched by the anomic corridor of the huge school.

There was an answer, and once again one sees it in cities like Paris and London, with schools of greater variety in size, under different auspices (generally religious), but rarely reaching the huge size that became the norm for New York. In a city with greater public discipline,

fewer new immigrants, lesser racial diversity, more famil-
ial control, as was true of New York in the 1930s and
1940s, this perhaps didn't matter. As all these conditions
weakened, the schools became disaster zones, as did
many housing projects built to enormous scale.

••

New York is in many ways an anomaly as the largest city
of the United States, the center of its mass media, its culture, its banking and finance, and, still in many ways, the
center of ideas. "New York is not America," we were often
reminded. And indeed, despite the fact that we are now
swamped by assertions that we are becoming a nation of
minorities, of nonwhite races, of immigrants, New York
was and is in many respects not America. The United
States is still less than 30 percent black, Latino, and Asian,
though the proportion rises, and only about 11 percent
foreign born. New York, by contrast, has a majority of
minorities and is 40 percent foreign-born. As a port city,
as a manufacturing city, it attracted immigrants of all
kinds. As a city of services, media, culture, it continues to
attract immigrants, from abroad and from the U.S. hinter-
land. New York, with 3 percent of the country's population, was in the 1980s and 1990s the first residence of 15
percent of the United States' immigrants. Nearly a hundred thousand immigrants a year settled in the city, and
that scale of magnitude has been maintained for two decades. This recent immigration has transformed the city.
One would expect the immigration to have been gov-
erned by the state of the economy, and that there should
have been a decline in the years when the city endured
hard times and a rising rate of unemployment; there have

been a number of such periods since the severe crisis of the 1970s. But there was no significant decline during hard times in the numbers of foreign immigrants settling in the city.

The immigrants have made an enormous contribution to the quality of life: they have restored decaying neighborhoods, filled empty storefronts in some neighborhoods, added to the mix of restaurants and street life that are so important to a world city. They have also added costs: their children flood the public schools, adding a heavy burden, in the way of crowding, of children of varied and often inadequate educational background who must be accommodated, and of varied language background for whom appropriate education must be devised. They add to the pressure on the hospitals and welfare services, and the resultant costs certainly affect the quality of life. Yet it is possible that the heaviest burden on our educational system and social and health services comes less from the recent immigrants, though they contribute, than from a large population that has been resident in the city for far longer than the new immigrants: native blacks originally from the South, and Puerto Ricans. All in all, the city and its quality of life would not, I believe, have been helped if the volume of immigration of the past thirty years had been a quarter or a third of what it was. Perhaps we should see the immigrants as somewhat like the miners' canaries, used to test the air: as long as they keep on coming, things are not as bad as we think they are.

The site made New York a great port; the port attracted diversity in immigration; immigrants and a growing population aided manufacture. Diversity attracted more diversity because it made for a tolerant city, and a city of enclaves in which immigrants of any kind could find a place to live, to work, to use their native language and experience some aspect of comforting connection to their native culture while learning a new language and a new culture. The foreign born, despite their great numbers, probably move out of the city at a rate not particularly lower than that we find among the natives, for New York has not been successful in creating or maintaining the quality of life that leads a growing family with children to find the city a desirable place to live.

When we speak of a city's "quality of life," we think of the elements that make a city gracious, pleasant, livable: the residential squares of London, the boulevards of Paris, the woods and lakes of Berlin. They are often featured on travel posters, but for New York, in contrast, we have skyscrapers—grand, but hardly contributors to quality of life. In that respect New York is poorer: what it has to offer is very far from the simply human, the accessible, the kind of cityscape a man or woman can walk in and enjoy, and which adds on to those necessities of urban existence—work, housing, transport, safety—something to lift the spirit and tell one, "I am a citizen of no mean city." New York has achieved great things in the past, which left a heritage that shapes the city today and without which it would be infinitely poorer: Central Park, Riverside Park, Prospect Park, the results of actions on a scale we seem incapable of today.

Our vision today is stunted, if it can be called vision at all. New York used to inspire visions more: one recalls Paul and Percival Goodman's *Communitas*, now more than fifty years old, with its amazing proposals for New

York. Restore the riversides, they said, to the people, for parks, for residence, for sport. (In modest measure that has been done in the most substantial enhancement of the city in the last two decades, Battery Park City.) They wrote before economic changes had made the river edges' role as a site for port facilities obsolete. Let us recall that all great cities have operated on more than economic motives. What is the economic justification for Central Park, or the parks of central London, or the extensive Imperial Palace grounds in the heart of Tokyo, or the green strips of Paris boulevards? It was the presence of kings and emperors that made it easier for the great cities that are now our competitors on the world stage to reserve, create, and maintain facilities that in our more commercial-minded civilization have been matched only with great effort by a host of civic-minded individuals. Yet matched they once were, and treasures were bequeathed to us that we are called upon to maintain, and, if we have the vision, to expand and add to. We struggle today with necessities rather than embellishments, yet a great city dies when it deals only with necessity.

••

The physical site of New York, whatever its contribution to some of the factors we have discussed, also, of course, offers virtues. We had to build great soaring bridges, the Brooklyn and the George Washington and many others. We built high because we lived in a crowded city, its center constrained by great waterways. (We also built higher because there was something in American culture that impelled us to build high—every city on the prairie, regardless of the great amount of space around it, has built high in the center, though none come close to matching New York's amazing built form.) But we have suffered costs.

I have been trying to make a case for physical planning, major public intervention for a common good. New York's development today is badly hobbled by a multiplication of authorities, powers, forms of regulation, opportunities for litigation; perhaps the day of great plans for the common good is over. The story of the five years since the World Trade Center disaster is not encouraging. There was no way of reconciling and satisfying for the common good the host of powers and interests that could intervene in the planning process. Admittedly it was no easy task to determine what redevelopment of that crucial site would add best to the city's life, its amenities and its economy. Determined private interests with a single objective, to make a profit, have been more successful in bringing their projects to completion, as in the case of Columbus Circle. With time and effort, they can make it through the regulatory and litigatory maze, and can take on the additional costs the authorities impose because the cost-benefit calculus works out for them. Determined cultural entrepreneurs can also bring great projects to completion, as in the case of the expansion of the Museum of Modern Art, but they must take the characteristics of the city and the limitations it imposes for granted: MOMA was content to snake its way as best it could through whatever parts of the block between 53rd and 54th streets it could buy.

But great city-shaping public projects have a harder time. How reasonable today seems Westway, the proposal for a new expressway with attached park on the

West Side of Manhattan, but it could not make it through the regulatory and litigatory maze, though it had strong support from top public officials. One is reminded of the exclamation of Senator Moynihan, contemplating the debacle of Westway, and asking, "How did we ever build the George Washington Bridge?"

Yes, New York's development should be unshackled, for it is far too bound by rule and regulation. But the unshackling should be combined with a vision of a better way of life. Unleash the productive forces, but then govern them by a larger sense of the public and common good than has prevailed in recent decades.

PART THREE

The Professions:
From Social Vision to Postmodernism

CHAPTER TEN

What Has Happened to the City Planner?

M ost observers of the city today would agree that the image of the planner in the public mind is not very defined or compelling, indeed rather dim. City planning, large-scale planning in general, is not in high repute these days, in the wake of the rout of Marxism almost everywhere by the principles of the free market. One can plan one's personal life; one can plan for the future of one's company; generals and defense department officials are expected to plan for future wars. But planning as it is generally understood in professional programs of city and regional planning—that is, the arrangement of space for the most effective and efficient performance of a variety of present and future functions in city, region, state, and nation—goes on, if at all, as a peripheral professional activity, in a city or state agency. Much greater attention is given to the plans of developers, which are more likely to reach realization than the plans of planners, and to the hopes of mayors and governors.

What can the common popular image of the planner be? A recent personal experience brought me in touch with professional planning in the City of Cambridge. I have been engaged in a remodeling project and have been astonished at how many restrictions there are on what I can do, though I am doing nothing exceptional. But un-exceptional as is my modest project to replace a crum-bling garage and connect the new structure to an ex-panded kitchen, I find I need to present a plot plan (which happens to be identical to the plot plan I acquired with the property), which cost me five hundred dollars; that I need an OK from the historical commission to demolish a cinder-block garage of roughly 1920s vintage (this is because it is more than fifty years old); that I need after that a demolition permit; that to get the demolition per-mit, I need a statement from a pest-control service that there are no pests in the garage; that I must inform all my neighbors of my plans even though the plans do not reach beyond the restrictive envelope on my property within which I am allowed to build (and who created that rather restrictive envelope on my property, I am led to wonder?); that I must, of course, get a building per-mit; that halfway through the construction the city sur-veyer must come back to attest that it conforms to the plans submitted—and so on. I am sure I have left out a few requirements.

Cambridge may be exceptional. I would guess, on the basis of the character of the city, that it stands high among cities in the use it makes of the services of professional planners and in its requirements for conformity to pre-viously set standards.

I wonder whom the annoyed house owner blames for all this, much of which he thinks is unnecessary, and how it affects his image of the city-planning profession. Of course if he stands back to think about the matter, the homeowner will realize that many of these restrictions come about because of some earlier popular protest to which the planner responded as a professional, rather than having been initiated on his own authority. The planner today, in an old city like Cambridge, if he is thought of at all, is expected to protect what one has, rather than project an image of the city that might or ought to be.

The salient characteristic of the popular image of the city and regional planner today is that he is no longer seen as a reformer. If one is feeling negative about what has happened when one comes into contact with the planner and his restrictions, he is seen as an obstruction. If one is attached to the objectives that the specific requirements are aiming at, he is seen as a facilitator. If one is attached to one's home and one's neighborhood, he is often seen as a threat, an ally of new development.

It is clear the dominant element in the image of the planner is no longer that of the reformer, the bringer of hope, which is what the image of the city planner, I believe, used to be.

There are probably two names that best capture what the public, the thinking public, has in mind when the idea of the city planner comes up. One is Lewis Mumford. The second is Jane Jacobs. Mumford thought of himself as a planner—after all, he was a student of Patrick Geddes, an early figure in the development of contemporary city and regional planning. But of course Mumford was not a professional planner—professional planning barely existed at the beginning of his career in the 1920s—and professional planners might think of him more as a prophet of planning than a planner. Jane Jacobs was also, of course, no planner, and she had as low an opinion of them as did her great antagonist, Robert Moses. Perhaps one ought to add Moses as a third name that would come to the public mind when it thinks about city planning.

It is an odd trio. The first, Mumford, was a great critic, a reformer and prophet. He denounced, as a biblical prophet would, the city that had come into existence under the shaping forces of industrialism and capitalism, and prophesied the city that should be. That city was visualized in an idyllic and pastoral section of a movie by Pare Lorentz, made for the New York City World's Fair of 1939, *The City*: a movie that has probably been seen by more people than any other that has been made on the theme of city planning. We would today find it prophetic only of the contemporary American suburb, which stands in high repute with few these days, except perhaps for those who live in it and some neoconservative defenders of existing bourgeois tastes.

The second in our trio is the great demolisher of the image of the ideal city for our contemporary society projected by the reforming mind of Mumford and other pioneers of the sensible, the human, the humane, the rational city. Jacobs lived in Greenwich Village and applauded what the city planners of her day deplored—crowding, diversity, the unexpected, the spontaneous, the unplanned—and insisted it all came together to make a better city than any the planners could design.

Moses's image today is shaped by the huge book on him by Robert Caro, *The Power Broker*, and by our disenchantment with the city made or reshaped by the freeways, though most of us live in that city and could not possibly manage to do so without the freeways. But once again, he was certainly no planner and rather despised them.

Pondering this trio—one could add others, but I can think of no one else of this level of eminence who would come to the public mind when it thinks of the city planner—one finds that the only one who remains a contemporary hero is Jane Jacobs. That does suggest that there is a considerable problem in constructing today a positive image of the city planner.

I believe a key moment in the transformation of the planner from admired reformer to professional came in 1961 and 1962. Perhaps I am so focused on that year or two because I was then in Washington working for the Housing and Home Finance Agency, which was soon to become the Department of Housing and Urban Development. There were high hopes for the new agency of housing and development that was shortly to come into being. The city was seen as in crisis; and Washington in the first years of the Kennedy administration was filled with self-confident people, politicians, officials, intellectuals, academics on leave, who thought they knew what to do about it. Robert Wood, the author of a widely read book, *Suburbia*, then a professor of political science on leave from MIT, was working on the reorganization of the agency and was later to become secretary of the new department. Charles Haar of the Harvard Law School was also in Washington working on urban problems for the Kennedy administration. Many of us would soon be involved in shaping the ideas that were in time to lead to legislation creating the Model Cities program.

I zero in on 1961–62 because a number of things happened then, or around then, that in time changed everything. One was the publication of Jane Jacobs's *The Death and Life of Great American Cities*. It dawned on many

Americans that they didn't like what had been happening
to their cities since World War II. A lot of good ideas—
public housing, urban renewal, suburbs built according
to the plats laid down by planners—seemed to be going
bad. Catherine Bauer Wurster, a major advocate of public
housing, which was then still seen by many as the model
of reform, had recently published an article on what had
gone wrong with public housing. Public housing, recall,
was the great reform of the 1930s. It was, for example,
what Mayor Fiorello LaGuardia had in mind as the ideal
of what reform meant for a city like New York. The
patches of well-designed and well-placed public housing,
it was hoped, would soon extend to cover most of the
city. What a disaster, we would now say.

By the 1960s, reformers were asking what had gone
wrong with this great urban reform. In 1962–63 I was
part of a committee pondering what to do with the huge
Pruitt-Igoe housing project in St. Louis, already a quarter
empty and plagued by serious social problems. In the
1970s, it became the first of the high-rise projects to be
demolished, and the astonishing picture of it being blown
up appeared on the covers of planning and architecture
magazines around the world.

And as I have indicated, another thing that was happening in 1961 and 1962 was that people who believed
in the power of ideas to transform society and fix what
had to be fixed had come to power, and wielded a kind
of influence that persons with such ideas were not to have
again in American government. John F. Kennedy was
president, and while he himself did not devote much
thought to cities and their problems, some around him
did. A poverty program was being launched. A big-city

antidelinquency program funded by the new and self-confident Ford Foundation was underway and was being embraced by the administration as a model for the new poverty program. (The president's brother, Robert F. Kennedy, was in charge of the antidelinquency program.) Federal programs to assist and expand the training of city planners were soon to be launched, along with programs that required the use of planners in all sorts of public planning. New forms of planning, such as transportation planning, were to become prerequisites to gaining access to the new programs, funded by the federal government, that were being launched for cities, and all these new forms of required planning meant that we had to have more professional planners.

The planner was being transformed from prophet and reformer into professional. It was the age of the expansion of a professional role and of confidence in what it could achieve. But it was not to last. The idea of what the planner was supposed to be underwent kaleidoscopic changes in the urban turmoil of the late 1960s and early 1970s. A 1974 cover of the *Journal of the American Institute of Planners* reflected the turmoil. One saw on it a monster, with what appear to be a number of heads, endless arms, branching tails. It is the monster of planning, or rather of contemporary planning theory. The chief slogans and themes that characterized the confusion in planning at the time could be read off along the branching and writhing arms and tails. One stocky branch began with "user need" and moved on to "disjointed incrementalism." Another read, "advocacy, common, and action planning," with little tags reading, "to the victor the spoils," "Don't blueprint America—just make money." Another branch reads, "National planning, jurisdictional planning, Feds., States, Counties. . . ." Another reads, "Functional planning—Econ* Soc* Poli Educ*—all together now," and goes on to "Future oriented." Perhaps the most robust branch reads, "Open-ended, future option (previously long-range), non-foreclosing" planning. We can also find "transactive planning," "learning environments planning," "planners anonymous," and "meta-multi-planning (formerly comprehensive)."

The artist was quite up-to-date on the various and confusing trends in planning education and planning theory, but he missed "post-industrial planning," introduced in a lead article in the same issue.

In the social turmoil of the period—recall the annual riots in the cities in the later 1960s—the central task of the city planner, space planning, was again and again challenged as inadequate, incomplete, unresponsive to the needs of the time. But what, after all, could replace it in the work of the planner? Advocating the interests of the poor? Many were doing that. Service to the political powers, whatever they were? That was not very inspiring. Professionalism? But what did that mean? Who was the client? The central conflicting images of what a planner in the heroic mode might be—Mumford, Jacobs, Moses—did not offer a professional role. They existed as possible models, but models who required action on a scale far beyond the professional role of the planner as he had come to be.

Moving forward to the present, one finds that the professionalization has only gone further. The planner today knows many details of many programs and the arguments that support one or another, but larger visions are beyond his responsibility. Consider, for example, what has happened to what used to be called public housing, that is, housing for the poor and for those who cannot pay for the housing provided by the unassisted private market. This was once a straightforward matter: one supported or opposed public housing. The original program proposed with vision and hope has morphed into a multitude of programs, federal and state and philanthropic. Few can follow any longer their complexity. I recently received an analysis from the Citizens Housing and Planning Council of New York—a name that conjures up an earlier, simpler, more hopeful period—of the crisis confronting one of the numerous forms of publicly subsidized housing that were instituted in the wake of the problems of the first type of public housing, the housing project. It makes various proposals on how the finances of this type of housing might be remodeled so it can serve its original ends. It is far too technical for anyone but a specialist to follow. An organization that started out in the 1930s as an advocate of subsidized housing for the working class, and of good planning, now finds it necessary to produce such reports. And as a corollary, we do not normally think of calling in the professional planner when we consider today what has gone wrong with the city and suburb, and what can be done about it. These days we call him in to help with the details.

In my search for the present contemporary image of the city planner, I have looked for examples in which the image of planning and the planner has impinged on the popular mind. A few years back, a cover of the *Atlantic Monthly* surprisingly featured city problems and planning. The cover was illustrating an article summarizing James

Howard Kunstler's book *Home from Nowhere*. The cover itself reads, "Home from Nowhere, How to Make Our Cities and Towns More Livable." It portrays a patch of nondescript but pleasant and traditional northeastern or midwestern town, with a few vernacular houses, a small apartment house, a patch of green, a steeple. It must mean something that this modest and traditional image makes the cover of the *Atlantic Monthly*. Planners and planning students would find what Kunstler is saying in this book (and in an earlier book, *The Geography of Nowhere*), familiar and quotidian. In both he is passionately attacking, as so many have, postwar American urban building, and denouncing what the city and the suburb have become. He blames traffic engineers first but planners at least second, or perhaps tied for first. He writes:

> Does the modern profession called urban planning have anything to do with making good places anymore? Planners no longer employ the vocabulary of civic art, nor do they find the opportunity to practice it—the term civic art itself has nearly vanished in common usage. In some universities, urban planning departments have been booted out of the architecture schools and into the schools of public administration. [This is what happened at Harvard, but the department has since returned to the Graduate School of Design.] Not surprising, planners are now chiefly preoccupied with administrative procedure: issuing permits, filling out forms, and shuffling papers—in short, bureaucracy. All the true design questions such as *how wide should Elm Street be?* and *what sort of buildings should be on it?* were long ago "solved" by civil engineers and their

brethren and written into the municipal codes. These mechanistic "solutions" work only by oversimplifying problems and isolating them from the effect they have on the landscape and on people's behavior.[1]

The Geography of Nowhere is one of the few recent books about cities that one might find in bookstores.

An even more widely read magazine, *Newsweek*, has also featured the problem of urban planning on its cover, in an article on the "new urbanism." This is the movement that advocates the design of new towns and suburbs so that they look traditional and have some of the virtues of older towns and suburbs—greater density, fewer wide streets for cars, more space for small stores, more opportunity and occasion to run errands and conduct life on foot, rather than requiring an automobile trip for each, and so forth. It was launched by Elizabeth Plater-Zyberk and Andres Duany and others, and is an approach that Kunstler admires. According to the well-informed Harold Henderson, writing in the professional organ *Planning*, it is "one of the few planning theories ever to grace the cover of *Newsweek*." One wonders whether there has ever been another featured on the cover of a major newsweekly. Perhaps Buckminster Fuller's theories were so fortunate fifty years ago. But isn't it striking that fifty years ago it would have been a futurist like Buckminster Fuller or a visionary like Le Corbusier who represented the new urbanism on the cover of a major newsweekly, while today the representative of "new urbanism" is an advocate of an older urbanism?

---

[1] James Howard Kunstler, *The Geography of Nowhere* (New York: Simon & Schuster, 1993), p. 113.

It is, over all, the failure of futurism and modernism to seize the public imagination, and the failure of a world encompassing some of the key elements advocated in that older futurist thinking—the city of skyscrapers and freeways—to capture public affection, that creates the cautious environment for today's professional planner. Looking backward, it seems, has become the most popular way of going forward.

What, after all, have been some of the most powerful movements affecting and shaping the city of the last thirty years, the city after Buckminster Fuller and Le Corbusier? There are four.

One is the preservation movement. In that stimulating period when I worked at HHFA in the early 1960s, the bankrupt Pennsylvania Railroad was preparing to tear down Pennsylvania Station in New York, a monument built to last a thousand years. I sought futilely to find a way to save it. At the same time, the Pennsylvania Avenue Planning Commission in Washington was proposing the demolition of the Willard Hotel, Hotel Washington, and the Old Post Office, all to create a square to overmatch Red Square in Moscow. It was a curator at the Smithsonian Museum of American History who started the movement "Don't Tear it Down!" that saved the Old Post Office, which now does more to bring life to Pennyslvania Avenue than anything new placed on that avenue. Alas, no one saved Pennsylvania Station, and its loss is now universally regretted. It was such vandalism, effected or proposed, that expanded the preservation movement and made it a power.

A second movement: the new urbanism of Plater-Zyberk and Duany and many followers and equivalents—

among them the Prince of Wales and an architect who planned a town for him, Leon Krier. This is the movement applauded and promoted with such enthusiasm by James Howard Kunstler.

A third: environmentalism. One of the most vigorous forms of planning in these latter days is the preparation of environmental impact plans, which are required now for almost all large projects. On occasion, environmental considerations may derail very large projects, as in the case of Westway, the intended replacement on filled land in the Hudson of the collapsed elevated highway on the West Side of Manhattan. Generally the required environmental impact study will support a project proposed by major developers and favored by major political figures—they will be able to exert influence on the findings of the environmental impact study—but it does offer an opportunity for opponents to enter the fray, and, through litigation on environmental issues, to stop or change the proposed development, which is what happened with Westway.

And a fourth: community advocacy, in all its forms, whose main thrust, almost everywhere and always, is, don't do it—don't tear down the old building, don't put in a new park, don't cut down the trees and widen the road, simply . . . don't.

Overall, the greatest influence on planning has come from the seminal work of Jane Jacobs and her allies, the defenders of the city as it has come to be, shaped by a host of participants and powers and with limited influence from planners. William H. Whyte, Jr., was one of Jacobs's allies, and himself wrote powerfully in defense of the kind of city that no planner would have designed or tolerated, but that has emerged from the complex forces of history and shifting economic needs and changing tastes. He comments on one of the roots of modern city planning, the work of Ebenezer Howard, founder of the "garden city movement," but his criticism would apply as well to a very different source of contemporary city planning, the vision of a city of skyscrapers and freeways of Le Corbusier and other futurists:

> The language of this kindly utopian [Ebenezer Howard] is not that of today's new town planners, but in their own more scientific way they are saying the same thing. They, too, are repelled by the city. New town proposals are generally prefaced with a sweeping indictment of the city as pretty much a lost cause. . . . [T]he city is a hopeless tangle. Medical analogies abound. The city is diseased, cancerous, and beyond palliatives. The future is not to be sought in it, but out beyond, where we can start afresh.
>
> The possibility of working with a clean slate is what most excites planners and architects about new towns. Freed from the constraints of previous plans and buildings and people, the planners and architects can apply the whole range of new tools. With systems analysis, electronic data processing, game theory, and the like, it is hoped a science of environmental design will be evolved and this will produce a far better kind of community than was ever possible before. . . .
>
> To offer all this, a new town would really have to be a city. . . . But there are not to be cities as we have known them. There is not to be any dirty work in them. There are not to be any slums. There are not to be any ethnic

concentrations. . . . Housing densities will be quite low. There will be no crowded streets. It will have everything the city has, in short, except its faults. . . . [But] you cannot isolate the successful elements of the city and package them in tidy communities somewhere else. . . . The goal is so silly it seems profound.[2]

Professional planners have played no great role in launching the movements I have described above—preservationism, the new urbanism, environmentalism, community advocacy—which have played so large a role in limiting what planners can do. One can, of course, find professional planners involved to some degree in all of them. Planners have given the people and the developers more or less what they wanted. After the fact, it turns out that is not quite what all the people wanted after all. But that is not the planners' fault. They had to accommodate the automobile; they had to respond to economic realities; they had to adapt to governmental requirements. The role of reformer or prophet had to be left to others. In time, the changes in sentiment effected by the reformers and prophets affected the work of planners. Perhaps that is the proper relationship between the large figures who have shaped the public's views of planning, and the professional planner.

Clearly if we want to find sharp and powerful images of planning and the planner, we will not go to the professional city planner. We should not be surprised by this. A profession has to routinize, systematize, organize, and it cannot take the position that only the most exceptional,

---

[2] W. H. Whyte, Jr., *The Last Landscape* (New York: Doubleday, 1968), pp. 256–57.

the most gifted, those with the reformers' instinct or the prophets' passion should be trained in the profession, or should be able to engage in it effectively. Fair enough. Not every doctor is going to be a Pasteur, every lawyer a Brandeis, every teacher a Debbie Meyer. But we need the prophets and reformers. They have shaped the image of city planning in the public mind, and they set the agenda with which the professional planner has to deal. That agenda will often limit and frustrate the planners, but it will also stretch them to better realize the many aims we seek to fulfill in the city.

The lesson of this look backward in considering the image of the city planner today is that there needs to be more of an interplay between the exceptional figures who do embody the image of the planner in the public mind, and the professional practice of planning.

CHAPTER ELEVEN

The Social Agenda of Architecture

A few years ago, I was asked to speak to the graduates of the 1950 class of the Harvard Graduate School of Design, at their fiftieth reunion in Cambridge. One sentence in the letter from Robert Geddes, the distinguished architect and former dean of the Princeton School of Architecture, suggested why an urban sociologist, who had only a layman's knowledge of architecture, would be asked to speak at such an event: "Our formative years as professionals were, as you know, during a period of optimism and a modernist faith in a social agenda." And the unstated question was, what happened? We are still in the epoch of modernism in architecture, even if we call it postmodernism, or some other variant of modernism. But what happened to the social agenda?

It is an important question, which has received surprisingly little attention despite the huge increase in interest in and writing on architecture in recent years. Fifty years ago one could still find a close connection between public social policy and architecture and planning. Architects thought their work could contribute to the amelioration of social problems. That was indeed an essential and ground dogma of modernism in architecture. Modernism in architecture began with social aims as strong as its aesthetic orientation, or stronger, but social objectives and interests have fallen away almost entirely, and aesthetic interests and judgment, ever more sophisticated and theory-based, have become predominant. The social objectives of leading architects in the twentieth century, whatever we may think of them now, were sometimes incorporated into designs for whole cities, as in the case of Frank Lloyd Wright and Le Corbusier, and in the case of Le Corbusier, one of them—Chandigarh in India—was actually built. A new capital for Brazil was built, following the design of major modernist architects.

It is hard to imagine that the architect stars of the present would dream today of devising a plan that expressed their vision of what a city should be. They do not think about or design utopias, an endeavor that was current in the middle of the last century. Consider the role and career of the book of Paul and Percival Goodman—Paul, a major social and literary critic; Percival, a major modern architect—*Communitas*. I read it at the time and was impressed by their ideas, which reflected a socialist tradition in which architecture, the physical form of buildings and a city, was linked to a social vision. Some of the Goodmans' ideas were rather wild, but they all emerged from a clear sense of how a city could contribute to the good life. For example, they proposed rebuilding Manhattan so it could make use of its riversides for parks and housing rather than giving them up for railroads and expressways. They seemed prescient enough to imagine that New York, then our greatest port, would have less need of its wharves and piers in the future. The main problem was that their plan meant rerouting freeways down the middle of the island through Central Park. That may not have been the best of their ideas. But there was certainly vision there, and indeed a social vision. They were thinking of how people on a crowded island could live better lives.

When I met David Riesman, in the late 1940s, at the beginning of the work that led to the writing of *The Lonely Crowd*—a book on which I collaborated and that ends with a description of a possible future social utopia—we were agreeably surprised to discover that we both knew and admired *Communitas*. Riesman had reviewed it at length for the *Yale Law Review*. A few years later, when I became an editor of the new Anchor Books, I was able to get the Goodmans to revise it and put it back into print. I wonder whether anyone in schools of architecture is now aware of it. No one is much concerned anymore with that kind of social utopia, which owes nothing to high-tech, virtuality, IT, and the like, but which rather thinks seriously about the relationship between physical forms and social consequences.

We do not see this kind of ambition or enterprise today, and one wonders why.

"Our formative years as professionals," to repeat Geddes's implicit question, "were . . . during a period of optimism and a modernist faith in a social agenda." I responded to that question because I had shared that optimism and that modernist faith, at a time when modernism in architecture was inextricably combined with a social agenda. Modernism, it was expected and believed, came hand in hand with social reform, was indeed essential in promoting important social reforms to overcome the misery of the poor and the working classes in the industrial city. The dominant figure of the time in the United States in spreading the modernist faith and its social agenda was the polymath Lewis Mumford, who, we should recall, on occasion called himself a sociologist—which emphasizes how seriously he took the social reform aims of modernism. (In those days, the distinctions demarcating the sociologist, the socialist, and the social worker were not as sharp as they were to become.) The link between a social or sociological critique of society and architecture and planning that was so potent in the 1950s and 1960s has now been reduced tu the thinnest of threads.

Mumford's case is a good example of this transformation. Mumford was the architecture and urban critic of the *New Yorker*. He appeared much more often and at much greater length than his successor, Paul Goldberger, who has not been allowed to play the role in the *New Yorker* that Mumford did. Mumford reviewed housing projects and new housing communities as well as important new buildings. We do not expect his successor to deal with such subjects. Mumford's magisterial books, *The Culture of Cities* in 1937, *The City in History* in 1961, poured scorn on all historicist and classicizing architecture, from the grand apartment buildings of Park Avenue to the Federal Triangle in Washington. He urged an architecture in which urban form was stripped of extraneous ornament and historical reference or symbolism, provided light and air and greenery for city-dwellers, and was adapted to the needs of families and children. He denounced the formal urban planning of the Baroque period and the American City Beautiful movement of the turn of the century as projects intended to celebrate princes and plutocrats and priests and to overawe the people. To him these grand creations were totally inappropriate for a democratic society, in which the common man and his interests should prevail. For Mumford (as I noted in chapter 5), the grand architecture of the past, from the Pyramids to the great tombs and memorials and monuments of our day, celebrated death. The New York Public Library and the Lincoln Memorial did not escape his scorn. We should celebrate life instead of death, welcome change and adaptation instead of building structures and monuments intended to last forever.

Another inspiration of our generation, as I noted earlier, was the wonderful movie *The City*, made by Pare Lorentz for the New York World's Fair of 1939, which contrasted the crowded and noisy industrial and commercial city with a future that could then be glimpsed in a few communities inspired by the Garden City enthusiasts of England. These by design separated family life from impinging business and commerce and industry, separated the roads that carried heavy traffic from the paths on which children and mothers could walk from home to school and shopping.

Mumford and *The City* represented a somewhat pastoral fusion of social reform and modernist architecture and design. Alongside it, and rather more influential among architects, there was also a big-city version of this fusion. The greatest architects of the day—Frank Lloyd Wright, Le Corbusier, Walter Gropius—pondered then what they could contribute to ameliorate the problems of the modern city. Their designs, whether for educational institutions or for cities, had as one objective the creation of settings that contributed to a more satisfying civic and communal life for students or workers. Major modernist architects of the time designed housing projects. The important Williamsburg Houses of Brooklyn, the first large project of the New York City Housing Authority, was designed by William Lescaze, an early modernist architect, and set the model and style, to a degree, for the public housing that was to transform vast sections of New York City. Twelve blocks of tenements were demolished to build the Williamsburg Houses, and superblocks were created, as the modernist urbanists of the time proposed, on which new buildings were placed. After all, who needed all those streets when they could be turned into green spaces and provide light and air to slum dwellers deprived of both? The buildings were spaced regularly and formally, ignoring the lines of the uniform street grid, and placed, so we thought, to get the most sunlight or best views.

I have already referred to the photograph taken from the air of the Williamsburg Houses, reproduced in many books on modern planning and architecture. They form a regular array of light-colored buildings, set amid a sea of tenements filling the surrounding blocks. The surrounding tenements are dark and somewhat varied in contrast to the regular and identical buildings of the new housing development, and each relatively small city block surrounds straggling scraps of open space, which contrast poorly with the regular large open spaces of the housing project. Looking at that picture fifty years ago, one thought, how wonderful it will be when that model spreads over the entire city, bringing its benefits to more than the lucky few who could gain entry to the Williamsburg Houses. Not only did a modernist architect design them, with some modernist aesthetic features, like horizontal bands of colored brick to suggest a continuous band of windows providing light, but a modernist painter provided abstract decorations for the public areas—they can be seen today in the Brooklyn Museum.

Minoru Yamasaki, one of the major architects of the 1950s and 1960s, the designer of the World Trade Center, also designed a major housing project, the large Pruitt-Igoe houses of St. Louis. Again, one could see the free-standing towers on the superblocks of modernism, giving greater access to light and air, allowing a larger amount of open space around them for greenery and recreation, as proposed by the greatest city-designer of modernism, Le Corbusier. Yamasaki drew from other parts of the repertoire developed by Le Corbusier, such as communal corridors within the building where the residents could gather, a kind of town square in a high-rise.

I am evoking a period whose time is well past, to set the stage for a consideration of why it is past, and what we have lost by its passing. Of course all the figures I have mentioned, the greater ones such as Frank Lloyd Wright and Le Corbusier, and somewhat lesser ones such as Lescaze and Yamasaki, were first of all architects, and as architects they were also—and primarily—form makers and image creators. But in contrast to their heirs and successors today—Frank Gehry, Daniel Liebeskind, Zaha Hadid, Peter Eisenman, and add who you will—one has to note that they seemed to eschew extravagance, sensation, and shock in form and image in favor of the creation of what they hoped would become a normal, accepted, and reproducible urban environment, indeed the ordinary environment, rather than an eye-popping intrusion into it. One is struck, contrasting these earlier modernist architects with contemporary star architects, by these themes of normality and reproducibility. Whatever we think of them now, they were models that their creators hoped would be reproduced and would become normal (and better) parts of the city. In contrast, their successors design walls that cant and lean, roofs that bubble and heave, buildings that look as if they are instantly ready to take off into space or collapse in a heap of tin. They are not models for a city: only models for what the architect hopes will be truly astonishing, something to hit a nerve of contemporary excitement that he can exploit.

Of course all architects are form makers, as Robert Gutman—the leading sociologist of how "users" respond to the buildings modern architects make—has reminded us a number of times. "[P]eople and their satisfactions," he has written, "are not the principal concern of architects. . . . The main thrust of architectural endeavor, the subject matter of architectural theory, has been architectural form itself." But Gutman then went on to say, "The evaluation of form by the designer and the justification of it to other architects and to the community at large have involved the discussion of user requirements."[1] The relative weight of the utilitarian and social as against pure design concerns can vary over time; we are now in a period of very reduced interest in the social and utilitarian when it comes to the leading architects of the day.

One example of this reduction in interest in the utilitarian and social is the decline of concern among architects with what sociologists and behavioral scientists

[1] "Human Nature in Architectural Theory: The Example of Louis Kahn," in *Architects' People*, ed. Russell Ellis and Dana Cuff (New York: Oxford University Press, 1989), p. 106.

themselves have to say. This was once a matter of great interest among architects. I recall that in Berkeley in the 1960s architects responded fervidly to Erving Goffman's classic book *The Presentation of Self in Everyday Life*, and I recall one leading architect describing how he had taken themes from that book into account in designing a restaurant. When I came to Harvard in 1969, a sociologist was on the faculty of the Gradual School of Design; there has been none, I believe, for these past thirty years. In 1974, Gutman could still write, "It is common knowledge that architects have become increasingly concerned with building evaluation in recent years. The growth of this concern probably stems from the architect's new interest in the user; instead of measuring his building against aesthetic standards, he now wants to measure it against utilitarian standards."[2] But that was thirty years ago, and the tide was already turning, with the rise of postmodernism and the increasing centrality of the modern aesthetic and its penchant for the surprising and startling. Only fifteen years after he wrote of architects' increasing concern for building evaluation and the interest of the user, Gutman observed, perhaps sadly, "We social and behavioral scientists must recognize that many of our intellectual orientations are not popular among architects now. Architects are less interested in designing buildings around user requirements and programmatic concerns. These orientations are seen as manifestations of a positivist and empiricist bias."

[2] Robert Gutman and Barbara Westergaard, "Building Evaluation, User Satisfaction, and Design," in *Designing for Human Behavior*, ed. Jon Lang et al. (Stroudsberg Pa.: Dowden, Hutchinson & Ross, 1974), p. 320.

Very different theories drawn from the social sciences and the humanities now interested architects. Gutman describes them as "traditions that emphasize the universality of social structural and mental forms (e.g., Gestalt psychology and structuralist thought), that investigate the role of symbolism in culture and society (e.g., symbolic anthropology and religious sociology), or that examine the impact of social change on culture (e.g., Marxist humanism and critical sociology)."[3]

I think Gutman was being too kind in describing the theories that then (and now too) seemed to interest architects. They were often scarcely comprehensible, and the less comprehensible, it appeared, the more they engaged architects' interests, but in any case they were no longer theories that envisaged the role of the architect as enabling and improving the life of ordinary or run-of-the-mill people and communities, as early modernism did. Despite the influence of quasi- and pseudo-Marxist thinking in these advanced contemporary theories, they had little interest in the improvement of the common social life and the circumstances of the working class or low-income families, or in the social reform that is consistent with some kinds of Marxism. Rather, they showed much more interest in the catastrophism, the apocalyptic character, that is a more important part of Marxism. The theories in favor today among advanced architectural theorists and students are those that emphasize, indeed celebrate, breakdown in society and meaning, often in obscure and contradictory language. But they do interest the avant-garde architect, and he takes them as some sort

---

[3] Ellis and Cuff, *Architects' People*, p. 106.

of guidance and justification for an architecture that also evokes these themes of the breakdown or explosion of social order and understanding.

II

So then, why this change? Architecture in recent years has turned away from the pragmatic social and behavioral sciences to the wilder reaches of critical theory because its early efforts to design better housing turned into a failure, not necessarily in terms of design or even usability, but a failure nevertheless in their endeavor to improve the city (See chapter 2). The involvement of architects in the planning of cities has a long history, but what was new in the 1920s and 1930s with the rise of modernism was that now architects concerned themselves with a subject that architects in the past had rarely dealt with, the housing of the poor and the working classes. Housing must make up a large part of any city, but the architects designing cities, up through the City Beautiful movement of the earlier part of the twentieth century, had rarely concerned themselves with this aspect of the city. They dealt typically with streets and avenues, with parks and vistas, with the placement of monuments and palaces and great public structures. Modernist architects turned away from the design of the monumental city, the city of vistas focusing on palaces or other great structures, and devoted themselves to the city of the common man. They were assisted and encouraged in this expansion of interest by large new programs after World War I and even more after World War II providing public funds for subsidized building, and offering architects the opportunity to design this basic element of urban form. Many of the great figures of modern architecture in their earlier years dealt with the problem of designing better communities. Even an architect as apparently remote from such considerations as Louis Kahn began as an architect with New Deal settlements and housing projects.

The modernist architects and urbanists who thought about the city and the common life believed that the better design of housing and the larger urban surround could contribute to social improvement. They could do better than the profit-inspired builders of housing for the working classes, crowding as much as they could onto the land available. It seemed to make sense, and indeed it made some sense. If people in the city were deprived of light, air, and greenery, that was a misfortune and their lives could only improve if these amenities were provided. It was a rare analyst of social problems who would have taken issue with this argument. The architect and the social scientist were in agreement on the proper course. Clearing away the buildings put up under early capitalism for workers, or other buildings that had become through change in the city crowded working-class dwellings, could only be an improvement. The sweeping away of such communities would provide opportunity for the modernist civic planner and the modernist architect to begin on a clean slate. He could strip away in his new designs the irrelevant ornament of the past, which was generally found then in crude form even in working-class housing. He could eliminate features that tried to evoke more expensive bourgeois and middle-class housing but offered no practical benefit. He could straight-

forwardly and directly accommodate human needs economically. In Europe, this process proceeded far, but in
time it could be seen at work in the United States, to some
extent in the New Deal era and on a greater scale in the
postwar period.

However, the matter, it turned out, was not so simple.
I have obviously not referred to the housing projects of
Lescaze and Yamasaki in all innocence. The housing project, which from one perspective seemed the fulfillment
of modernism in planning and design, from another
turned out to be the Achilles' heel in the link between
social reform and modernism. The environmental argument was sound. But there came along with it a social
expectation that the lives of the poor and working classes,
removed from dwellings deficient in light, air, and greenery, and in newer housing that repaired these defects,
would improve in other respects too. There was, as one
writer has put it, a degree of "architectural determinism"
in this expectation. "[T]he belief that the designed environment has a major impact on social behavior is deeply
rooted in the polemic of the modern movement in architecture. . . . As Albert Mayer once noted: `We all naively
thought that if we could eliminate the very bad physical
dwellings and surroundings of slums, the new sanitized
dwellings and surroundings would almost per se cure social ills. We know better now.' "[4]

There were sociologists interested in studying this
hoped-for transformation that would come as the result

[4] Mayer in *The Urgent Future* (New York: McGraw Hill, 1967), p. 20,
quoted in Lang, *Designing for Human Behavior*, p. 5.

of an improved physical environment. These sociologists were not skeptics to begin with; indeed they appreciated architects and urban designers and worked with them, but they found in their empirical investigations that there were significant losses in these programs of radical clearance and rebuilding. Two sociological classics, in particular, drew attention to these losses: Michael Young and Peter Willmott in their *Life and Labor in East London* in 1957, and Herbert Gans in *The Urban Villagers* in 1959. They both discovered virtues in what urban planners and their political supporters had labeled slums. Whatever their origins as housing for workers or downgraded middle-class housing, the poor and the working classes could, despite the constraints of their economic weakness, create communities within them, with the key features that define a community: the ability of people close to each other through relationship to also live close to each other physically, and to have access to institutions that served them—churches and social agencies, and the small businesses that catered to their needs. Clearance for rebuilding destroyed these communities, and the bureaucratic requirements that had to govern large projects built under public rules made it difficult to re-create them.

And there were other rumblings from sociologists: I wrote an article in *Architectural Forum*, in June 1958, for one of the then editors, Jane Jacobs, that bore the somewhat sensational title "Why City Planning Is Obsolete." There I criticized the Corbusian approach to city rebuilding, as exemplified (in debased and corrupted form, if you will) in the public housing towers of American cities. Catherine Bauer Wurster, who had first brought the news about working-class housing in Europe to the United

States in the thirties, published her influential article on the social problems that were developing in public housing that I have already referred to (see chapter 7). Jane Jacobs—who could have called herself a sociologist had she wished to, just as Lewis Mumford did—published *The Death and Life of Great American Cities*, which became the coup de grace to the modernist approach to the improvement of cities. Lewis Mumford's attack on that book in the *New Yorker* could do nothing to save the alliance between the social agenda and modernism.

But if modernism could do nothing for social problems, if the expectations of architectural determinism were naive, the architect could then conclude, why bother? Let us devote ourselves to architecture itself, to design, to form.

The criticism of architectural determinism came in both soft and hard forms. The soft form was that architecture did nothing to deal with the social problems that came along with poverty for the working classes of advanced industrial societies. The hard form was that it made things worse. The hard form turned architectural determinism on its head. In the soft form, it could be agreed that the improved environment and the improved quality of the building itself, a new one that had replaced an old and ill-maintained one, was a change for the better. In the hard form, a reverse architectural determinism insisted that not only did the architecture not contribute to a better social life, but it had the opposite effect: it led to a social life and social problems worse in many respects than those in the slums the new architecture had replaced. Here the specific attributes of modernism in the city came under attack, and particularly those aspects of it that Le Corbusier had promoted: the high-rise itself; its placement in large open space; the separation from the street; the hostility or indifference to a varied environment that included commerce, workplaces, amusements; and the focus on total design that made no place for the many simple accidents or innovations in urban life that can emerge in the leftover or older spaces of the disorderly unplanned city.

Those possibilities could not be provided for in the modernist city, yet they have always been considered an essential aspect of the successful city. As an early writer on civil architecture noted, "There must be regularity and whimsy, relationships and oppositions, chance elements that lend variety to the tableau, precise order in the details, and confusion, chaos and tumult in the whole."[5]

The hard architectural determinism that zeroed in on the physical features of the modernist aesthetic as a cause of social problems did go too far, and it ignored how class affects the varying influences of planning and design on people. Upper-class people were often quite happy in high-rises, and even lower-middle-class people without access to summer homes in the country for release could find high-rises quite congenial. Co-op City in New York may look like New York City public housing, but it had few of its social problems, since it was inhabited by teachers and firemen and accountants rather than by poor families headed by single mothers. Further, the argument from physical form ignored the important financial and

[5] Manfredo Tafuri, "Toward a Critique of Architectural Ideology," quoting M. A. Laugier, *Observations sur l'Architecture* (1765)–and Francesco Milizia, *Principi di Architettura civile* (1813), to the same effect–in *Architecture Theory since 1968*, ed. K. Michael Hays (Cambridge: MIT Press, 1998), pp. 8, 13.

political and administrative factors that affect the fate of a modernist urban environment, as of any environment, quite independent of its design characteristics. The financial arrangements for housing projects did not take seriously enough the costs of maintenance. Political factors affected their placement and often resulted in their being sited too far from the more desirable areas, or in places where social links with the social or ethnic group from which public-housing tenants were drawn could not be maintained. The administrative arrangements made it hard to establish stores and meeting places and places for a variety of social associations.

The attack on the high-rise and the housing project generally as the root of social problems was naive. Nevertheless, it was effective. It relieved architects from thinking about how their designs might improve social life. And it was effective in other ways that removed architects from the social agenda. The public money that had gone into large public housing projects and which might have engaged the interest of major architects—despite the inevitable limits imposed on expenditure in building public housing for the poor—now began to flow into other means of assisting the poor with their housing that did not require major public design, such as voucher programs in which the poor were given money and left to fend for themselves in the private sector.

III

High modernism was condemned for making a bad city, and not only because of housing projects. Much that could be attributed to other causes—the automobile, the desire of people to own their own homes located on their own private plots of ground, the public policy that accommodated these interests—was blamed on modernism in urban design and building. While there seemed no escape from modernism when it came to office or shopping developments and other major buildings, when it came to housing, the traditional forms prevailed and resisted modernism. Modernism could no longer play a significant role in the housing of the poor, the workers, or the middle classes, and was limited to housing for some of the wealthy who appreciated its aesthetic. In the 1970s, the Pruitt-Igoe project of Yamasaki was dynamited, and in the 1990s there was more dynamiting of high-rise projects in other cities. The government had long since given up the effort to design communities for the low-income and the poor, an enterprise that we can trace back to the early New Deal: better to give them the vouchers and let them find housing on their own in the private, commercial sector, which was free of any grand effort at planning.

I have perhaps given too great attention to the story of the housing project in considering why the connection between social reform and modernism in architecture has been ruptured, but I believe it is at the heart of the matter, at least for the United States. (One could see the same links elsewhere, too, as one notes the criticism of the design of the new towns around Paris and other French cities as a cause of the social conditions that led to severe riots in 2005, and the fate of public housing estates in the United Kingdom.) The sociological critique of the replacement of the complex and dense urban fabric of the city of capitalism by the planned city of modern intelligence served to disconnect modernism from its most substantial effort to relate to social reform. It was indeed a shock to modernists that the housing put up by small entrepreneurs with no social objectives in mind, except to make a profit, could develop advantages over time that housing specifically designed to provide environmental advantages to low-income groups did not. But there was a powerful argument, and not only in Jane Jacobs, that this was the case. *The Death and Life of Great American Cities* became the most influential book on planning and the city of the last half century.

Public subsidy for housing for the poor continued, in some respects expanded, but in ways that gave no scope to modernism. New York City rehabilitated or built 200,000 units for low-income residents in the 1980s and 1990s. They were no longer in projects designed by modern architects, however, but in rehabilitated tenements and apartment houses, and in small developments, often of modest row town houses, that drew on no great or sophisticated architectural intelligence. It is understandable why low-income housing, a key aspect of the social agenda of modernism, now plays little role in the thinking of architects.

The city is more than housing, important as it is, and in connection with these other aspects of the city modernism had no better record. It is in particular when one considers what we distinctively have in mind when we summon up images of the city and urbanism—complexity, variety, the unexpected, the sophisticated, the varied, "chance elements that lend variety to the tableau, . . . confusion, chaos, and tumult," to quote our previous authorities—that modernist city planning failed. Architects in the past had designed a framework for the city; the modernist architect wanted to design the complete city.

It was rare that he could succeed, but Chandigarh and Brasilia are two examples, both designed by major modernist architects, the first by Le Corbusier himself. And it appeared to most observers and to many of the inhabitants that some important aspects of cities had been suppressed in these designs. When one considered these other aspects of cities—the surprising, the unexpected, the accidental, all that made for urbanism and urbanity in a wider sense—modernism had no contribution to make.

The long history of the relationship of architects to the design of cities seems to have come to an end, or at least a temporary stop. Architects no longer design cities, and they are not being asked to. A relationship between architects and the design of cities that goes back to the Renaissance and perhaps before, and continued through the American City Beautiful movement and through early modernism, is for the moment in suspension.

The pastoral modernism that can be traced back to the Garden City has come off better, both in criticism and in relation to behavioral science. This kind of modernism placed less emphasis on aesthetics, much greater emphasis on the creation of a good community. Social scientists were called in to help design James Rouse's projected city of Columbia in Maryland in the 1960s, and the developer Ray Nasher added social scientists to the team designing Flower Mound in Texas in the 1970s. I wonder whether this kind of relationship has continued in the design of new towns in the 1980s and 1990s.

Whatever remained of a social agenda in the cities became divorced from high modernism and from the frontiers of architectural thought and practice. And so we have housing programs that emphasize vouchers and the use of the private sector, the rehabilitation of older buildings, contextual adaptation to what exists, all of which has nothing to do with modernism. We have had a movement for "community architecture," in which the architect suppresses his taste and sophistication to favor that of the uneducated client. Most currently, we have the "new urbanism," which tries to reproduce the form and the look of older traditional neighborhoods, which of course owe nothing to modernism.

Modernism no longer provides an architecture for normal, quotidian urban use and life. Housing tastes remain traditional; present-day modernism expresses itself in advanced and experimental architecture that has become reserved most typically for museums or cultural centers or concert halls where the architect can count on a sophisticated elite client. Characteristically, it has become an architecture that we associate with world's fairs, something put up to amuse or astonish the multitude, the kind of building that looks as if it should be taken down after a year or two. Unfortunately this kind of shock architecture is now used also for major permanent public buildings. The architecture of ordinary life has gone into permanent opposition against modernism.

And can one argue with this stance? From attempting to design an environment that reflected rationality and good sense and economy, modernism evolved into something that wanted to surprise, to astound, to disorient, perhaps to amuse. That was fine on occasion—at the World's Fair, on vacation, in the fun fair. But it was not an architecture for ordinary life, and ordinary life has fled from it.

Index

Adams memorial, 110, 129
Adams, Michael, *Harlem, Lost and Found*, 218
African American Museum, Washington, 119
AIA Guide to New York City, 215
Air and Space Museum, Washington, 103
Alexander, Christopher, 35, 65
American Indian Museum, Washington, 118
Anderson, Marian, 95
Andrews, John, 31
Annan, Noel, *Our Age*, 5–6, 11
Arp, Hans, 133, 134
Art Deco, 13, 94, 217
Astaire, Fred, 220
Astor Place, New York, 205
Atherton, Charles M., 153n6
Atlantic Monthly, 263–64

Bacon, Henry, 143
Baker, Josephine, 220
Ballston, Virginia, 91–92
Banham, Reyner, 147
Barnard College, 242
Barr, Alfred A., 122
Bartholdi, Frédéric, 98
Bartók, Béla, 220
Battery Park City, New York, 249
Bauer (Wurster), Catherine, 4, 49, 121–22, 180–81, 260, 284

Beard, Rick, *Greenwich Village*, 218
Bedford, Steven McLeod, *John Russell Pope: Architect of Empire*, 121–22
Benton, Thomas Hart, 220
Berlage, Hendrik, 12
Berlowitz, Leslie Cohen, *Greenwich Village*, 218
Bethesda Fountain, Central Park, 69
Betjeman, John, 5
Blake, Peter, 4
Bloomberg, Mayor Michael R., 243
Bochum, Germany, 79, 83–84, 86–87
Bois de Boulogne, Paris, 51
Boston, 105
Boston City Hall, 32
Boston Public Library, 32
Brancusi, Constantin, 133
Brazilia, 290
Breyer, Stephen, 159
Broadway, Manhattan, 68
Bronx, The, 78–79
Brooklyn Bridge, 214, 231
Brooklyn Museum, 277
Brooks, Michael, *John Ruskin and Victorian Architecture*, 25n4
Brown, J. Carter, 138
Bugs Bunny statue, Boston, 105
Bulfinch, James, 31
Burke, Edmund, 66

Buskirk, Martha, *The Destruction of Tilted Arc*, 85n
Butts, Calvin, 221

Cafritz, Gwen, 135
Calatrava, Santiago, 3
Calcutta, 170
Calder, Alexander, 89, 100, 134, 135
Calvert, George, 184
Cambridge courthouses, 31–32, 33
Cambridge, Massachusetts, 255–56, 257
Campbell, Robert, 141
Canary Wharf, London, 34
Caro, Robert, *The Power Broker*, 258
Cathedral of St. John the Divine, New York, 40
Catskills, 70
Central Park, 68, 69, 70, 72, 88, 230
Chandigarh, 290
Chanin building, New York, 211
Charles, Prince of Wales, 1, 4, 11, 29, 34, 48, 49, 66, 267
Chase Manhattan building plaza, New York, 198
Chauncey, George, *Gay New York*, 218
Childs, David M., 154, 157
Chrysler building, 14, 211, 223, 229
Citizens Housing and Planning Council of New York, 263
City College of New York, 205
City Hall station, New York, 212
City Journal, 225

Clarke, Gilmore, 122
Columbia, Maryland, 290
Columbia Presbyterian Hospital, New York, 242
Columbia University, 242
Columbian Exposition, Chicago, 123
Columbus Circle, New York, 205, 250
"Community architecture," 291
Conwill, Houston, 208
Coolidge, Charles, 29
Coolidge, Shepley, Bulfinch, and Abbott, 29
Co-op City, New York, 286
Craig, Lois, *The Federal Presence*, 156–58
Crimp, Douglas, 86–87
Customs House building, New York, 146, 243

Danto, Arthur, 144–45
Deleuze, Gilles, 74
Dennis, Norman, *People and Planning*, 55–57, 66
Di Suvero, Mark, 160n
Dionne, E. J., 178
Dole, Robert, 107
Dolkart, Andrew S., *Morningside Heights*, 218
Domosh, Myra, *Invented Cities*, 218
Drennan, Matthew, 225–26
Duany, Andres, 265
Dubuffet, Jean, 89

East Harlem, Manhattan, 69, chap. 7
East River, New York, 231
Eastern Parkway, Brooklyn, 68
Eiffel Tower, 97–98

Eisenhower memorial, 119, 139
Eisenman, Peter, 143
Emerson Hall, Harvard, 30, 31, 32
Empire State Building, 14, 223, 229
Erie Canal, 232

Faneuil Hall, Boston, 105
Farrakhan Louis, 93, 95–96
Federal Triangle, Washington, 160–61
Feiss, Carl, 122
Fermi, Enrico, 220
Fifth Avenue Hospital, New York, 167
Fishman, David, *New York 1960*, 217
Flower Mound, Texas, 290
Fogg Museum of Art, Harvard, 29, 32
Fortune magazine, 229
Franklin D. Roosevelt Memorial, 103–4
Fuller, Buckminster, 128, 265

Gabo, Naum, 133
Gans, Herbert, *The Urban Villagers*, 59–60, 174, 178, 284
Garden City, 268, 290
Geddes, Patrick, 257
Geddes, Robert, 271, 273
Gehry, Frank, 3
General Services Administration, 113
George Washington Bridge, 249, 251
Giacometti, Alberto, 133
Gibbon, Edward, 25
Giedion, Siegfried, 131

Gilbert, Cass, 146, 161
Gilfoyle, Timothy J., *City of Eros*, 218
Gill, Richard T., 105
Gilmartin, Gregory, *New York 1900, New York 1930*, 217
Giuliani, Mayor Rudolph, 214
Glazer, Nathan, 204, 284
Goffman, Erving, *Presentation of Self in Everyday Life*, 279
Goldberger, Paul, 274
Goldhagen, Sarah, *Louis Kahn's Situated Modernism*, 130
Goodman, Paul and Percival, *Communitas*, 248–49, 272–73
Grand Central Station, New York, 45
Grand Concourse, The Bronx, 68
Greenwich Village, New York, 258
Gropius, Walter, 275
Grumbach, Antoine, 16
Guastavino tile, 212
Guattari, Felix, 74
Gund Hall, Harvard, 31, 36
Gunn, David, 205
Gutman, Robert, 278–80

Haar, Charles, 259
Hadid, Zaha, 3
Hamlin, Talbot, 122
Harlem River, New York, 231
Harvard Graduate School of Design, 30–31, 271
Hays, K. Michael, *Architecture Theory since 1968*, 16, 286n
Hegel's owl, 213
Heins, George, 203–4
Henderson, Harold, 265

Hiss, Tony, *The Experience of Place*, 90–91
Hofstadter, Richard, 221
Holocaust memorial, Berlin, 103, 144–45
Holocaust memorial museum, Washington, 100, 133–34
Homburger, Eric, *Historical Atlas of New York City*, 218
Hood, Clifton, *722 Miles*, 206–7
Hope Community, East Harlem, 184
Horsky, Charles, 153
Howard, Ebenezer, 268
Hudnut, Joseph, 122, 138
Hudson River, 231
Huxtable, Ada Louise, 141, 157
Hyde, Henry, 142

Indian museum, New York, 243
Izenour, Steven, *Learning from Las Vegas*, 4

Jackson, Anthony, *A Place Called Home*, 177
Jackson, Kenneth T., *Encyclopedia of New York City*, 212–27
Jacob Javits Federal Building, New York, 81
Jacobs, Jane, 11, 124, 174, 178–79, 181, 257–59, 285, 289
Jefferson memorial, Washington, 120–21, 138, 143
Jefferson, Thomas, 34, 36
John Harvard statue, Harvard, 105
Johnson, Philip, 32
Journal of the American Institute of Planners, 260–61

Julliard School of Music, New York, 242, 243

Kahn, Louis, 282
Kallmann and McKinnell, 32
Katzmann, Robert, *Daniel P. Moynihan: The Intellectual in Public Life*, 147n
Kelly, Ellsworth, 100, 133
Kennedy Airport, New York, 214
Kennedy, President John F., 103, 150, 151, 152
Kennedy, Robert F., 261
King, Martin Luther, Jr., 95, 117, 119, 139
Klein, Woody, 169
Kohler, Sue A., *The Commission of Fine Arts: A Brief History*, 123n
Kohn Pedersen Fox, 159
Koolhaas, Rem, 3
Kopp, Anatole, 7n
Korean War Memorial, Washington, 110
Krauthammer, Charles, 103
Krier, Leon, 267
Krinsky, Carole, *Rockefeller Center*, 200–201
Kunstler, James Howard, 263–65, 267
Kyoto earthquake memorial, 137

Laboulaye, Édouard de, 98
Lacy, Bill, 159
LaGuardia, Mayor Fiorello, 168, 170, 171, 260
Lamb, William, 122–23
Lancaster, Osbert, 140

Lang, Jon, *Designing for Human Behavior*, 279n, 283
Laugier, M. A., 286n
Le Corbusier, 9, 193, 265, 272, 275, 286, 290
Legacy, 228
Léger, Fernand, 131
Lescaze, William, 122, 276, 283
Lever House, New York, 198
Levittown, 61, 62
LeWitt, Sol, 100, 133
Library of Congress, 34
Liebeskind, Daniel, 3, 202
Lin, Maya, 110, 141
Lincoln Center, New York, 173, 190
Lincoln Memorial, 95–96, 98–99, 125, 126, 143
Lorentz, Pare, *The City*, 48, 158, 275
Lowell, Guy, 30

Mall, Central Park, 69
Mall, Washington, 93–94, chap. 5
Mallgrave, Henry Francis, *Modern Architectural Theory*, 9, 13n
Manhattan, plan of, 68
Manhattan Bridge, 214
Manhattan Institute, 115
Marcantonio, Vito, 168, 178
Marx, Karl, 87
Massengale, John, *New York 1900*, 217
Mayer, Albert, 283
McKim, Mead and White, 30, 32, 117, 123, 242
McMillan Plan, 117–18
Meier, Richard, 3, 159

Mellins, Thomas, *New York 1930, New York 1960*, 217
Metropolitan Museum of Art, New York, 201, 226
Mies van der Rohe, Ludwig, 4, 38n, 198, 199
Milizia, Francesco, 286n
Millennium Dome, London, 128
Mills, Nicolaus, *Their Last Battle*, 139–41
Model Cities Program, 172, 259
Mondrian, Piet, 221
Moore, Henry, 89, 100, 109, 134
Moses, Robert, 173, 232, 233, 257–58
Mount Sinai Hospital, New York, 167
Moynihan, Daniel P., 47, 107, chap. 6, 214, 251
Mumford, Lewis, 41, 48, 57, 122, 123–28, 175, 239, 240, 257–58, 285
Muschamp, Herbert, 71, 72–73
Museum of Modern Art, New York, 219
Museum of the City of New York, 167, 242, 243

Nasher, Ray, 290
National Gallery, London, 29
National Gallery of Art, Washington, 121, 138, 143
Nelson, George, 130
"New Urbanism," 165, 266–67, 291
New York Academy of Medicine, 167, 242

New York City Housing
   Authority, 169, 175, 180,
   182, 276
New York City subways,
   203–13
New York City subway graffiti,
   204–5
New York Public Library, 125,
   126, 203, 219
New York University, 242
Newman, Oscar, 186–87
Newsweek, 265
Nixon, President Richard M.,
   153

O'Casey, Sean, 199–200
Old North Church,
   Boston, 105
Oldenburg, Claes, 89, 112
Olmsted, Frederick Law, 67,
   69, 70, 72–75, 123
Olmsted, Frederick Law, Jr.,
   117, 123
Owings, Nathaniel, 154

Parkinson's law, 213
Paul Revere house, Boston,
   105
Peck, Robert A., 147, 155
Pei, I. M., 138
Pelham Bay Park, New York,
   68
Pennsylvania Avenue,
   Washington, 150–52
Pennsylvania Station, New
   York, 45, 106, 159–60, 222,
   266
Perot, Ross, 142
Piano, Renzo, 3
Picasso, Pablo, 89, 100, 133
Plan for New York City, 171–72

Plater-Zyberk, Elizabeth, 265
Pompidou Center, Paris, 77–78
Pope, John Russell, 121, 138
Port of New York Authority,
   233
Post, Langdon W., *The Chal-
   lenge of Housing*, 169
Prospect Park, Brooklyn, 68,
   90–91
Prudential building, Buffalo,
   147
Pruitt-Igoe housing project, 5,
   260, 277, 288

Queensboro Bridge, 214

Radcliffe Camera, Oxford, 34
Rapoport, Nathan, 109
Reagan, President Ronald,
   103, 142
Richardson, Henry Hobson, 32
Riesman, David, 273
River of Time, 212
Rizzoli, 88
Robinson Hall, Harvard, 30
Rockefeller Center, New York,
   199–201, 202
Rockefeller, John D., Jr., 200
Ronald Reagan Building,
   Washington, 105–6, 160–61
Roosevelt, President Franklin
   D., 120–21
Rose, Frederick, Daniel, and
   Elihu, 219
Rosenberg, John, *The Darken-
   ing Glass*, 25n3
Ruskin, John, 24, 25, 35,
   37, 41
Russert, Tim, 147n
Rybczynski, Witold, 112, 141

Saarinen, Eero, 18
Safdie, Moshe, 19n, 50
Safire, William, *Lend Me Your Ears*, 160n
St. Florian, Friedrich, 139–41
Sandon, Valerie, 212
Sant'Elia, Antonio, 12
Schlesinger, Arthur, 221
Schultz, George, 154
Scott, Geoffrey, 24
Scott-Brown, Denise, 4, 77, 82
Seagram building, New York, 150, 198, 199
Seine, 231
Senate office buildings, 161
Senie, Harriet, 86n9, 111, 112, 113
Serra, Richard, 77–89, 100, 113, 133, 144
Sert, Josep Lluis, 131
Sever Hall, Harvard, 32
Shapiro, Joel, 134
Sharpton, Al, 221
Shefter, Martin, *Capital of the American Century*, 219
South Bronx, New York, 189
Speer, Albert, 82, 140
Spirn, Anne Whiston, *The Granite Garden*, 70
Statue of Liberty, 98, 223, 229
Stein, Clarence, 48
Stella, Frank, 134
Stern, Robet A. M., 195, 217
Stirling, James, 30, 31
Stookey, Lee, *Subway Ceramics*, 203–4
Sullivan, Louis, 13, 161
Sumida, 231
Sunderland, England, 54–57
Sydney Opera House, 18

Tafuri, Manfred, 16n5
Taylor, William, *Inventing Times Square*, 218
Terminal (Serra sculpture), 79, 80, 81
Thames, 231
Thomas, Dylan, 221, 222
Tiber, 231
Tilted Arc, 77–89, 113
Tompkins Park, New York, 187
Transit Museum, Brooklyn, 212
Tufino, Nitza, 209
TWA Terminal, 18
Tweed Courthouse, 243

Union Theological Seminary, 242
University of Virginia, 34, 36
Unrau, John, *Looking at Architecture with John Ruskin*, 35
Utzon, Jorn, 18

Valhalla monument, 125
Van Cortlandt Park, New York, 68
Vaux, Calvert, 70
Venturi, Robert, 4, 38n, 77, 82
Victor Emmanuel Monument, Rome, 125, 126
Victoria and Albert Museum, 7–8n
Vietnam War Memorial, 99–100, 110, 112, 115–16, 136–37, 141–42
Vimy Ridge monument, 125, 126
Vitruvius, 24

Wallock, Leonard, *New York: Culture Capital of the World*, 219

Walton, William, 153
Ward, David, *The Landscape of Modernity*, 218
Washington, D. C., subway, 212
Washington Houses, New York, 170, 175–76, 183
Washington Monument, 119–20
Washington Square, New York, 187
Westway, 250–51, 267
Weyergraf, Clara, 78n
Weyergraf-Serra, Clara, 85n
Whyte, William H., 193, 240, 267–69
William James Hall, Harvard, 36
Williamsburg Bridge, 214
Williamsburg Houses, 51, 175, 278
Willmott, Peter, *Life and Labour in East London*, 284
Wilson, Richard Guy, 122n2
Wolfe, Tom, 5, 109
Wood, Robert, 259

Woolworth Building, 211
World Trade Center, 30, 197, 202–3, 250
World Trade Center memorial, 128
World War II Memorial, 103, 117, 135, 139–43
Wotton, Henry, 23
WPA art, 94
WPA Guide to New York City, 216
WPA Guide to Washington, 93, 94
Wright, Frank Lloyd, 13, 122, 272, 275, 277

Yamasaki, Minoru, 30, 31, 277
Yeshiva University, New York, 242
Young, James E., *Texture of Memory*, 109–10, 114
Young, Michael, *Life and Labour in East London*, 284

Zunz, Olivier, *The Landscape of Modernity*, 218